CARLYLE AND THE IDEA
OF THE MODERN

Studies in Carlyle's Prophetic Literature And Its
Relation to Blake, Nietzsche, Marx, and Others

by
ALBERT J. LaVALLEY

NEW HAVEN AND LONDON
YALE UNIVERSITY PRESS, 1968

Copyright © 1968 by Yale University.
Designed by Marvin H. Simmons,
set in Baskerville type,
and printed in the United States of America by
Vail-Ballou Press, Inc., Binghamton, N.Y.
Distributed in Canada by McGill University Press.
Library of Congress catalog card number: 68-13916

To
A. Dwight Culler
and
Charles Feidelson, Jr.

Mentors and Friends

ACKNOWLEDGMENTS

I am principally indebted to A. Dwight Culler and Charles Feidelson, Jr., to the former, for acquainting me with Carlyle and directing an early version of this book as a dissertation and in particular for his excellent suggestions concerning this manuscript; to the latter, for acquainting me with the idea of the modern in our joint course at Yale a few years ago—and for all the good discussions that followed from that endeavor.

I also want to thank my colleagues at Yale for their encouragement and suggestions over the years, principally Michael Cowan, Michael and Susan Holahan, and Martin Price.

I am also deeply indebted to Wayland Schmitt and Kathleen Roberts of the Yale Press who as editors did service worthy of *Sartor* in pruning my Teufelsdröckhian style and building a bridge across chaos to the public.

When I first began to study Carlyle "organic filaments" were spun forth from suggestions of John Galm, Richard Sullivan, and Paul Robinson; in the background, encouraging me in my task, were my parents and my friends Thomas McCarthy, Peter Rose, James Christie, Christopher Givan, and Scott McIntosh. To them and to Lee Patterson, Harry Berger, Rosalie Colie, Leo Braudy, Joseph Graham, and Eric Havelock, I am also indebted for interest in professing "Things in General." Last, I want to thank all those Yale students who retired after

class with me and over a "tumbler of Gukguk" heard my river of utterance in New Haven's Grüne Gans, in particular Victor Chen, Walker Buckner, Stuart Kiang, Steve Kany, Thomas Holahan, Douglas Yates, Ned White, Michael Fishbein, Elizabeth Francis, Tom Will, Iver Kern, John Waxman, Danny Gottlieb, Mark Howson, Tim Thompson, Charles Niles, George Adams, and Jeff McGrath. My friends Peter Kornblum and Randall Byrne deserve thanks for their proofreading and making this manuscript finally "resartus."

A. J. L.

CONTENTS

Acknowledgments   vii

Abbreviations   xi

Introduction   1

PART ONE: SELF-DISCOVERY AND SELF-CONSOLIDATION

Chapter 1
Preparations for *Sartor:* The Discovery of a Voice   17
    The Masks of Schiller, Goethe, Richter, and
    Voltaire   17
    Achievement and Failure in *Wotton Reinfred*   44
    New Soundings in "Signs of the Times" and
    "Characteristics"   56

Chapter 2
Sartor Resartus: The Prophet Finds His Literary
Role   69

PART TWO: LONDON—VARIETIES OF SOCIAL PROPHECY

Chapter 3
The French Revolution: Change and Historical
Consciousness   121

Chapter 4
Past and Present: Apocalypse and Full Vision   183

CONTENTS

Chapter 5
    Hunting for Heroes: The Flight from Reality   236
        Hero-Worship: Everlasting Adamant or Solac-
        ing Fact?   236
        Cromwell and *Frederick:* Problems of Power
        and Futility   253
        Toward the Totalitarian Self   278

        PART THREE: RETURN TO SELFHOOD

Chapter 6
    Limited Heroism: *John Sterling*   303

Chapter 7
    Conclusion, with a Glance at the *Reminiscences*   328

A Basic Bibliography   337

Index   345

LIST OF ABBREVIATIONS

All texts, with the exception of *WR,* are from the American variant (New York, 1903–04) of the Centenary edition (London, 1896–1901) of *The Works of Thomas Carlyle,* ed. H. D. Traill.

C	*Oliver Cromwell's Letters and Speeches with Elucidations*
E	*Critical and Miscellaneous Essays*
FG	*History of Frederick II of Prussia called Frederick the Great*
FR	*The French Revolution: A History*
H	*On Heroes, Hero Worship, and the Heroic in History*
LDP	*Latter-Day Pamphlets*
PP	*Past and Present*
R	*Reminiscences*
S	*The Life of Sterling*
Sch	*The Life of Friedrich Schiller*
SR	*Sartor Resartus*
WR	*Wotton Reinfred* (in *Last Words of Carlyle*)

INTRODUCTION

> For us in these days *Prophecy* (well understood) not
> Poetry is the thing wanted.
>
> Carlyle,
> *Letters*

The title of this book implies a special angle of vision
on Carlyle. I attempt to demonstrate his central role in
a dominant modern tradition, that of the artist as problematic prophet, the seer who is himself a quester into
self and society. This demonstration takes two general
forms: first, a close aesthetic study of Carlyle's writings,
their tone, their stylistic import, their thematic interrelationships, and especially their author's shifting sense
of roles or "masks" in the forging of his vision; second, a
comparison of Carlyle with authors more generally assumed to be "modern," a comparison which, I believe,
attests to his pioneering importance in "the modern
tradition" [1] and one which can illuminate not only Carlyle but also the authors to whom he is likened.

It is this "aesthetic" and "modern" Carlyle that has
been neglected by much of the excellent present criticism, which generally approaches him by placing him
only within the Victorian context, examining his atti-

1. For a discussion of this topic, consult the bibliography at the
end of the book under the "Idea of the Modern." See especially
the anthology by Richard Ellmann and Charles Feidelson, Jr., eds.,
The Modern Tradition: Backgrounds of Modern Literature (New
York, 1965) .

1

tudes toward social issues in comparison with Mill, Arnold, and Ruskin or studying the roots of his thought in German Transcendentalism, the romantic experience, or his Calvinist heritage. Yet Emerson, Carlyle's contemporary, friend, and champion, sensed the aesthetic importance of this pioneering role and its peculiar relationship to a new kind of society and literature.

> Carlyle's style is the first domestication of the modern system with its infinity of details, into style . . . . Carlyle's style is the first emergence of all this wealth and labor with which the world has gone with child so long. . . . This is the first invasion and conquest.[2]

Emerson's comments here and elsewhere—particularly in his lengthy correspondence with Carlyle—always suggest a host of modern themes and attitudes. They note Carlyle's excitement, verve, daring freedom, rebellious and adventurous voice, and drollery and humor in his capacity for play and literary experiment. Emerson underlines Carlyle's unique attempt to extend the frontiers of art into new arenas, worlds opened up by the industrial revolution—urbanization, new ways of living, the dynamics of machinery, and the excitement of change. Carlyle's writings show that new possibilities of selfhood emerge as man engages with the complexities of the modern world and discovers new complexities within self and society.

Despite his admiration, however, Emerson tends to scant the Janus face of the modern which Carlyle so strongly emphasizes. To Carlyle's excited discoveries must be added his acute sense of fear and uprootedness in a society deprived of all traditions and certainties. He particularly fears the loss of religious traditions, the

2. Ralph Waldo Emerson, *Works, 12* (Centenary ed. 12 vols. Boston and New York, 1883) , 390.

atomization of the individual within the whirlpool of the city, the alienation of man from his work and from his fullest self, the giddiness of rapid social and technological change, the destruction of the classes, and the unleashing of greed in the anarchic pursuit of money. An incipient sense of crisis and doom pervades all his work and threatens both self and society with disintegration and ruin.

By virtue of his acute embodiment of these dualities, Carlyle is peculiarly modern. He celebrates the dynamics of change, the possibilities of the new society, but he laments the loss of roots and fears the mechanization of man and a world governed by self-interest and greed. He brings art adventurously into new areas, but in each area he futilely seeks some final note of ultimate authority to replace the stability of the religious finality he has lost. He strives for the rich public voice of a prophet who redefines what is enduring in the old traditions for a modern age, but in his very prophecy he embodies the problematic, the tentative, the doubtful, the negative, the skeptical and self-questioning, and even the futile. In both his style and the variety of his efforts, he seeks to encompass all the variety of modern existence, but the multiplicity of industrial society, the rapidity of change, and his own endless striking out into such varying directions frequently create a sense of restlessness, desperation, and incipient chaos. Even in his mythmaking of heroes, where his voice is most assertive, the tormented note shows through in the strident tone and the desperation of the social solutions.

Emerson's stress on the adventurous note in Carlyle is valid, of course, for his total work reveals a striking variety, novelty, and openness to a wide arena of interests and is especially courageous—and often artistically successful—in its admission of doubts and the darker dualities of nineteenth-century existence. It is in this sense of

experimentation and variety, this very process of forging a full public and private voice, that this study of Carlyle finds its center. By stressing the author's own involvement in the making of his vision, by charting the varying public and private roles or "masks," and by emphasizing the problematic, the tentative, and the exploratory, my interpretation of Carlyle differs from those which stress either the personality of the sage, the critic of society's aberrations, or the completed and fixed messages of the restored self, of heroism, of duty and work, that he utters as a solution to social ills.

The emphasis upon variety and experimentation, however, does not imply chaos (though this indeed is always a threat that Carlyle himself acknowledges), for behind the variety of areas that are explored—history, economics, politics, selfhood, industry, the mythology of heroism, or class struggle—some deeply felt central concerns provide the creative thrust. Unlike the messages or doctrines for which Carlyle has become known—and occasionally infamous—these concerns are rarely overtly stated or adumbrated, but their pressure, united under the search for a full self and society, provides the dynamics of exploration. In uncovering these central pressures, the techniques of literary criticism rather than those of intellectual history, philosophy, or biographical scholarship can be most useful, for these concerns are revealed not so much in Carlyle's life or in his message-making per se as in the implications of his style, imagery, tone, and presence in the works themselves.

For introductory purposes, I shall distinguish four central concerns which lie behind all of Carlyle's work. Obviously these topics are always closely interrelated and frequently merge into one another, and even more obviously my labels are too precise. Nevertheless, the concerns can be denominated loosely as a concern with the unconscious; an exploration of alienation in indivi-

dual and society; the awareness of multiplicity; and, finally, the urge to unify these concerns through mythmaking activity.

A concern with the unconscious. The term "unconscious" occurs frequently throughout Carlyle and is examined in the early essay "Characteristics" (1831), where he opposes the values associated with the conscious side of life to the true silent organic growth associated with the unconscious. Yet elsewhere his conception of what is hidden beneath abstractions, systems, false forms, and consciousness is rarely a silent unconscious. Like Wordsworth, Carlyle seeks to remove the barriers of habit and custom, to delve beneath the superficial, the intellectual, and the analytic in order to reach deeper realms of feeling, emotion, and significance; but, unlike Wordsworth, his sense of what is covered over is generally far more turbulent and violent and occasionally even awesomely amoral. Furthermore, his fury at repressing forces and their social dominance, his anger at what impedes the release of instinctual energy, precipitates a revolutionary manner which dynamically charges the very instinctual nature of man that he uncovers. At the center of Carlyle's conception of art, selfhood, and nature is an idea of burning energy that unites the three realms and provides both the surest evidence of truth and the source for what must be fully realized individually and socially. Since his theorizing deals mainly with organic growth, it is easy to credit him with more Wordsworthianism than he actually possesses; but the variety of the works, their deliberate raggedness, their wild inventiveness, and their surging style suggest that the unconscious is a field that can be invaded from multiple directions.

Carlyle's style probably has its psychological roots in his intuitive feeling of force and unconscious energy (obviously supported by the power of its "pulpit" pre-

decessors to move him as a youth). In its wide and sweeping capacity to adduce examples, exploring seemingly every cranny of a subject, always seeing things from new perspectives, it suggests a bold comprehensiveness, a cosmic unity, a field of force that seems to hold the perceptions together. In each example the same natural force is shown as alive and significant. Furthermore, in its freedom from the usual rules of grammar, its deliberate syntactic dislocations, its coinages, and its vocal pitch, what may be termed his anti-style suggests rebellion, the destruction of spurious grammar and the modes of thought fostered by such containment, and the revelation of the very inner forces of feeling and perception, Carlyle's central fire of creativity itself. Carlyle's style tends to pack pressure upon objects—much as Lawrence was later to do—until the real natural force behind them bursts through upon the reader: the words cease to act as mediators as the ground of force behind them asserts itself. There is an ever-present wish for deep participation and frequently a desire for the book to disappear.

Nevertheless, Carlyle's unformulated program of the unconscious is not without a kind of drama, though not of the neat Aristotelian kind. Carlyle now champions, now fears the unconscious. He heralds the capacity of the dynamic unconscious to destroy false social and religious forms, to crush repressing forces, and to connect man with his ultimate nature, but then he quickly withdraws from too strong an endorsement, fearing the groundlessness of the unconscious, its unexplored terrain, possible amorality, and the psychological and social chaos it may prelude. He fears that he will ultimately be led to an extreme skepticism worse than that of Locke, Hume, and the utilitarians he is seeking to correct.

Frequently Carlyle smooths out his difficulties not by

avoiding the unconscious, but by hypostatizing it in a fashion akin to the German Transcendentalists—or, what may be more familiar today, to the psychological writings of Carl Jung. Such celebration of the unconscious as a super-personal and social pool of redemption rather than an individual and personal dynamic easily closes off trials and complexities by offering, with a simplistic concern for the depths of myths and heroes, a flight from history and its burdens. In treating the unconscious this way, Carlyle inaugurates not only a concern but also a pattern of prophetic identity making that besets a host of other "instinctual" writers who follow him and who also attempt to destroy outmoded and repressing social institutions, to recall man to his roots, and ultimately to reconstitute society. Certain totalitarian aspects of the later Nietzsche easily come to mind, as well as the Lawrence of *The Plumed Serpent*. And Diana Trilling has shown how the novels of Norman Mailer, a contemporary who closely resembles Carlyle, oddly end up with hints of a fascism far more severe than that they originally sought to destroy.[3] Carlyle's drama of the unconscious, of energy and instinct, is never resolved and finally dissipates into other concerns and methods. But inasmuch as it finds a kind of chronological conclusion in the embodiment of the heroes Cromwell and Frederick, it approximates, though in a rather halfhearted fashion, the more intense concern with instinctual heroism in Nietzsche, Lawrence, and Mailer.

An exploration of alienation in self and society. The concern with the unconscious presupposes to some extent the concern with alienation, for the unconscious is that from which men are principally alienated. Carlyle constantly uses the word "alienated" in its most modern

3. Diana Trilling, "The Moral Radicalism of Norman Mailer," *Claremont Essays* (New York, 1964).

7

sense, but he is also concerned with a variety of its forms and effects, both personal and social. Among the more obvious social forms of the problem—the alienation of man from his political, social, and religious traditions as he is catapulted into the new industrial society of the nineteenth century—he focuses primarily on man's alienation from work, the ground in which his deepest, most natural, and most religious instincts were previously animated.

As Carlyle depicts the effects of such alienation upon society and charts its origins, he simultaneously explores his own alienation from both the past and the present, orienting this exploration toward psychological methods of healing that very personal estrangement. He is one of the first to speak of alienation with the voice of alienation, and throughout his writings his voice renders us aware of his peculiar sense of isolation, of being different, of not fitting in with other people—or conversely, of the need to go it alone, to be unique, to accept the pressures and identity crises of forging one's own destiny. The personal roots of his alienation act like a catalyst for the variety of roles and voices in the later writings. The early letters, the first volume of J. A. Froude's "Life of Carlyle," or the "symbolical-myth" sections of *Sartor Resartus* all show his basic timidity; his untamed and repressed energy often issues in scorn and more frequently in self-pity and the sense of victimization. His failure to find himself in any of the traditional professions, his departure from his evangelical upbringing, his sense of being thrust from a rude country environment, solid and stable, into the complex change and turmoil of Edinburgh and London—all of these create a sense of being uprooted and apart that is never resolved in any final fashion. When Emerson commented on the strange mixture of humor and despair in *Sartor*, Carlyle replied:

You say well that I take up that attitude because I have no known public, am *alone* under the Heavens, speaking into friendly or unfriendly space; add only that I will not defend such an attitude, that I call it questionable, tentative, and only the best that I in these mad times could conveniently hit upon.[4]

Thus, doubt, self-criticism, and negativity actually invade Carlyle's major works, and *Sartor* sounds a new note in literature, which has since become a hallmark of the modern, the radical self-questioning of the principal voices themselves. What emerges, however, is not merely tentativeness, but a dialogue of variant aspects of self-hood, a mutual criticism or dialectic of the "masks" of selfhood. These masks usually cluster around polarities, one an outsider, an editor, the other a mode of ideal but unattainable fulfillment, a prophet, literary artist, leader, or hero. Through their critical action a new self is gradually defined and a new kind of self-questioning literature is born.

Carlyle's conquest of alienation is not a constantly progressing drama, however, but a history of rises and falls, with new problems always adding new complications. For instance, once the public role of prophet to Victorian society has been achieved, new difficulties and new kinds of alienation make themselves felt. Calling members of a society to reformation and difficult truths is to court rejection by that society. Furthermore, Carlyle's conscious sense of mission, his need for final beliefs, his conflicts with his more immediately felt apprehensions of life, and his fear of compromising his increasingly public vision intensify the pressure not to admit doubts, skepticism, and complexities.

4. Letter of Carlyle to Emerson, 12 Aug. 1834, *Correspondence of Emerson and Carlyle,* ed. Joseph Slater (New York, 1964), p. 103.

Ironically, Carlyle's resolution of the problem of alienation seems most effective in the private sphere which he grew more and more to discount. Both *Sartor* and *The Life of Sterling* seem to me to handle the problem in a way that is both literarily and psychologically rich and successful and to be filled with possibilities for creative development that were used by later artists. In the light of this success, I have ventured to reassess *The Life of Sterling*, which Carlyle himself tended to view as a minor work, and to show how it plays back over much of Carlyle's major material, offering the promise of a resolution of a limited and redefined heroism to his search for selfhood. Ironically, too, the alienation is greatest in the histories of Cromwell and Frederick and the *Latter-Day Pamphlets*, where the message to society is most public, affirmative, and clear. The note of the alienated prophet is partly glimpsed here, as in Nietzsche and Lawrence in a similar vein, by the intensity of the tone, the violence of the argument, and the extremity of the social remedies. But Carlyle's alienation is primarily revealed by his constantly intruding note of futility, his very awareness of the great gap between himself and the "masks" of his heroes and between himself and his contemporaries. While the social writings increasingly shut off the critical and exploratory note in favor of reiterated demands and messages, the alienation persists beneath the heroic masks and makes itself felt —and it is this strain which is explored in the later personal writings of memoirs and biographies.

In the social proposals of the later Carlyle, and in both Nietzsche and Lawrence as well, the problem of alienation finds expression in a kind of totalitarian and fascistic program and personal pose. While the word "fascism" is unfortunately charged with the recent horrors of Nazism, from whose programs it is obviously important to disassociate these authors, we cannot over-

look, gloss away, or "reinterpret" the common syndrome that lurks behind such proposals, the common note of desperation, the extremity of solution to an extreme sense of deprivation. Inasmuch as all of these authors stress instinct, blood, and race as a basis for the continuity of social traditions, inasmuch as they preach a hardened or ascetic selfhood as a personal solution and militarism as a social one, they are fascistic in their leanings and obviously approach the more radical statements of Nazism. That they would not share the extreme gestures of Nazism goes, I think, without saying, and that they merely "approach" this program in similarity through some possibly not too important aspects seems equally obvious. Yet the fascistic implications which do appear in the works should not be palliated. Carlyle and Nietzsche have both suffered for their fascism, whether lauded and made all-important or condemned and used as an occasion for dismissing their seriousness of purpose. An attempt at perspective is needed, for the fascistic role is a common temptation to the isolated and fiery prophet of the modern age—even the liberal one—and Carlyle is one of the first to assume its voice, only to discover the role as a step toward self-destruction and increased alienation.

The awareness of multiplicity. Alienation within the self implies division and multiplicity, of course, and I have already shown how Carlyle used this division within the self for self-exploration, whether as editor of Teufelsdröckh in *Sartor,* admirer of his heroes in *Cromwell* and *Frederick,* or biographer of Sterling. Another kind of multiplicity within the self is evidenced by the difficulty in affixing a label to Carlyle. "Prophet," "man of letters," or "sage" seem too amorphous. It is easier to think of Carlyle in a variety of roles, no one of them final—historian, philosopher, political thinker, social propagandist, preacher, religious thinker, autobiogra-

11

pher, essayist, orator, military chronicler, social reformer, and so on. But this variety of roles is developed to
embrace and contain another kind of multiplicity, the
variety and complexity of the nineteenth-century world
with its disrupted traditions, shifting values and classes,
and widening possibilities. Again Emerson is the best
commentator on this new note in Carlyle's writings.
Speaking of "The Diamond Necklace," he says:

> I thought as I read this piece that your strange
> genius was the instant fruit of your London. It is
> the aroma of Babylon. Such as the great metropolis,
> such is this style: so vast, enormous, related to all
> the world, & so endless in details. I think you see as
> pictures every street, church, parliament-house, bar-
> rack, baker's shop, mutton-stall, forge, wharf, &
> ship, and whatever stands, creeps, rolls, or swims
> thereabout, & make all your own. Hence your ency-
> clopediacal allusion to all knowables, & the virtues
> & vices of your panoramic pages.[5]

Nothing, in fact, is so distinctive of Carlyle in both
style and content (of which Emerson seems here to be
attempting an imitation) as his drive toward embracing
everything, no matter how painful, confusing, humorous, chaotic, ridiculous, or bleak, and his simultaneous
need to reduce the multiplicities to order, plan, and
harmony, to bind them into acceptance through humor,
and to bring them within the totality of art and a recon-
structed self and society. From this drive, in its most extreme form, arise the deliberate pursual of confusion,
raggedness, formlessness, and randomness for the sake of
the new totality in *Sartor;* the movement backward into
the apocalyptic moment of history and the destructive
fragmenting impulses behind the French Revolution;
the opposition of medievalism and stability to indus-

5. Letter of Emerson to Carlyle, 31 Mar. 1837, ibid., p. 161.

trialism and rapid change in the conflicting worlds of *Past and Present;* and the counterpointing of memory and present reality in *Sterling,* its careful study of oppositions in friendship and in time.

Emerson once again, however, does not stress the duality of Carlyle's treatment of multiplicity as much as he does the optimistic note. Carlyle, even while he celebrates expansion, variety, and change, laments the loss of stability and fears the loss of identity and values that the disappearance of tradition and the new multiplicity create. For multiplicity implies disruption of both self and society, unmooring the self from its traditions, casting man adrift, and even, as in *Sterling,* forbidding friends who once could have worked under the same banner any real mutuality of interest. Excitement, adventure, self-development, and challenge are all a part of multiplicity, but so too are bleakness and emptiness, pain and separation, giddiness and the odd humor of man's new plight.

The urge to unify these concerns through mythmaking activity. Carlyle's mythmaking is of two varieties. The less important sort is the more overt concern of the writings—the need to make a tradition (often at any price), to redefine the stable aspects of the past and make them available for contemporary existence. Carlyle's highly selective and individual approach to medievalism, his philosophy of history, tenets of heroic vitalism, and pantheon of heroes are all a part of this lesser sort of mythmaking, but of greater importance is the central act of mythmaking itself, the development of a new kind of artist and a new kind of self. What have usually been considered the basic "tenets" of Carlyle must be merged with the drives and concerns I have been investigating and united under the urge to define a total self and a new society. From this perspective Carlyle's hero-worship is only one part of the central act of

mythmaking, a limited though complicated and fascinating development. Priority must be given to the aesthetic quest, to the discovery of art, society, and selfhood launched in the early essays and *Sartor* and carried on with both adventurousness and strange disruptions through *Sterling* and the later histories. Looking at the totality of Carlyle's writings in this manner, as an extraordinary quest into new methods of self-definition, new literary forms, and new visions of society, we may say of him as Joyce obliquely does in his parody of Carlyle's style in *Ulysses,* "Thou art, I vow. the remarkablest progenitor barring none in this chaffering all-including most farriginous chronicle." [6]

6. James Joyce, *Ulysses* (New York, Modern Library, 1946), p. 416.

PART ONE

SELF-DISCOVERY AND SELF-CONSOLIDATION

ᛥ 1 ᛥ

PREPARATIONS FOR *SARTOR:*
THE DISCOVERY OF A VOICE

THE MASKS OF SCHILLER, GOETHE, RICHTER, AND VOLTAIRE

How changed in these new days! Truly may it be said, the Divinity has withdrawn from the Earth . . . . Not Godhead, but an iron, ignoble circle of Necessity embraces all things; binds the youth of these times into a sluggish thrall, or else exasperates him into a rebel . . . . At the fervid period when his whole nature cries aloud for Action, there is nothing sacred under whose banner he can act . . . the invincible energy of young years wastes itself in sceptical, suicidal cavillings; in passionate "questionings of Destiny," whereto no answer will be returned.

Carlyle,
Characteristics

Long before Carlyle came to the notice of the world with the publication of *Sartor Resartus,* he had been readying himself for the prophetic mantle he was later to wear. That this process of self-education was a painful one is indicated by both the letters, with their insistent complaints, and the early essays, with their equally insistent praise of willpower, mastery, and self-direction. The first stage of the process follows the familiar story of the thwarted and alienated young genius,

17

culturally disinherited, uprooted from his peasant background, and unable to find a field in which his talents could be activated—a frustrating situation greatly amplified in the nineteenth century by the general sense that all the old institutions, where prophets could traditionally wear their mantles with ease and power and authority, were desiccated, outmoded, and rapidly dying. Carlyle's early letters document not only his intense awareness of his genius and his basic Calvinistic sense of a religious mission, but also his frustration, despair, and bitterness about his own failure to find a place in the traditional niches of the church, the law, and education. The times are chaotic, social institutions are in flux, a peasant populace is rapidly being shifted into industrialism, old beliefs and trades have grown obsolete, and Carlyle, torn from his Scottish country moorings, is cast adrift.

This first stage closes with the decision to become a man of letters; Carlyle's religious mission will fulfill itself henceforth in the realm of literature. But he then faces the problems of how to become a man of letters and what new kind of man of letters the new times, with their special problems of unbelief, lack of traditions, and social upheavals, demand. With the growth of a larger reading public and with the demand for nostrums in a time of social unrest, the urge to compromise is pressing. To find a new voice, to unfold his own originality in a proper organic growth, is time-consuming, spiritually anguishing, and financially unrewarding. Nevertheless, Carlyle chooses the difficult way; he retreats to Craigenputtock in the bleak country of Scotland and there readies himself for his future social role.

The path is not clear-cut, of course, and the letters continue to voice the same discontent, the same yearning for some permanent employment, the difficulty of

bringing any literary plan to fruition, and, worst of all, the hatred of the public and an accompanying need to prove his genius, even by force. Even at Craigenputtock Carlyle had to make some moves to support himself by his profession of man of letters, but he could scarcely be content with compiling the biographies of Montesquieu, Montaigne, and other "M's" for *Brewster's Encyclopedia* or with the more original but still derivative book reviewing for British magazines. All of these efforts seemed paltry when he recalled his lofty ideal of the man of letters, the hero who was supposed to bring belief back into the nineteenth-century world. But if the dedication to his religious vision was strong and pressing, never allowing him either to be satisfied with what he was writing or to compromise, the content of that vision was obscure and the methods and vehicles by means of which he could present it were unclear. The exposure to skeptical thought in Edinburgh and the wider currents of intellectual interest he encountered in his education made any return to childhood faith impossible, and though he may have overcome his deepest despair before a hostile mechanical universe, Carlyle had no means for realizing that vision artistically.

Imperceptibly the withdrawal to Craigenputtock, with his insistent refusal to become merely a man of letters, provided an answer. The note of joy in his acceptance of Francis Jeffrey's offer to "Germanize the public" [1] in the *Edinburgh Review* is not simply a response to some more permanent form of reviewing; from a social pulpit Carlyle could formulate and promulgate the new doctrines of his vision. More than he may have realized, his new post provided a method whereby he could come closer to those authors who had demonstrated to him

1. Letter to his brother John, 4 June 1827, *Letters of Thomas Carlyle, 1826–36*, ed. Charles Eliot Norton (London, 1889), p. 46.

that faith was still possible in a world that science and utilitarian philosophy had seemingly emptied of all value. Craigenputtock may have been a retreat from a world in which Carlyle felt it compromising and difficult to move and live, but his was a strategic withdrawal in the fullest sense of the word, a search for a way to rebuild a lost faith or at least the vision of man that that faith had once provided. This was a period of spiritual stock-taking, of reading in the German authors who could point the way to liberate man from the skepticism and spiritual darkness launched by Locke and Hume.

Before the Craigenputtock retreat Carlyle had already sensed the possibility of spiritual liberation that came from Germany. His biography of Schiller in which he so closely identified with Schiller's perplexities, so similar to his own, had launched a correspondence with Goethe, who had translated the biography into German, and soon Carlyle found himself more deeply immersed in German authors. Goethe became his patron saint, having overcome similar doubts and trials and having reached a condition of harmonious peace and well-being. Kant's conception of Reason—and, as Carlyle read him, a very mystical form of Reason—over Understanding provided a new basis on which to argue against the skeptics and against Lockian and Humean insistence on sense data. The joint appeal of Kant and Goethe to being within the self, to man's innate mystery and nature, congenially met with Carlyle's religious sense of the importance of duty, will, and self-mastery.

The critical writings of Carlyle's early career should neither be dismissed as ephemeral and insignificant (as he himself was often eager to do) nor be salvaged as valuable literary criticism. C. F. Harrold has approached these writings and the reading from which they spring in his masterly study *Carlyle and German Thought*,[2]

20

still perhaps the best serious introduction to Carlyle. He establishes sources for almost every one of Carlyle's early thoughts and shows how Carlyle understands, amplifies, or distorts those sources in favor of his own beliefs. Unfortunately, however, the Carlyle that Harrold portrays is rather unliterary, very much oriented toward ideas, and stodgily Calvinistic.

Harrold's ideas can be amplified and in some sense recast by stressing the aesthetic activity of these early essays. From this point of view another Carlyle appears, a figure often quite modern, who continues the role of the German heroes but transforms it into a new function suitable to the literary man of the nineteenth century. Carlyle is at once both like his sources but also very different from them, uniquely Carlyle.

These writings then are best viewed as essays in the root sense of that word, attempts at a voice and role, studies of models after which Carlyle might shape himself in his own manner. Not primarily critical writings, they are autobiographical acts of self-discovery, closely analogous to Carlyle's mode of letter writing or notebook jotting. As he tries on one mask after another to see where it fits and where not, his once depleted deposit of truth is gradually refilled and redefined until the author of *Sartor Resartus,* with his own voice and mission, emerges. But, unlike letter writing and notebook jotting, these articles are public acts. They enable Carlyle simultaneously to study his German heroes and to expound their vision to a sluggish and materialistically oriented British public. This is the literary origin of his principal creative role, that of the seer who quests, the prophet who is searching for the new vision. Though Carlyle tended to regard even "Germanizing

2. Charles Frederick Harrold, *Carlyle and German Thought, 1819–1834* (New Haven, 1934; reprinted, Hamden, Conn., 1963).

the public" as a second-rate form of creativity, his principal literary manner, voice, and methods arose from this initial collocation of self-educator and educator-editor. He became a prophet, but a problematic one, a figure who pores over the tumult and complexities of the century and the mysteries of both other poets and himself in order to discover the possibility of pattern and vision.

In this chapter I shall glance at several of these early writings in order to show, not the sources of Carlyle's ideas, but the kinds of self-identification he effects, the aesthetic acts of self-definition that occur within them. I should stress, as a background against which this theme must be explored, the fact that Carlyle is not modeling himself literarily in any direct manner upon any of these figures. He is always the reviewer, another kind of artist, and often he is tempted to consider this a lesser role; but, at the same time, he quite openly admits that in literary method the new forms of those authors have already proved outmoded. Even his beloved Goethe, whom he calls "the greatest of contemporary men," he recognizes "is not to have any follower, and should not have any." [3]

Carlyle's failure to become as interested in art and literature in these essays as he is in the character and life of the author has often been attributed to his Puritan distrust of art. In part this objection is valid, but it is also reductive. Carlyle lived with a greater sense of social and religious crisis, than his literary forebears, with a greater fear that all vision would be extinguished, which accounts in large part for his demand for a new voice, a new style, a new art, and a new kind of man of letters. "For us in these days *Prophecy* (well understood) not *Poetry* is the thing wanted; how can we *sing*

3. Letter to his brother John, 1 Oct. 1833, *Letters, 1826–36*, p. 378.

and *paint* when we do not yet *believe* and *see?"* [4] In his writings he seeks a more direct relationship with his public than any of his authors did, while at the same time he seeks their full and harmonious organic self-development. Throughout these early essays, he is always more insistent on seriousness, fact, moral truth, order, and coherence than any of his authors are, yet he responds to them to the extent that they respond to the complexities of the contemporary world and share his quest for a vision of the whole.

It is equally reductive to see Carlyle merely extracting moral nuggets from these literary figures. What is actually occurring, though in a muted manner not to be fully revealed until *Sartor Resartus,* is the individual appropriation of this material within a voice and style, an art uniquely his own. The omnivorous, encyclopedic, allusive manner is already in evidence, and gradually Carlyle's role as editor emerges, so that by the time of the essay on Novalis a greater degree of self-consciousness and awareness of the possibilities of this voice appears. *Sartor Resartus* serves as the transition in which this voice works upon itself instead of upon other authors—the development from the feeling of the voice as a mere commentator, that of a figure shut out from the great successes of his predecessors and from their literary forms, to an awareness of this voice as a new manner of art, a new way of prophecy that unites public address with individual self-exploration. The mood changes from despair through pain to discovery, and the writings move from the uncreativeness of translations, notebooks, and book reviews through the dim creativity implicit in "Germanizing the public" to the full fledged creativity and self-discovery of *Sartor Resartus.* Carlyle's own actions over this period include the withdrawal to Craigenputtock, the growing awareness of the value of Craig-

4. Ibid.

enputtock's possibilities, the overcoming of intense alienation, and, finally, the movement of the prophet to London, paralleling the emergence of Teufelsdröckh in *Sartor* into the contemporary social scene.

This period of literary self-discovery was actually launched before the withdrawal to Craigenputtock with *The Life of Friedrich Schiller*, written in 1823–24, serialized in the *London Magazine* in 1825, and finally published anonymously, an act symbolic of its author's dissatisfaction with it. Partly for this reason, and partly because *Schiller* seems to provide no direct source of ideas or imitation for Carlyle, the biography has received scant critical attention. It is certainly true that this is a young man's book. Schiller is everywhere over-idealized, and his problems mainly consist in overcoming the obstacles of a stern necessity that seeks to fetter him, much in the manner that social forces oppressed the young Carlyle. Once the initial struggles with education, religion, law, medicine, and various illnesses are over, Schiller soars into the empyrean and there receives his homage from Carlyle. One senses throughout that Carlyle hopes he can reach the same fulfillment.

Despite the obvious simplicity of this account and the book's failure as biography, the intensity of identification between Carlyle and Schiller gives it a value beyond that of the other German essays. Indeed, in retrospect, after a reading of Carlyle's total work, *Schiller* appears as a rehearsal not only for the themes of *Sartor* but for all of Carlyle. From this perspective Schiller himself seems to drop out of the picture altogether, to function for the purposes of self-identification alone or at best as an impetus toward Carlyle's clarification of goals. The biography appears as a full-scale programmatic sounding of the major themes that will occupy Carlyle throughout his career.

24

Though thematically *Schiller* is wide-ranging and rich, stylistically it offers little evidence of the Carlyle to come. In calling its tone "affected, meagre, bombastic," [5] Carlyle must have been aware that he was not attaining the originality and freedom he desired. In fact, the writing contains little of what has come to be known as "Carlylese"; its tone is often more suggestive of a neo-classical manner. The sentences are generally balanced and formal, lofty and abstract, as though Schiller's life were being used to illustrate vast general moral truths.

Despite this un-Carlylean tone, however, there is still a certain richness of voice. Because the book has no firmly defined central problem, it offers possibilities as a kind of pastiche, picking up now one problem and voice, now another. Within the general air of grandiloquence, Carlyle appears in several guises, more in fact than in the more firmly controlled later essays, where he finds sharper literary definition as an editor. Occasionally he is the translator, offering large samples of Schiller's plays in his own rather awkward verse. Then he becomes the generalizing moralist, lofty in tone, expatiating on the values of Schiller's conquests over his problems. Next he is the indignant Carlyle, protesting against "Necessity," mechanism, and the formalism of a dead society; then the champion of force, power, rude energy, and rugged earnestness as sources of self-value. He appears as the philosopher, as the moralist, as the strong social voice condemning society's limitations and denial of genius, and occasionally even as the questing voice poring over the tumultuous world of Kant's philosophy and trying to find the rays of sense and religious wonder.

5. *Two Note Books of Thomas Carlyle from 23rd March 1822 to 16th May 1832,* ed. Charles Eliot Norton (New York, 1898), p. 21.

The first part of the book could almost as easily be Carlyle's biography as it is Schiller's. As Schiller's explosive sense of selfhood and genius bursts through the fetters of society, he emerges with an individual direction to his life as a man of letters. Carlyle's identification with Schiller is extreme, even to the point of special events and character traits. Like Carlyle, Schiller was

> of an ardent and impetuous yet delicate nature; whilst his discontentment devoured him internally, he was too modest and timid to give it the relief of utterance by deeds or words. Locked up within himself, he suffered deeply, but without complaining. (*Sch*, 9)

Portrayed here are not only the brooding young Carlyle but also the socially shy and timorous figure of *Sartor*'s Aesthetic Tea. Throughout the book Schiller is every bit as unable to communicate with society as Carlyle is and appears at ease and natural only with his private circle of friends. Schiller's experiences as a student also parallel Carlyle's; the Stuttgart School, with its stiff formality of military drilling that roots out natural growth, forecasts the Hinterschlag Gymnasium of *Sartor*.

Like Carlyle, Schiller's shyness and sensitiveness in response to these situations is not a weakness but the surface of a great and accumulating strength. The deepest aspect of Carlyle glories in Schiller's bursting of such bonds, in the breakthrough of an assertive, titanic, and rebellious energy that is the foundation of the full self. Already in *Schiller*, this sense of force seems proleptic of all Carlyle's work.

> his natural timidity gave place to indignation; he threw the paper of exercises at the feet of the messenger, and said sternly that *"here* he would

26

choose his own studies." But Schiller was no ordinary character, and did not act like one. Beneath a cold and simple exterior . . . there was concealed a burning energy of soul which no obstruction could extinguish . . . the time was now come when the gyves of school discipline could no longer cripple and distort the giant might of his nature; he stood forth as a Man, and wrenched asunder his fetters with a force that was felt at the extremities of Europe. (*Sch,* 13)

Like Blake, however, Carlyle is aware of the destructive force that is potential within man's released energy, but even more overtly and with more fright than Blake, Carlyle sees the need for reason, mastery, self-direction. Reason can be a fetter, a hindrance, when it violates nature, but it is also a necessity to direct an otherwise unchanneled force. The man of letters is the channel through which this force flows. For Schiller the content of this channel has been completed; for Carlyle it has not.

Thus Parts Two and Three of the biography show a Carlyle who is an outsider looking in on Schiller's life, finding its central thread of direction and coherence (again the role as editor-quester), contemplating through Schiller the temptations that will eventually befall him as a writer. Even after Schiller reaches a measure of freedom and serenity as a man of letters, he must still combat new and serious chronic illnesses, temptations by the public, isolation and loneliness, and the trials of success for the suffering genius. Carlyle rightly visualizes through this projection his own future problems and steels himself against them through Schiller's example.

But Schiller's career is closed to him. Carlyle can

never summon up much interest in Schiller's central works, the plays. He has trouble overcoming his Puritan distaste for the theater. Those plays to which he does respond are either the forceful and energetic heroic dramas, such as *The Robbers* and *Don Carlos,* or those with strong peasant heroes with whom he can identify. Joan of Arc provides an exemplum of the noble grandeur of the "lowly herdsmaid" bursting forth against obstructions, of Mind over Fate (*Sch,* 157). William Tell provides a study of the "salubrious" mountaineer forced to become a shedder of blood against the tyrant Gessler (*Sch,* 177), a note to be heard again in *The French Revolution* and *Cromwell.*

What fascinates Carlyle about Schiller is his loftiness of tone, the grandeur of his general powers over his poetic genius (*Sch,* 194), his sense of strength and vastness, and the possibilities of combining fieriness with tenderness, a strong dualism he feels in himself. Striving for these virtues himself, Carlyle places strong emphasis on the "half-poetical, half-philosophical imagination" (*Sch,* 192) as Schiller's greatest strength. Yet he finds the plays too poetical and the histories too general. His own histories will differ from Schiller's by more feeling, more fact. The aesthetic and philosophic treatises of Schiller are also treated rather cursorily by Carlyle, almost as if he were incapable of understanding them except as milestones on the way to religious faith. Carlyle's need for feeling, fact, and heart is just as strong as his need for clarity, organization, and intellect. But he wants neither extreme alone. Schiller does not provide for Carlyle the balance that he seeks for himself.

This role of Carlyle as outsider, admiring onlooker of Schiller's success, tends toward an overidealized Schiller —serene, harmonious, almost ethereal in his removal from the concerns of men and their faults, a uniter of religion, art, and literature. Yet Carlyle also identifies

28

closely with the tempestuous Schiller of the early years, and that figure finds an extension in another kind of Schiller, one filled with boundless energies, who achieves considerably less unity and serenity. In one of his most extraordinary statements Carlyle actually removes a definite goal and perhaps even the harmony and unity he attributes to Schiller by espousing a "process" Schiller who is committed to the process of self-discovery alone.

> The primary disposition of his nature urged him to perpetual toil: the great aim of his life, the unfolding of his mental powers, was one of those which admit but a relative not an absolute progress. New ideas of perfection arise as the former have been reached; the student is always attaining, never has attained . . . . The restless ardour of his mind is evinced by the number and variety of his attempts; its fluctuations by the circumstance that all of them are either short in extent, or left in the state of fragments. (*Sch,* 81–82)

Usually Carlyle more overtly distrusts and suppresses his awareness of a continual questing as the content of the quest, of the need for a multiplicity of roles, styles, literary works and voices in order to gather together the multiple strands of a dislocated century. Here, however, the concepts of force and energy provide an infinity of power within the self, a way of meeting the chaos without submitting to it.[6]

6. Dostoyevsky plays with the same idea far more mordantly and cheekily in *Notes from the Underground* (trans. Andrew R. Mac-Andrew [New York, Signet paperback, 1961]) :
> But man is frivolous and unaccountable and perhaps, like a chess player, he enjoys the achieving rather than the goal itself. And who can tell, perhaps the purpose of man's life on earth consists precisely in this uninterrupted striving after a goal. That is to say, the purpose is life itself and not the goal, which,

One can almost see Carlyle looking over both his book and Schiller's career, discovering that there is no strong central line of development, but a uniting of many activities—playwriting, philosophy, aesthetics, history. The only central line that binds these is the infinite possibility of the imagination, of the creative faculty itself. At the book's close this is the Schiller who dominates; in summing him up, Carlyle prophesies more accurately about his own career than anywhere else.

> On the whole we may pronounce him happy. His days passed in the contemplation of ideal grandeurs, he lived among the glories and solemnities of universal Nature; his thoughts were of sages and heroes, and scenes of elysian beauty. It is true, he had no rest, no peace; but he enjoyed the fiery consciousness of his own activity which stands in place of it for men like him. (*Sch*, 203)

Carlyle was one of those "men like him."

If Schiller provided an exemplum of the fiery consciousness always open to its powers and possibilities, Goethe offered the stronger vision of the seer who had passed through trials and doubts and now dwelled in unity of being, harmony, and peace. But for Carlyle this second role would always remain an ideal, a projected goal, often a tenuous hope enabling him to stabilize powers that threatened to dissolve into chaos or multiplicity of intent. In the study of the friendship between Goethe and Schiller, it is Carlyle who plays Schiller to Goethe. Goethe is described as

---

of course, must be nothing but twice two makes four . . . . He loves the achieving but does not particularly enjoy what he achieves. Funny, isn't it? (pp. 116–17)

an all comprehending spirit . . . tolerant of all; peaceful, collected; fighting for no class of men or principles; rather looking on the world, and the various battles waging in it, with the quiet eye of one already reconciled to the futility of their issues . . . . The other is earnest, devoted; struggling with a thousand mighty projects of improvement; feeling more intensely as he feels more narrowly; rejecting vehemently, choosing vehemently; at war with the one half of things, in love with the other half; hence dissatisfied, impetuous, without internal rest, and scarcely conceiving the possibility of such a state. (*Sch,* 90–91)

Carlyle needs the ideal of harmony, of the philosophic visionary who surveys existence quietly, if only as a brake to his own destructive rage and irony. But it will remain a kind of vision, for even in Teufelsdröckh it is clouded with more of the ambiguities implicit in Schiller than in Goethe.

The essays on Goethe and his works, the translations, and even the correspondence with him are labors of devotion and love. Goethe is Carlyle's patron saint, often hailed as father or patriarch and always treated with a curiously distanced and remote tone, a certain stiffness and formality. With the early Goethe, as with the early career of Schiller, Carlyle strongly identified, but the Goethe of *Wilhelm Meister* remains curiously out of reach, however much Carlyle longs to model himself on him.

Nevertheless, Carlyle sees himself as inheriting Goethe's mantle. Having gone through the trials of unbelief and emerged with a serene vision, Goethe provides a role for Carlyle. Later in *Sartor* Carlyle will tell himself to close his Byron and open his Goethe; in his first Goe-

the essay he points out that the English are still in the state the Germans were in before Goethe, searching for a way to cast off the incubus of oppression. Here as elsewhere, Byron is likened to the early Goethe, and the implication is that Carlyle is here discovering that he is going beyond Byron, no longer quarreling with existence but refusing to submit to necessity or delusion. He too is presumably moving toward the mature Goethe. Yet Carlyle never fully becomes the serene seer. Walter Houghton has rightly pointed out that Carlyle remains more like Byron than Goethe.[7] Even when he quietly praises Goethe for restoring the "forgotten nobleness" of the poet, he cannot resist adding "even in these trivial, jeering, withered, unbelieving days" (*E, 1*, 228). Thus the criticism of the times nearly overpowers the praise of Goethe, and the second note remains the longer lasting.

Goethe nevertheless remains a major influence; the tug toward the visionary seer is a strong one, and Goethe provides a constant image, however unattained it actually is. What he primarily offered to Carlyle was a cure for his skepticism—or, in a more liberal vein, a justification for it. Carlyle constantly praises Goethe only as a moralist and philosopher, treats only the moral and religious philosophy in his lengthy citations from the works, and in general regards those citations as if they were scripture. In fact, his use of such Goethean phrases as *Entsagen* and "the divine worship of sorrow" suggests a kind of devotion to them as spiritual anchors in troubled times.

In both a psychological and literary way Goethe probably became for Carlyle a father replacement, for as Carlyle outgrew the religion of his own father and found that he could not harmonize its teachings with

7. Walter Houghton, *The Victorian Frame of Mind, 1830–1870* (New Haven, 1957), p. 252.

the new science and philosophy of the Enlightenment, he needed a new source of authority. Gradually he would locate this source of authority in the self and nature, but Goethe provided a transition in which his career and attitude and words became a kind of scripture for Carlyle. He offered the possibility of squaring religion with skepticism, of maintaining belief in the divine origin of nature and the self along with belief in the new science and the contemporary world. He enabled Carlyle to escape an outmoded sentimentality and provided a way of defending old beliefs in new molds. Goethe is praised for uniting head and heart, for maintaining the belief of a saint with the clearness of a skeptic, the devoutness of Fénelon with the gaiety, sarcasm, and shrewdness of Voltaire (*E, 1,* 210–11). Transforming the barrenness of the nineteenth century into beauty, but not by hiding the skepticism and science of his day or by any recourse to superstition, he provides for Carlyle a way out of his extreme cultural alienation and a mode of entry into his own time. After the voice of authority in Goethe becomes Carlyle's own, the image of Goethe disappears, but the ideal of himself as a contemporary seer does not: ironically enough, once the modernity has been accepted, Carlyle as the seer can revert without qualm to the much more dogmatic Calvinistic voice from which he felt culturally disinherited.

In Jean Paul Friedrich Richter Carlyle finds a much more congenial subject for meditation and self-discovery than he did in Goethe. He is not attracted so much by what Richter says as by how he says it: "So fantastic, many-coloured, far-grasping, everyway perplexed and extraordinary is his mode of writing" (*E, 1,* 5). He sees Richter's style as the perfect expression of the man—and this is a man that Carlyle wants to imitate most closely, primarily in a literary manner. It is not so much the

subject matter as the tone and manner that attract him. This "style of his own, full of wild strengths and charms, to which his natural Bayreuth accent often gave additional effect" (E, 1, 7), conveys to Carlyle the sense of someone different, someone unique—and perhaps someone from the "outside," like Scotland. The rugged quality of the style itself is regarded as a testimony to a certain freedom, a breakthrough of convention and formality, and a witness to the sources of self and nature, impeded by no false conventions and none of the glitter of a false and crumbling society. Freedom, naturalness, self-fulfillment are the chief virtues of this style, but when the voice is heard amid society, its virtues are apt to brand the writer as a "strange crackbrained mixture of enthusiast and buffoon" (E, 1, 7). "Tried by many an accepted standard, Richter would be speedily enough disposed of; pronounced a mystic, a German dreamer, a rash and presumptuous innovator" (E, 1, 11).

Richter already appears here as the bizarre side of Teufelsdröckh; but in the Carlyle who tries to fathom him, who reveals his consistency, his direction, his coherence within his wild tumultuous style and forms, one can already see the editor of Sartor attempting to understand Teufelsdröckh. In treating figures like Richter, with whom Carlyle feels a kinship that he cannot completely comprehend because it does not fulfill itself in ideas alone, and like Kant, who requires great patience to understand, the editorial voice comes to the fore. Like the editor of Sartor, Carlyle becomes one with the figure he expounds, absorbing the vision he seeks to understand and give to the public. A sense of mystery of an editor voyaging over a tumultuous infinitude is conveyed, but also a feeling of discovery, of significance, for the editor and his public. In the essay on Richter the need for messages, paradigmatic careers, and ideational

34

solutions gradually disappears, and the editorial voice as both learner and teacher begins to emerge with real clarity as a central concern; the book review becomes a literary form of some subtlety and flexibility, a quest, a creative enterprise in its own right.

Two concerns tap Carlyle's excitement in this essay, fostering an identification of imaginative methods stronger than any the other essays provide. The first is Richter's style and its significance and possibilities; the second is the rooting of that style in the character trait and literary tone of sport or humor, a reconciler of vehemence and tenderness, criticism and love. It is significant that one of the earliest examples of "Carlylese" has as its subject matter the problem of style. It has long been debated whether Carlyle accurately describes Richter's style in this famous passage and whether that style influenced him or not. A more important consideration, however, is that the passage is quite clearly both a description of what he responded to in Richter's style, of what excited him imaginatively, and an example of that style.

Not that he is ignorant of grammar, or disdains the science of spelling and parsing; but he exercises both in a certain latitudinarian spirit; deals with astonishing liberality in parentheses, dashes, and subsidiary clauses; invents hundreds of new words, alters old ones, or by hyphen chains and pairs and packs them together into most jarring combination; in short, produces sentences of the most heterogeneous, lumbering, interminable kind. Figures without limit! indeed the whole is one tissue of metaphors, and similes, and allusions to all the provinces of Earth, Sea, and Air; interlaced with epigrammatic breaks, vehement bursts, or sardonic turns, interjec-

tions, quips, puns, and even oaths! A perfect Indian jungle it seems; a boundless, unparalleled imbroglio; nothing on all sides but darkness, dissonance, confusion worse confounded! (*E, 1, 12*)

Here the style itself provides the very sense of dislocation, shock, confusion, extension of vision, newness, excitement, and heightened imagination that it is discussing.

The first sentence is a means of dealing with astonishing liberality. Its grim defiance of any rhetorical balance, its spilling out of clauses, conjures up a titanic and godlike author transcending the rules of grammar because it is his nature to be unique. The godlike image is abetted by the veiled church metaphor in "latitudinarian" and by the implications of the verb "deals," which suggests a figure who has all grammar under his control and can choose to dispense it or dispense with it. The independent clauses of the opening seem to collapse as the subject disappears, leaving only the verbs of creative activity piling up more closely upon each other: "deals with . . . invents . . . alters . . . or chains and pairs and packs." The summarizing clause also sums up the structure of the sentence: "in short, produces sentences of the most heterogeneous, lumbering, interminable kind." The piling up of long adjectives and the jarring of the Anglo-Saxon "lumbering" with the Greek "heterogeneous" and the Latinate "interminable" give a feeling of Miltonic and epic scope and suggest a visionary seer who captures everything within his sentences. Even the summary "in short" leads to a lengthy conclusion.

The next sentence begins with a subject without a verb but soon looks like an exclamation, conveying a feeling of excitement with which in fact the sentence does conclude, "Figures without limit," and then the spilling out of ideas like a torrent begins again. The

"tissue of metaphors, and similes, and allusions" actually produces a cosmic allusion, for the jarring together of elemental provinces suggests that similar kinds of conflicts are occurring within the style, that a new verbal cosmos is being formed, one which encompasses "all the provinces of Earth, Sea, and Air." The interlacing with "vehement bursts, or sardonic turns, interjections, quips, puns, and even oaths!" is designed to show that the excitement, the pitch, of the author is always present in the style, that he is never controlled by its regulations, but that it is a living testimony of his personality, vision, and freedom, his cosmic scope. "Even oaths!" is almost an oath itself, containing the excitement about the style that the style manifests. Personality, style, and vision all collapse into one whole.

The last sentence leads into a complexity which can in fact suggest chaos, loss of direction, but which Carlyle will later reveal to be actually a complexity that reflects the real plan of life in the nineteenth century and not a formal, mechanical version of it. Metaphors and allusions are deliberately mixed for mutual intensification. The Indian jungle merges with the Italian strangeness of "imbroglio" and both with the Miltonic allusions to Satan's Hell in the "darkness, dissonance, confusion worse confounded." The reader is expected to be mystified, to lose his bearings and direction, but Carlyle regards this initial befuddlement as the prelude to full vision. In the next pages, perhaps with too much desire for seriousness, order, and plan, he proceeds to deal with that vision.

> Let us not turn from him after the first cursory glance, and imagine we have settled his account by the words Rhapsody and Affectation . . . . There are rays of the keenest truth, nay, steady pillars of scientific light rising through this chaos; or may it

be that our eyes are of finite, not of infinite vision,
and have only missed the plan? (*E, 1,* 13)

It is possible, perhaps, to sense in this a fear of vision,
a dread of the powers of the untrammeled imagination
and the free style; the stress on plan may be an insistent
demand for order, for the insistence that makes itself
felt here in a dim manner will fulfill itself in Carlyle's
later demands for order at any cost and dismissal of almost everything else as cant. Carlyle is always fearful of
chaos and of the imagination's powers; even in "Signs of
the Times" he states that undue cultivation of the inward powers, of dynamics, the very act he is there
espousing, will lead to superstition, frenzy, a lack of
realism, "visionary, impracticable courses" (*E, 2,* 73).
His skeptical side is always very prominent—a voice of
the anti-superstitious Voltaire, a clarity of intellect—
and perhaps it is because he is so baffled by the enigma
of figures like Novalis and Kant that his editorial voice
comes to the fore so strongly. Novalis and Kant, far
more than Richter, give the promise, similar to Goethe's, of messages, and Carlyle is always ready to pursue
such a hope; like Richter's, however, their significance is
cloaked in obscurity. Many of the possibilities of message-making embodied in Kant and Novalis are later
transferred to the figure of Teufelsdröckh in *Sartor,*
where they are similarly encased in a "mysticism" that
may be moonshine or the answer to the world's secret.
Similarly, the editor of *Sartor* hovers between annoyance
at the mysticism of Teufelsdröckh and the serious act of
imaginative sympathy with hopes for untangling the
riddle.

"Richter," however, seems an advance over the essays
on Goethe and Novalis and the frequent investigations
of Kant because it has practically abandoned the chim-
era of messages and focuses on the aesthetic bases, both

psychological and literary, of Richter's style. Carlyle finds the source for Richter's creation and harmony in his humor, "the ruling quality . . . as it were the central fire that pervades and vivifies his whole being" (*E, I,* 14). This quality, whose essence is sensibility and love, allows Richter to be in touch with significance at all times and yet to be a "Titan in his sport" (*E, I,* 14). Humor allows him to treat the universe as a plaything, yet to regard it not with anarchy but with a purpose: to bring out the faces of all men, to feel pathos and pity for his living beings, and even to transform his aversion into a form of love.

> The essence of humour is sensibility: warm, tender fellow-feeling with all forms of existence. Nay, we may say that unless seasoned and purified by humour, sensibility is apt to run wild; will readily corrupt into disease, falsehood, or, in one word, sentimentality. (*E, I,* 16)

Humor is the measure of insight and flexibility; as the embodiment of fire and the central imaginative force, it molds opposites or unlike things together, producing, in its style and vision, a new manner of looking at existence. With Teufelsdröckh the utilitarian "clothes" will lead through humor to the transcendent vision which will return the reader to a new awareness of the everyday. Humor embraces the cosmos, through sensibility melting it into one unity, and provides the writer with the maturity and range of its own flexibility.

For the first time Carlyle offers an aesthetic attitude (which is also a moral one) as the basis for a significant world view and for an art that will produce living beings in a full universe. This is an important step toward *Sartor Resartus* and toward an aesthetic attitude that is assumed throughout most of Carlyle's work—the element of aesthetic sport or play as an end in itself. Such

an attitude heralds the Nietzschean view in its perception that harmony can be found in the world and its contradiction, "nay finding in this very contradiction new elements of beauty" (*E, 1, 17*). Certainly such an attitude is important for the self-contained imaginative quality of *Sartor*, something which still strikes readers as most impressive and allies the book with such totally imaginative constructs as *Tristram Shandy, Moby Dick, The Counterfeiters,* and more recently, Nabokov's *Pale Fire.* Even such an immediate and pamphleteering work as *Past and Present* is given strength, buoyancy, and significance through this attitude.

The reflections on humor in "Richter" are accompanied by a denunciation of irony as shallow, lifeless, soulless, and unfeeling. The purpose of this attack is not only to exalt Richter's humor; it is also part of a larger campaign throughout the essays to purge Carlyle's own aggression against the world and his denunciation of it. In fact, it is an attempt to take that aversion up into a more loving kind of humor, a more aesthetic and imaginative form of play, a method for vision. Carlyle tried to lift himself by Richter's bootstraps, and it is probably fair to say that he only occasionally reached the ideal of humor that he sketched for himself in the essay on Richter. In fact, the very irony he denounced and polarized against Richter's humor came far more easily to him. To his credit, however, it must be said that even in those essays which might be called ironic—the study of the German playwrights, or in "Richter" of the mechanical biographical methods of Döring, or in "Werner" of the playwright's absurd and incoherent dramas—Carlyle is always capable of great imaginative sympathy and invariably eschews strong denunciation and satire even when he is most moralistic.

The essay on Voltaire shows other aspects of the problem of irony and humor. As we might expect, Carlyle

finds Voltaire wrongfully choosing the humor of wit (a king of irony) instead of real humor, electing a gaiety of head over heart. Such a failure left Voltaire with the familiar defects of those heroes who went astray, Burns and Byron—lack of deep vision and real insight, absence of moral earnestness, failure in strength, and worship of public opinion. Carlyle sympathizes—rather surprisingly—with Voltaire's mission as far as it went, but he realizes that it did not pierce the depths of reality. "He earns abundant triumph as an image-breaker, but pockets little real wealth" (*E, 1,* 413).

Yet the essay on Voltaire is basically an attempt to go beyond him; in its quiet manner, it reveals more sympathy with Voltaire's mind, style, and mission than Carlyle openly admits. "We may consider him as having opened the way to future inquirers of a truer spirit" (*E, 1,* 459). Voltaire wrought little good and caused mainly dislocation, but he cleared the world of superstition, ironically pricked false social forms, became a hero as a man of letters, and—Carlyle would like to think— passed the mantle on to him, the truer spirit. Carlyle often comes quite close to Voltaire's ironic role (perhaps this is why he protests against it so much) and readily admires his clarity of intellect, skepticism of cant, modernity, and acceptance of the new science that allowed him to reach a large modern public. Goethe was praised as uniting the skepticism and clarity of Voltaire with the devoutness of Fénelon, and Carlyle also hopes to represent a similar combination of powers. In his essay on Voltaire he seems to be not so much denying Voltaire's wit as trying to lift it to a higher plane, where it will be no longer merely destructive. Voltaire after all was not a shallow ironist; he was the "greatest of all *Persifleurs* . . . morally speaking also, he is the best" (*E, 1,* 436).

Carlyle's ambivalent attitude toward Voltaire is tes-

timony of an ambivalence within himself—the need for belief and the need for skepticism. It shows, as Robert Langbaum has suggested, that while romanticism is a reaction against eighteenth-century empiricism, it is nevertheless absorptive of that empiricism, in fact is a corrected empiricism.[8] At the same time, it indicates an aspect of Carlyle's consciousness that forbids him merely to imitate Richter's art and style, however congenial these may be. Voltaire, with his clarity, skepticism, and distrust of cant, has erased superstition, and Carlyle also has much to destroy; he too envisions a mission against outmoded forms of society and, consequently, sees himself as the heir of Voltaire in England. Furthermore, Voltaire's clarity is an important fact of the modern world, an important part of the modern consciousness. The historical process can not be reversed. The nineteenth century is inevitably the heir of Voltaire. There can be no retreat into dreamy mysticism, sentimentality, or visions; clarity of intellect must be reunited with imagination to produce a new kind of art. The voice of the understanding editor of *Sartor* must always accompany the vision of Teufelsdröckh.

Carlyle's attitude toward Voltaire may be profitably compared with Nietzsche's attitude toward Socrates in *The Birth of Tragedy*.[9] Here again it is possible to argue that Nietzsche both hated and admired Socrates.

8. Robert Langbaum, *The Poetry of Experience: The Dramatic Monologue in Literary Tradition* (New York, Norton paperback, 1963), p. 22.

9. See Nietzsche, *The Birth of Tragedy*, trans. Francis Golffing (Garden City, Anchor paperback, 1956), secs. 12–17, pp. 76–108. For the ambivalence in the denunciation of Socrates, see esp. pp. 90, 95. Also see Walter Kaufmann, *Nietzsche: Philosopher, Psychologist, Antichrist* (New York, Meridian paperback, 1956), Chap. 13, "Nietzsche's Admiration for Socrates." As usual Kaufmann is overly corrective. See also his introduction to his new translation of *The Birth of Tragedy* (New York, Vintage paperback, 1967).

Nietzsche rails against the hypertrophy of logic in Socrates, an overgrowth that made him distrust all poetry and thus destroy through his influence the Apollonian-Dionysian balance of art previous to him. But the modern world for Nietzsche is unfortunately the heir of Socrates' logic—just as for Carlyle it is the heir of Voltaire's piercing clarity and eradication of superstition—and while he does not openly admit any identification with Socrates, it is clear that he too suffers from the same hypertrophy of intellect that makes art difficult or impossible to create. He too knows that the process of history is irreversible (even though he later tries out a doctrine of eternal recurrence), that the old art of the Apollonian-Dionysian duality has been irrecoverably lost, and that the new art demands a rebirth of Dionysos and the union of the Dionysian Nietzsche with the Apollonian Nietzsche, the merger of the Greek tragedian with the Socratic logician, exposer of false values. Thus *The Birth of Tragedy* becomes that new kind of art for a particular historical situation. *Sartor Resartus* will be the same, something very new, something very original, a modern mixture of Dionysian feeling and Apollonian intellection.

In its own aesthetic activity *Sartor Resartus* will fuse the results of Carlyle's Craigenputtock reading and writing. Its form will emerge from the book review and will still feature a rather baffled reader studying the works of a sage. Teufelsdröckh will evolve from the figures of Goethe, Kant, Schiller, and Richter, and especially from Carlyle's own autobiography, though transmuted into "symbolical myth." [10] The book as an aesthetic act of self-discovery finds its basis in the imaginative romantic literature of self-discovery of the previous years, but its

10. As Carlyle styled it; see James Anthony Froude, *Thomas Carlyle: A History of the First Forty Years of His Life, 1795–1835* (2 vols. London, 1882), *1*, 81.

own special mode along with its public platform has been prepared for in the book review. The kinds of humor it utilizes will find their sanction in the odd use of this form in the light of the discussions about the humor of Richter and Voltaire.

But before I turn to *Sartor Resartus* in detail, I must discuss Carlyle's gradual development of two further aspects of this work. The first is the autobiographical one and its relation to the romantic quest. The second is the intensification of the public voice as it meets larger and more immediate social problems on its own and finally bursts out of Craigenputtock entirely.

ACHIEVEMENT AND FAILURE IN *WOTTON REINFRED*

> I make no grain of doubt that in time I shall pene-
> trate the fence that keeps me back, and find the place
> which is due to me among my fellow-men.
>
> Carlyle,
> *Early Letters*

In 1827 Carlyle made an abortive attempt to create an original imaginative work, a romance entitled *Wotton Reinfred*. However unsuccessful that work may be as literature, it is as fundamental as the essays in the creation of the literary method and vision the mature Carlyle was to display in *Sartor Resartus*. Indeed, to readers acquainted with *Sartor, Wotton Reinfred* may appear simply a preliminary sketch for the biographical section of Teufelsdröckh in Book II. Unlike that later treatment of Teufelsdröckh's childhood, education, love, and spiritual crisis, the earlier version fails with its flimsy romantic vehicle to sustain a continuous narrative progression. The romantic form is constantly dissolving into autobiographical or biographical recollection and philosophic debate or dialogue.

44

Since the book is so little known, it will be wise to outline its action here. The opening scene presents the hero, Wotton Reinfred, complaining about his unhappiness to his cousin, a doctor, and his "last link . . . with the living and loving world" (*WR,* 11). Scientific study and readings in skeptical philosophy have killed belief in Wotton, and in his mind "the world is whirling like a sick man's dream" (*WR,* 3). His despair is augmented by his loss in love; Jane Montagu has chosen Walter, the "tiger-ape," instead of him, "darkness rather than light" (*WR,* 6). Though the reasons for her choice are cloaked in mystery, the loss is there, and when it is combined with a loss of belief, Wotton's grief can only voice itself in groaning and complaint. The doctor, serving as a foil to such despair, claims that complaint is nature's method of purging itself, urges a course of action and affirmation, and by his arguments persuades Wotton to take a journey into the world and once again to mingle with society.

In Chapter Two, Wotton is already somewhat more buoyant as a result of arranging plans for action. This chapter turns into a long biographical account of Wotton's childhood joy, the beginnings of his imaginative life with his discovery of the *Arabian Nights,* and the religious practice inculcated by his devout mother. School is shown as a great trial in which the sensitive Wotton is despised and attacked by other boys, though upon occasion he responds with a wild but short-lived fury. At the university his character achieves its present state with the loss of faith and its accompanying mental instability, though at the same time the qualities of the artist, "a keen and painful feeling of his own weakness, added to a certain gloomy consciousness of his real intrinsic superiority" (*WR,* 21), become apparent. When Wotton turns to the study of science in order to regain his lost faith, to find a center to his universe, his at-

tempt is only momentarily successful and provides no continuing spiritual sustenance. He finds himself in a state of utter negation, "dreary stagnancy" (*WR*, 24). "Among his fellow-men he felt like a stranger and a pilgrim—a pilgrim journeying without rest to a distant nowhere" (*WR*, 25).

At this point Bernard Swane, an optimistic and believing youth, appears and by his friendship saves Wotton from madness. With the meeting of Jane Montagu, arranged through Bernard, Wotton's despair is conquered by love. But the curtailment of the romance at the wish of Jane's mysterious aunt only plunges Wotton into deeper despair. Bernard plans a journey to bring Wotton out of darkness into daylight, convinced, like the doctor,[1] that Wotton's noble nature will find a resolution through his perseverance and love of truth.

Having set out at last on their journey, Wotton and Bernard meet a stranger in the mountains who invites them to the mysterious House of the Wold, a secluded spot in perfect harmony with nature, inhabited by a group of intellectual inquirers representing the various facets of the contemporary British philosophical currents. In the ensuing debate on the nature of happiness and the aim of life, Dalbrook, a Kantian, delivers a mystical paean on the value of the unseen over the seen, "reason" over "understanding," while Burridge, the "atrabiliar philosopher," supports a mild utilitarianism, and Maurice, the host, urges a philosophy of self-denial, humility, and action.

The next morning Wotton questions Henry Williams, a jovial skeptic, whom he has understood from the first; Wotton hopes to probe the mysterious significance of the inhabitants of the House. Williams praises his host,

1. The separate identity of the doctor and Bernard Swane is not clear in the present state of the text.

PREPARATIONS FOR *SARTOR*

Maurice Herbert, for his philosophy of action but questions Dalbrook's mysticism, which, he feels, is "discord [that] may in part be harmony not understood" (*WR*, 80). Dalbrook's inability to turn his mysticism, his dreams, into actions limits and qualifies the praise for his philosophy; he "revolves rather than advances" (*WR*, 80). Burridge, the utilitarian, is criticized as a worshipper of the devil Necessity but he is redeemed by his loving heart. When Wotton assures Williams that "surely of all the men I have ever met with, you seem the most free from cant" (*WR*, 84), Williams makes a defense of the necessity of cant and the inability of all men to free themselves from it. Wotton sees Williams, nevertheless, as positively oriented, loving, gay, and kind—but not without a kindly contempt for man and his actions, his own included.

> For an instant the gay sceptic has become a worshipper and a rapt enthusiast. These, however, were but momentary glows, reflexes of a strange glory from a world he had never dwelt in, which he knew not, and soon lost in the element of quiet kindly derision and denial where he lived and moved. (*WR*, 87)

Filled with philosophical contradictions, he had not resolved them and was, in Wotton's opinion, "professedly a sceptic, unconsciously a believer and benefactor" (*WR*, 87).

After this conversation, the two return to the House, where, in the harmonious peace of the evening, a discussion of the poet as seer takes place. Goethe's *The Sorrows of Young Werther* and Byron's works, notably *Childe Harold*, are condemned as products of the "arsenical school" (*WR*, 92), and modern poets are seen as

47

falsely channeling their energies into a sensual philosophy of the self or into mechanical "Profit-and-Loss" philosophy. Burridge alone defends the right of these poets to voice their complaints, to make articulate the loss of the age and its failure to find a symbol of the infinite. The tide of the conversation is against him, however, and Dalbrook and Maurice end with a vision of the poet as a believer in the invisible, a "man as harmonious and complete in his reasonable being" (WR, 100) as a warbling blackbird is in its instinctive being. Even Burridge is seen as a worshipper of the invisible, since he respects honor, a spiritual quality. The discussion ends with a defense of the poet as maker, Wotton supplying the example of Phidias giving birth to the symbol through chance artistic inspiration.

The next morning, as Wotton and his hostess, Dorothy Herbert, are inspecting pictures in the House, the peace is shattered by the arrival of Wotton's rival, Edmund Walter. Wotton is curiously drawn to Walter and yet repelled by him; he admires his force and control, his power, but fears his pride, isolation, and calculation. Together they inspect a picture of Cromwell. Walter, Dorothy observes, wants devoutness and reverences only power. "It is not the pure ideal but the exciting real that you look for" (WR, 111), she comments on his preference for portraits of eminent men and his scorn for Charles, the martyred king. Wotton defends the idea of power and notes its presence as the basis of all religion, but he censures its abuse, the murder of Charles. Dorothy, uniting head and heart, makes a plea for the presence of love as an equally important factor in religion; she sees that Wotton can be converted from his errors while there will be no salvation for Walter. The rocks and abysses of Walter's mind, however carefully concealed, are wisely noted by Dorothy, who envisions the future shipwreck they will cause.

48

At this point, upon the introduction of Isabella, a shallow and giddy woman who worships only the passing moment, Wotton makes a quick escape. His mind is in turmoil; new thoughts have introduced new complications. Under the effect of the wild and expansive scenery, and with a resolute maintenance of his own integrity, he defies death and experiences a renewal with nature, a vision in which nature is seen as a fairyland, as his mother, and as divine. This renewal is followed by the sudden and mysterious appearance of Jane Montagu, riding an Arab horse, and the possibility of the renewal of love after the conquest of metaphysical despair becomes apparent. Wotton accompanies Jane and her cousins to an inn where she begins to relate her life story, but before she can explain the mysterious machinations of her aunt, the story breaks off.

If the reader is left in a state of confusion regarding the further progress of the romance, he is perhaps even more confused with the material he has already been given. Certainly all the familiar Carlyle themes and problems are here, even the extraordinary forecast of Cromwell and the problems of hero-worship. And there is multiplicity in plenty as well as patterns. But where amid all these disparate and heterogeneous threads can a unifying factor be found? There is clearly no unity of result, as Carlyle himself recognized. It almost seems as though it were his mind, not Wotton's, that was seized by turmoil and that he consequently put the romance aside. Ultimately, it is a unity of aim and intention that significantly allies *Wotton* with both the essays and *Sartor Resartus,* all of which reflect the drive toward spiritual wholeness.

In the journey from spiritual negation to spiritual affirmation, *Wotton Reinfred* begins just before the point where Goethe's *The Sorrows of Young Werther* leaves off. While the earlier German novel, so strongly

condemned here, depicted the intense psychological struggle of a young man whose hopes to attain his ideal, Charlotte, were frustrated by a rival, as well as by life and necessity itself, Carlyle's tale opens with the beloved ideal already lost to the rival. Any forward movement must be toward a conquest of spiritual frustration and emptiness, toward affirmation, which remains a possibility because of the conventional evil quality of the rival, the use of which Goethe eschewed. Werther ended a suicide in the logic of negation; the world's scheme was not his, and only through such an act could he affirm the validity of his ideals and, at the same time, allow the world scheme its way in the continuity of Albert's devotion to his wife Charlotte. In contrast, the possibility of Wotton's victory is apparent from the start in the words of encouragement from the doctor and from Bernard Swane, in the constant references to Wotton's love for truth, his perseverance, and his noble nature, and in the very possibility of the quest and journey itself.

This unity of aim and intention is shattered from the very beginning, however, by the separation between metaphysical despair and the renewal of belief, on the one hand, and despair in love and love's renewal, on the other. Goethe's Charlotte is seen only in the images Werther forms of her, and those images present the metaphysical problems of meaning as well as problems of life, love, and action.[2] Carlyle, it is true, sees the two as somehow connected—that is why he depicts both of them—but the exact nature of the connection remains unexplored. First the hero is seen buried in metaphysical despair; life and nature are meaningless to him. Then he is immediately rehabilitated by his love for Jane Montagu, only to be plunged back into despair

2. *Werther,* however, has also been severely criticized for its plot division between fulfillment in love and in social action.

again with the forced severance of the romance. Because of this separation of themes, the romantic vehicle, the journey in search of the ideal and the triumph over obstacles must itself be split.

All the plot incidents—Jane's mysterious break with Wotton, the discovery of Wotton's picture in the locket, the appearance of Walter at the House of the Wold, the strange and inexplicable journey of Jane in the mountains—are connected with the first manifestation of this vehicle, the search for Jane as fulfillment in love. The very genre of the novel, a German romance, indicates that this should be the controlling structure, yet none of these incidents appears linked to one another; each is as inexplicable as the preceding one. The technique is fictional, but there is apparently no causal connection between the incidents.

The energy of the novel does not lie in its love situation but resides in the other manifestation of the romantic vehicle, that major portion that deals with the larger problems of meaning and truth and self. But not only does this search for an ideal, this quest for meaning and spiritual fulfillment appear separated from (though strangely joined with) the search for fulfillment in love; it also fails to find fictional techniques for expression. Instead, it manifests itself in dialogue with sympathetic opponents like Bernard Swane or the doctor; or it splits the self into several possibilities, such as the varied inhabitants of the House of the Wold, and generates answers through debates; or, lastly, it turns to recollection and autobiography, as in the extensive recounting of Wotton's background in Chapter Two. Because this theme does not easily associate itself with the methods of the traditional romance, the intrusion of such fictional techniques as the appearance of Walter and the break with Wotton appears forced, melodramatic, and calcu-

lated, militating against the very grain of any real thematic development.

The real thematic development is carried by the process of self-discovery in the methods of autobiography and debate. These latter recall the techniques and themes of *Wilhelm Meister's Apprenticeship*, which Carlyle had translated in 1823–24 and which he read as a portion of Goethe's spiritual autobiography in which, by quelling the turmoils of *Werther*, the German had finally arrived at spiritual peace. The static quality of the action, the emblematic significance of settings, and the semiallegorical role of characters point to such an influence. The House of the Wold clearly resembles in its emblematic quality the castle of the Prince through which the currents of life flow in *Meister*. Isabella, the votary of changing fashion, seems to be directly modeled on Philina, a player whose heart is given but for a moment. It is almost as though Carlyle first had striven to become Goethe then, by translating *Meister*, sinking himself into its ambience, and then, when this had failed, had actually tried to rewrite *Meister* for himself. The image of Goethe was for Carlyle an almost obsessive ideal.

But the discovery of the self through autobiographical reflection and debate militates against the discovery of the self through a romantic love plot, even though Carlyle senses that thematically both are connected. When the final chapter of the book erupts into an extravagant display of romantic melodrama, the reader feels that Carlyle has discovered that his method and content are at variance, that he is forgetting his central theme, that he is unable to say what he wants to say, and, finally, that the process of self-discovery cannot be poured so easily into the traditional forms of romance or even the Goethean ones.

Wotton Reinfred, then, though it ends as a failure, is

nevertheless important because it clearly introduces the autobiographical theme to be fully developed in *Sartor Resartus*.[3] Its very failure helped to make Carlyle aware that the theme of self-discovery needed its correlate, the literary process of self-discovery. While autobiographical techniques and the creation of personas could be an aid in solving these problems, as the essays and *Sartor* reveal, the use of romance plots with independent characters who participate in the action and/or serve as possibilities of the self could only cause confusion.

Critics have been misled by the intensely autobiographical opening chapters of *Wotton* into just such confusion. One can find direct parallels in Carlyle's letters to his attitude toward his mother, his inability to tell her he had lost his belief, his friendship with Edward Irving (Bernard Swane), the introduction to Jane Welsh (Jane Montagu), and the like. Perhaps there is even an interesting Freudian suggestion in the portrait of Wotton's "dead" father who, while alive, gave Wotton "a vague unpleasant impression . . . of restraint and awe" (*WR*, 14). But it is a mistake to read the entire novel as a roman à clef, as some critics have the latter portion, and then attempt to pin tags onto the various figures in the House of the Wold. Though these figures may also have a living contemporary basis, it is

---

3. See, for instance, Augustus Ralli, *Guide to Carlyle* (2 vols. London, 1920).

The book must be ranked as a study for Sartor, the first hasty overflow of a rich mind, rather than an independent work. From the success or failure of its parts Carlyle learned to coordinate his powers, to heighten and recast his thoughts, to fix the subject previously in his mind and work outwards in ever widening circles. He learned also the limitations of form, and that he must eschew the novel—for, unlike George Eliot, he could not bend his philosophical intellect to small things. (*1*, 57)

best to read them as potentialities in Carlyle, positions which interested him and which he wished to argue out. This view is supported by the general flatness of these characters and their tendency, after a brief introductory portrait, to move off into the realm of abstract ideas. There is little life to anyone in the House of the Wold, and the one person who is portrayed with some vividness, Henry Williams, the skeptic, is the image to which Carlyle feels closest, almost an alter ego. He is the one man whom Wotton could really understand, the only one who receives unstinted, unqualified praise; he is the only person with whom Wotton discusses the other inhabitants of the House of the Wold and his own nature. Williams represents a positively oriented, though still skeptical, Carlyle.

Walter, the rival lover, though he belongs to the romantic plot, also makes his appearance at the House of the Wold with suggestions of a darker side of Carlyle's nature. Even though he represents those unconscious and negatively destructive undercurrents, he exercises a powerful attraction upon Wotton.

> To Wotton, again, deeply as he reckoned himself entitled to detest and dread this Walter, there was a singular dominion in his presence; a power, which, whether it were benignant or the contrary, you could not but in part respect . . . his compact, sinewy frame impressed you in its soldierlike repose with an idea of strength beyond his stature, which, however, was tall and portly; while the thick black locks clustering in careless profusion round that face . . . all bespoke a character of singular vehemence and vigor, a striking union of passionate force with the strictest self-control. Yet this self-control did not invite you, but rather silently beckoned you away; for this, too, seemed passionate, the

result not of love, but of pride; not of principle,
but of calculation; its very strength seemed dangerous. (*WR*, 108–09)

From this point on the condemnation is explicit, but
the encounter is sufficient to disrupt Wotton's mental
repose and to send him fleeing into the mountains.

This use of the double as a process of self-discovery
seems to be one of the most effective and original things
in the novel (Wotton, Walter, Williams: the three
"W's" may provide an interesting unconscious linkage).
As one of the most common literary techniques of the
nineteenth century,[4] it undergoes constant modifications
throughout Carlyle's works. Its presence here seems almost accidental and unconscious, however, and it remains for later works to take up the theme with more
literary awareness and maturity.

Wotton Reinfred, Carlyle's only novelistic venture,
will scarcely qualify as the traditional German romance
he apparently hoped it would be. While it possesses
techniques and themes of Goethe's *Werther* and *Wilhelm Meister's Apprenticeship,* it remains a pastiche of
the two, containing elements of both yet lying some-
where between them with neither the violent psychological turmoil of the former nor the steady progress toward peaceful serenity of the latter. Carlyle rightly put
the novel aside to explore his themes and techniques
and their interrelationship in the essays I have already
discussed, but when he was ready to write *Sartor Resartus,* he returned to *Wotton*'s autobiographical sec-

4. It appears most explicitly in works such as Poe's *William Wil-
son,* Dostoyevsky's *The Double,* and Stevenson's *Doctor Jekyll and
Mr. Hyde;* less explicitly, it is the organizing method in works such
as Goethe's *Faust,* Melville's *Moby Dick* and *Billy Budd,* and Kierkegaard's *Either/Or.* It is, of course, related to the device of projection that comes to the fore in *Heroes* and the later social and
historical works of Carlyle.

tions and debates because they had represented the most personal and central subject of self-discovery.

NEW SOUNDINGS IN "SIGNS OF THE TIMES" AND "CHARACTERISTICS"

Some chance wind of Fame blew your name to me perhaps two years ago as the author of papers which I had already distinguished, (as indeed it was very easy to do,) from the mass of English periodical Criticism as by far the most original & profound essays of the day the works of a man of Faith as well as Intellect sportive as well as learned & who belonging to the despairing & deriding class of philosophers was not ashamed to hope & to speak sincerely.

Emerson,
Correspondence of Emerson and Carlyle

Before embarking on a detailed analysis of *Sartor Resartus,* two long essays, "Signs of the Times" (1829) and "Characteristics" (1831), should be examined. Each offers new qualities of Carlyle's voice and methods which the essays and *Wotton Reinfred* could not allow and which play an important part in the makeup and problems of *Sartor.*

In each of these essays Carlyle is his own philosopher. No longer merely a student of German literature, he is now shaping his own religious vision and prophetic role. Working with such simple polarities as mechanics vs. dynamics in "Signs of the Times" and the silence of the unconscious vs. the noise of the conscious in "Characteristics," he allows each of his terms to move out over a wider social framework and utilizes them to examine all of society's institutions. Both essays offer ironic visions, satiric extensions of mechanism and consciousness, as these evil forces make their way into all human enterprises, gradually eradicating the vitality and spirituality

that once filled them. We are reminded of Pope's *Dunciad*—and the constant references to Pope throughout these essays and the book reviews show that Carlyle had this poem and its vision very much in mind when analyzing the threats to his age.

As we shall later see, however, Carlyle's own voice is more problematic than Pope's, for he is more involved in the activity that he condemns. Though he laughs at the possibility of a Review of Reviews, he himself is a book reviewer. Though he opposes a science of mechanics, he nevertheless seeks a science of dynamics. He despises consciousness but must work with its tools for a new "theory" of the universe. The sense of ambivalence, the problematic aura, the increased feeling of nightmare, crisis, and frenzy are all more suggestive of the desperation embodied in such contemporary satires as *Catch*-22 or *Dr. Strangelove*. A weird blend of realism and fantasy, an immediate sense of a threat to the self emerges.

Hartley's vibrations and vibratiuncles, one would think, were material and mechanical enough; but our Continental neighbours have gone still farther. One of their philosophers has lately discovered, that "as the liver secretes bile, so does the brain secrete thought"; which astonishing discovery Dr. Cabanis, more lately still in his *Rapports du Physique et du Morale de l'Homme,* has pushed into its minutest development. The metaphysical philosophy of the last inquirer is certainly no shadowy or unsubstantial one. He fairly lays open our moral structure with his dissecting-knives and real metal probes; and exhibits it to the inspection of mankind by Leuwenhoek microscopes, and inflation with the anatomical blowpipe. Thought, he is inclined to

hold, is still secreted by the brain; but then Poetry and Religion . . . are "a product of the smaller intestines"! (*E, 2, 65*)

Similarly, the listing of reviews, pamphlets, and societies in "Characteristics" points away from Pope's more unified threat of dunces, writing to make a reputation and fortune, toward the modern nightmare city, a computerized, paper society, like the one described in Lewis Mumford's *The City in History,* in which the people who have designed machines to help them are finally the victims of the machines.

As these negative terms, mechanism and consciousness, are allowed to widen, so too the positive terms, dynamics and unconsciousness, are more broadly contemplated—but in a different fashion, with a tone of lament at their passing and a glance at their original idealization in old institutions. Each of the terms is played over all the segments of society—politics, education, literature, religion, metaphysics, economics. Each offers a new perspective on these areas and a way of showing how they are linked within certain trends and impulses, a sense of the common fate that dooms them.

As philosophy this polarization of terminology and its rather indiscriminate application may not be very subtle, and it would obviously be easy to point out all the logical fallacies in these essays: the revision, illegitimate extension, and obvious self-contradictions of terms at certain points. But these essays do not convince logically. Their rhetorical and aesthetic conviction stems from the ability of the terms to pick up new applications and deepen in significance. The rhetorical strategy is akin to Schopenhauer's *The World as Will and Idea,* which, while philosophically argued, convinces, not by its terminology or logic, but by the number of examples and applications of the idea of will, the power of the vi-

58

sionary seer who can perceive this vast movement in human enterprises. The metaphor of clothes will work in the same manner in *Sartor*.

The polarization, to be sure, has an initial disadvantage, much as Schopenhauer's does: it furnishes a kind of fixed opposition in which one set of terms will triumph over the other—dynamics over mechanics, unconsciousness over consciousness, will over idea. In Carlyle's case the denigration of mechanism and consciousness produces at the beginning of each essay a general sense that Carlyle is very reactionary, a preacher recalling men to old truths that they have forgotten, a foe of anything modern. He laments that nothing seems to be done "by old natural methods" (*E*, 2, 60), and he glamorizes the feudal medieval society when action was spontaneous, not conscious (*E*, 3, 8).

Yet while these idealizations of the past, recalls to primitive truths, are always an important part of Carlyle's thought, they are never an ultimate program. In fact they usually serve only as a model for redefinition, for the recovery of relevance in the past. The essays, split at the beginning with their polarities, present the workings out of a new voice that will include both mechanism and dynamics, unconsciousness and consciousness. At times they suggest merely an inversion, a return to inwardness, vitality, and natural force as the source of all impulses within the self; at other points they convey an equipoise, a balance; and, in an even more complicated vein, they occasionally portray a warring dialectic, something entirely new, like the warfare between reason and energy in Blake, a sense of contradictions as the goad of energy itself.

The rhythm of each essay, however much its logic may be distorted, is that of an initial lament for lost truths, an attempt to induce in the reader the sense of being shackled. This is followed first by a recall to those prim-

itive truths and then by a modulation in which the mixture of the new and the old is tolerated and even seen as a way to higher growth, as part of the irreversible historical process itself. At the end of each essay the voice of the prophet becomes "upbeat"; he absorbs both the threats of the conscious and the mechanical and glimpses the new society in a final vision.

"Signs of the Times" is the simpler and the clearer of the two essays. Its tone is more optimistically hortatory, its satire less troubled by anguish than that of "Characteristics." Its aim is more simply that of a warning, an Ecclesiastes-like lament, that there is "a mighty change in our whole manner of existence. . . . Men are grown mechanical in head and heart, as well as in hand. They have lost faith in individual endeavour, and in natural force, of any kind. . . . We may trace this tendency in all the great manifestations of our time" (*E, 2,* 62–63). Carlyle simply aims to tell men that there is a "science of *Dynamics* in man's fortunes and nature, as well as of *Mechanics,*" and that it "treats of, and practically addresses, the primary, unmodified forces and energies of man, the mysterious springs of Love, and Fear, and Wonder, of Enthusiasm, Poetry, Religion, all which have a truly vital and *infinite* character" (*E, 2,* 68).

Though there is little exploration in the essay, and far more preaching and prophecy, Carlyle nevertheless emerges eventually with a kind of marriage of heaven and hell. Undue cultivation of the outward and mechanical is obviously a cause of ill, but by the essay's end it is clear that "undue cultivation of the inward or Dynamical province leads to idle, visionary, impracticable courses, and especially in rude eras, to Superstition and Fanaticism, with their long train of baleful and well-known evils." The streak of skepticism in Carlyle's attitude toward Voltaire and the distrust of mysticism in

his attitude toward Kant and Novalis have already been noted, and if Carlyle, like the editor of *Sartor,* feels a loyalty to the traditions of the English past, his vision is not of a return to that past but to its virtues transformed by modernity. He is perfectly aware that "by our skill in Mechanism, it has come to pass, that in the management of external things we excel all ages" and that this contains the possibility of vision and excitement. He may hate machines if they threaten to invade the inner life, but the contemplation of a steam engine can produce a highly charged sense of power within as well as outside of the self. Thus, as the essay advances, Carlyle practically abandons any attempt to define the limits of each of his terms, so hopelessly have they become intertwined, for they "work into one another, and by means of one another, so intricately and inseparably" (*E, 2, 73*). In the "upbeat" ending of the essay—partly determined, no doubt, by its sermonistic form, but partly also by his excitement about action, increased force, multiplicity, and upheaval as a carrier of the new society—Carlyle exclaims that "this age also is advancing. Its very unrest, its ceaseless activity, its discontent contains matter of promise" (*E, 2, 80*). Mechanism is no longer merely a foe, but an active principle of force itself, propelling life onward. Carlyle reaches the same conclusion as Blake in *The Marriage of Heaven and Hell,* and, like Blake, he does not explore the exact relationship or limits of his dialectical forces.

Those two hostile influences (mechanism and dynamism) which always exist in human things, and on the constant intercommunion of which depends their health and safety, had lain in separate masses, accumulating through generations, and France was the scene of their fiercest explosions. (*E, 2, 82*)

Here, in fact, there is a glimpse of the Blakean Carlyle of *The French Revolution,* for whom force is not merely the static underlying power of nature and self but a conglomeration of fierce dynamic energies, repressed by a dead and hypocritical civilization. Noticeably Carlyle's metaphors of mass and explosion seem more specifically scientific than Blake's.

"Characteristics" begins in a quieter vein, endorsing a health which is silent, un-self-conscious, in touch with the silent springs of nature. But, though it might be called less dynamic than "Signs of the Times," the essay is fundamentally more troublesome and points to many of the thematic problems in *Sartor.* In its constant re-definition of terms, its glib attempts to cover up differences that threaten to destroy a harmonious vision, it also shows Carlyle's weakness as a systematic philosopher and thinker. Change is affirmed as the basic principle behind social forms, but any of the possibilities of meaningless flux, any of the dissolutions of self-identity, that such a philosophy might imply are quickly covered over by an assertion of the transcendence of eternity upon which change must rest. By the end of the essay Carlyle has chosen to be the preacher, not the thinker.

Carlyle again begins by polarizing the two forces and ends by fusing them. But since he is more conscious than mechanical, the fusion is stronger and more significant. Fraught with implications about Carlyle's art, it points to an odd mixture of preaching and thinking that will become even more strange in *Sartor.* The world of the vital unconscious is soon dismissed as a dream of paradise, "an impossible dream . . . some luxurious Lubberland" (*E, 3, 28*). Carlyle seems to locate it in a world of innocence, analogous to Blake's, or in a childhood harmony like Wordsworth's when "we knew not that we had limbs, we only lifted, hurled, and leapt" (*E, 3, 2*). This dream has passed, however, and to

revive it is to flee into the Blakean state of Beulah, not to reenter Eden. "We stand here too conscious of many things: with Knowledge, the symptom of Derangement, we must even do our best to restore a little Order" (*E, 3, 3*). This is not only the herald of the voice of the editor of *Sartor,* working with the tools of a utilitarian, self-conscious age to establish his vision; it is also the prelude to a Teufelsdröckh, who also suffers from self-consciousness and some derangement, and who will extend society's sense of diseased consciousness by going one step further along the line of compendiums, reviews, philosophies, and moral systems by publishing a Philosophy of Clothes and by being a Professor of Things in General. Teufelsdröckh will participate in the disease even as he attempts to uproot it. We must remember that he writes both a philosophy of *clothes,* which themselves embrace the highest and the lowest in a unitive vision, and a *philosophy* of clothes, an unsystematic system that continues the work of the philosophers. Carlyle seeks to join the two principles of consciousness and unconsciousness as he had mechanism and dynamism. He wants both a science of *dynamics* and a *science* of dynamics.

Just as consciousness as a polarity in this essay covers more troublesome problems than mechanics did, so too does the unconscious absorb more problematic areas. Part of the difficulty is merely logical; the term begins to cover contradictory ideas. But some of the difficulties point to darker problems; consciousness begins to appear as a kind of gift, wisely letting us see only the surface of nature, hiding us from a mysterious, unconscious, and often occult universe, filled with mystery, doubt, and governed by ceaseless change and death.

But Nature, it might seem, strives, like a kind mother, to hide from us even this, that she is a mys-

tery: she will have us rest on her beautiful and awful bosom as if it were our secure home; on the bottomless, boundless Deep, whereon all human things fearfully and wonderfully swim, she will have us walk and build, as if the film which supported us there (which any scratch of a bare bodkin will rend asunder, any sputter of a pistol-shot instantaneously burn up) were no film, but a solid rock-foundation. Forever in the neighbourhood of an inevitable Death, man can forget that he is born to die. (*E, 3, 3–4*)

Soon even doubt, which appeared to be the foremost villain of consciousness, of diseased metaphysics, becomes identified with the vital mystery of the unconscious in nature. The picture of the universe is obviously supposed to suggest grandeur, mystery, perhaps the power of a terrible God as in Jonathan Edwards' similar picture of sinners in the hand of an angry God of a more orthodox age. Yet this uplifting sense of infinity pales before the darker overtones.

We, the whole species of Mankind, and our whole existence and history, are but a floating speck in the illimitable ocean of the All; yet *in* that ocean; indissoluble portion thereof; partaking of its infinite tendencies: borne this way and that by its deep-swelling tides, and grand ocean currents;—of which what faintest chance is there that we would ever exhaust the significance, ascertain the goings and comings? A region of Doubt, therefore, hovers forever in the background; in Action alone can we have certainty. Nay, properly Doubt is the indispensable, inexhaustible material whereon Action works, which Action has to fashion into Certainty and Reality; only on a canvas of Darkness, such is man's

way of being, could the many coloured picture of our Life paint itself and shine. (*E, 3, 25–26*)

Blake would find in this Carlyle the worship of nature as Urizenic mystery, a lowering of man's powers of imagination, indeed a retreat back to the Newtonian mechanical universe. But if the overt message of action recedes and the uplifting grandeur of infinity subsides, still another kind of grandeur does emerge—a troubling and problematic vision that will occasion more exciting aesthetic methods in *Sartor*. Beneath the world of consciousness, nature becomes a troublesome world of darkness and death and doubt, an undifferentiated all, a current of flux and will. In such a picture, man can easily become the victim of a remorseless force, losing his identity as he is enslaved by time and trapped by ceaseless change.

Schopenhauer saw the world in much the same light in *The World as Will and Idea*. For him man was a floating speck in a remorseless all-devouring nature. With his more self-conscious and philosophical imagination, however, he also saw that man alone of all creatures had an idea of that force, that aesthetically through art man could contain a vision of that will and heighten his existence by joining with it and thus triumph over it, that ascetically through sainthood man could kill that will in himself, could renounce the will to live and therefore defeat it.

Like Schopenhauer's universe, Carlyle's is fundamentally one of process, movement, change. "All human things are, have been and forever will be, in Movement and Change" (*E, 3, 37*). But Carlyle recoils from what he fears, the "dark shoreless sea of Pyrrhonism" (*E, 3, 38*), the aimless and hopeless human condition such a fundamental belief would entail. Change is not the noumena, but merely another phenomenon, the body of

the soul. The past does not depart, for "Time itself reposes on Eternity" (E, 3, 38).

It is partly true that here Carlyle looked into the abyss and then suddenly clamped a lid over it. Certainly the earlier essays all contain condemnations of wanderers, people of noble soul who found no center to their lives, who ended like Werner or Byron or Burns in dissolution, in that very world of ceaseless flux and change that destroyed their identity. But, despite this fear, Carlyle's fundamental drive is toward a universe of process and change defined by energy, vitality, and force. The "upbeat" ending of the essay returns to the active possibilities inherent in change, "the product simply of *increased resources* which the old *methods* can no longer administer; of new wealth which the old coffers will no longer contain . . . the increase of social resources . . . the new omnipotence of the Steam-engine . . . the real increase, increase of Men; of human Force" (E, 3, 39). Thus Carlyle's action philosophy, his clarion call to duty, is on the one hand a shutting off of speculation, doubt, the fear of change, but on the other hand a way of allying the self actively with the very fundamental fact of the universe, energy, motion, action.

In a brilliant essay on Schopenhauer, Thomas Mann has characterized him—and we may apply this to Carlyle too—as a pessimistic humanist whose "reverence for the mission of man . . . outweighs all misanthropy and supplies the corrective to (his) loathing of humanity." For Schopenhauer is of "a bipolar nature, full of contrasts and conflicts, tortured and violent; after its own pattern it must experience the world: as instinct and spirit, passion and knowledge, 'will,' and 'idea.' " [1]

1. Thomas Mann, "Schopenhauer," *Essays* (New York, Vintage paperback, 1958), p. 297. See also Books Two and Four of *The World as Will and Idea* (Garden City, Dophin paperback, 1961). Mann's essay is, I think, the best comprehensive account of Schopenhauer's philosophy and its relation to modern literature and psychology.

Mann locates this torment in Schopenhauer's all-devouring sexual urge as it conflicts with his mighty intellectu-
ality; in short, he sees the problem of nature as also one
of Schopenhauer's interior nature. Certainly each of
these polarities is far less active in either Carlyle's
universe or self, but the analogy seems apt nonetheless,
for the fundamental polarities are equally at work in
Carlyle—the need to see the world as energy, motion,
drama, change, power, and the need for order, coherence, belief, principles of action. The drive toward fact,
time, reality is contrasted with the drive toward spirit,
eternity, infinity.

Carlyle's torment is less polarized, less painful than
Schopenhauer's, and his solution exists in another more
optimistic and humanly available dimension. Mann has
shown how Schopenhauer was never the ascetic and only
aspired to be such in his philosophy; he was in fact the
artist. Carlyle's solution is only partly ascetic and partly
philosophic, stoic; it is almost entirely aesthetic. The
soldier, who hovers on the brink of sainthood, may recall Schopenhauer's final triumph of the saint who shuts
the remorseless will out by killing it, but Carlyle's saint
and soldier, who can also be the artist like himself, is
open to that will and united with it in action. Carlyle's
soldier is closer to Schopenhauer's artist, the lonely man
of genius who at moments succeeds in uniting himself
with the world will and understanding it intuitively in
his art. Carlyle's fundamental move is toward the act of
soldiering itself—an ideal which he will later take quite
literally—but at this point the gap between action and
writing is not so severe. He too is a soldier of a special
sort.

To summarize, then, these two essays are important
steps forward because they provide a widening of terms
in which key words absorb and accrete new meanings, a
fundamental technique of Carlyle's method in *Sartor*,
where the idea of clothes dislocates old perceptions,

sharpens new ones, and leads into imaginative vision. Through this very widening the essays provide a larger social platform: problems of politics and economics are touched on significantly for the first time and are shown to be akin to the previous themes that occupied Carlyle. Finally, each of the essays, particularly "Characteristics," shows how Carlyle's methods enabled him to approach increasingly complex problems which then generated new imaginative techniques for the exploration of multiplicity. These are not merely calls to static truths of a rather conservative cast but are workings out of extremely problematic situations in the light of those truths and ultimately are total redefinitions of them. The essays clearly reveal that Carlyle is not fundamentally a philosopher, but a special kind of artist who moves his readers to new awareness not by the philosophical statements, epigrams, allusions, and quotations in his works, but by his aesthetic manipulation of this material within a deeper and more personal exploratory manner.

◄§ 2 §►

SARTOR RESARTUS:
THE PROPHET FINDS
HIS LITERARY ROLE

Can it be that this humour [of Teufelsdröckh] proceeds from a despair of finding a contemporary audience & so the Prophet feels at liberty to utter his message in droll sounds.

Emerson,
Correspondence of Emerson and Carlyle

You [Emerson] say well that I take up that attitude
because I have no known public, am *alone* under the
Heavens, speaking into friendly or unfriendly space;
add only that I will not defend such an attitude, that
I call it questionable, tentative, and only the best that
I in these mad times could conveniently hit upon.

Carlyle,
Correspondence of Emerson and Carlyle

Sartor Resartus, Carlyle's great creative work produced
during the years of seclusion at Craigenputtock, is the
fitting climax to his period of withdrawal. In it he unfolds the new dynamic vision to the fullest multidimen-
sional explanation of man's self, nature, and society.
Even its first chapter, "Preliminary," though the tone is
often satiric, presents the Clothes Philosophy as the necessary complement to present-day science and heralds it
as the beginning of a new order to be achieved by
"planting new standards, founding new habitable col-

onies, in the immeasurable circumambient realm of Nothingness and Night!" (*SR*, 4/7).[1]

The Clothes Philosophy is dynamic not only in its content but also in its method of presentation. *Sartor Resartus* is deliberately unsystematic. As a philosophy of wonder and experience, it resists all "Attorney-Logic" which allows one to " 'explain' all, 'account' for all (and) 'believe' nothing of it" (*SR*, 54/69). The Philosophy of Clothes makes a virtue of its surface chaos in order to comprehend more fully the total nature of life. With its intuitive, imaginative method, it attempts at every point to embrace a kind of totality. Carlyle understood this quality of the work when he presented a version of Book One to *Fraser's Magazine* in 1830 and described it in a Shakespearean phrase as "a very singular piece, I assure you! It glances from Heaven to Earth and back again in a strange satirical frenzy, whether *fine* or not remains to be seen." [2]

When Carlyle decided to expand the original "Thoughts on Clothes," he saw his task primarily as an expansion of the Clothes Philosophy through all forms of life. "I can devise some more biography for Teufelsdrock [sic]; give a second deeper part, in the same vein, leading through Religion and the nature of Society, and Lord knows what." [3] From the perspective of clothes, he could view human experience, religion, and society dynamically and could thus achieve unity. This perspective did not neatly pigeonhole these dimensions of life in a static mechanical system but sought to grasp their

1. The second page reference here is to the Odyssey Press edition of Charles Frederick Harrold (New York, 1937). This edition has copious annotations which give the sources of most of Carlyle's German quotations and variations.

2. Letter to his brother John, 21 Jan. 1831, *Letters, 1826–36*, p. 183.

3. Ibid.

organic unfolding in time, to delineate a natural history of mind and civilization, and to show how each finally grew into a system of interrelationships, of "organic filaments," into a complete garment in which "Nature (was) not an Aggregate but a Whole" (*SR*, 55/71).

The idea of clothes and the naked man beneath them also suggested the distinction between phenomena and noumena in Kant's philosophy and, as Carlyle read Kant, a distinction between a rather utilitarian Understanding and a deeply religious Reason. He sought no Kantian system, however, and no dogma, but rather the progressive unfolding of the various forms of life from an initial concrete level in which clothes are really clothes (fig leaves, aprons) to a final abstract plane wherein "all Symbols are properly Clothes; that all Forms whereby Spirit manifests itself to sense, whether outwardly or in the imagination, are Clothes" (*SR*, 215/270). Though the Clothes Philosophy unfolds progressively into larger and more abstract dimensions, the empirical plane is not abandoned. Rather, it is seen as pointing toward the total symbolic vision which at every moment includes it. All of life simultaneously blends the infinite with the finite and both conceals and reveals the godlike force operating through the symbols. "Those ages . . . are accounted the noblest which can the best recognize symbolical worth, and prize it the highest" (*SR*, 177/222). Since the Clothes Philosophy strives to unite simultaneously all reality, empirical and imaginative, external and internal, the level of the concrete and the specific can never be denied.

Carlyle did not merely turn his weapons of satire, irony, and invective against the mechanists, the system builders, and the utilitarians. He also sought to meet them head on with his own vision and to incorporate them within it. Because the philosophy of mechanism, espoused by logic acting independently, if accepted as

one's total method and vision, leads only to death, "Not our Logical, Mensurative faculty, but our Imaginative one is King over us" (SR, 177/222). It is this logical philosophy, pursued to its limits, which brings Teufelsdröckh to a spiritual death wherein he sees "the Universe . . . all void of Life, of Purpose, of Volition, even of Hostility; it was one huge, dead, immeasurable Steam-Engine, rolling on, in its dead indifference, to grind me limb from limb" (SR, 133/164). Mechanism alone as a philosophy of life leads only to a "descendentalism" in which man appears like the jacketed Gouda cows (SR, 45/57) and "a forked straddling animal with bandy legs." [4] Transcendentalism, the Clothes Philosophy, does not deny the truths of descendentalism but transforms these truths into a basis for building a vision of man as "also a Spirit, and unutterable Mystery of Mysteries" (SR, 44/57).

An overall view of the book reveals clearly that the movement of the Clothes Philosophy is organic. (The work's haphazardness will be discussed later; for the moment it is easier to emphasize the organic strand in isolation, since it coincides with the book's more overtly stated vision.) Clothes as a metaphor provides a method of attaining a vision that is at once concrete and abstract, flexible and organically formative. Thoroughly grounded in empirical realities, the image of clothes expands, absorbing such worlds as mechanism, mathematics, industrialism, nature, and religion until it nears an ideal of unitive knowledge and wisdom.

Beginning in "Werden (Origin and successive Improvement) of Clothes" (SR, 39/51), the exposition remains, for a time, on a concrete, often lighthearted historical level, a whimsical historical fashion plate. From this selection of curiosities, it moves into a "Speculative-

4. With references to origins in Swift and Shakespeare's *King Lear*.

Philosophical portion, which treats of their *Wirken*, or Influences" (*SR*, 40/51). In this section of Book One, the "moral, political, even religious Influences of Clothes" are explored, and "Society" is shown to be "founded upon Cloth" (*SR*, 40/51). Here the real clothes are stripped from man, and society stands naked before Teufelsdröckh. "The Clothes fly-off the whole dramatic corps; and Dukes, Grandees, Bishops, Generals, Anointed Presence itself, every mother's son of them, stands straddling there, not a shirt on them" (*SR*, 48/61). But such a descendentalism is only a preparation for a final vision of transcendentalism; man is stripped only that he may be exalted "beyond the visible Heavens, almost to an equality with the Gods" (*SR*, 51/65). Frequent allusions recall Lear and the Fool upon the heath, their divestment and preparation for transcendence. Clothes now take on a relative quality; they even become the flesh garment that reveals the inmost godly force behind man. Man, life, nature, time, heaven, and earth all become vestures of the eternal. "Whatsoever sensibly exists, whatsoever represents Spirit to Spirit, is properly a Clothing, a suit of Raiment, put on for a season, and to be laid off" (*SR*, 58/74). Then, in one final burst, the metaphor of clothes leaps beyond sensibilia and embraces the totality of existence.

> Thus in this one pregnant subject of CLOTHES, rightly understood, is included all that men have thought, dreamed, done, and been: the whole External Universe and what it holds is but Clothing, and the essence of all Science lies in the PHILOSO- PHY OF CLOTHES. (*SR*, 58/74)

Book Two, containing the autobiography of Teufelsdröckh, is the necessary complement to the clothes volume and the fulfillment of a true *Lebensphilosophie*. From a vision of wholeness in the innocence of child-

hood the hero falls into despair and isolation, a victim of false love and the monsters mechanism and skepticism. But this reduction, like the reduction of man to naked nothingness by descendentalism, is only a preparation for a more exalted vision. The Everlasting No precedes the Everlasting Yea. In his spiritual rebirth, Teufelsdröckh discovers that "the Universe is not dead and demoniacal, a charnel-house with spectres; but godlike and my Father's" (SR, 150/188). In the Everlasting Yea, he fully awakens to "a new Heaven and a new Earth" (SR, 149/186). This experience suddenly merges indistinguishably with the Clothes Philosophy itself, but not without contributing its quality of lived experience to that philosophy. The editor has discovered that Teufelsdröckh's autobiographical fragments are "partly a mystification . . . some more or less fantastic Adumbration, symbolically, perhaps significantly enough, shadowing forth the same," only "hieroglyphically" authentic, and not "literally so" (SR, 161/202).[5] While it is true that such an admission tends to collapse the hoax by indicating that both Teufelsdröckh and his philosophy are aspects of the author Carlyle, it is also true that it points to an archetypal, mythical, and paradigmatic quality of action in the life of Teufelsdröckh, pushing it further into the direction of philosophy instead of life, but with the suggestion that the new source of the new myth is within the self rather than external to it.

The full expansion of this philosophy is properly postponed because it needs its autobiographical basis in Book Two. Book Three then returns principally to the philosophy itself in its most mystic significance—society, tradition, politics, and especially religion, "the inmost

5. Already referred to in note 10, p. 43. See Froude, *First Forty Years*, *1*, 81. "Nothing in 'Sartor Resartus' [Carlyle says] is fact; symbolical myth all, except that of the incident in the Rue St. Thomas de l'Enfer."

Pericardial and Nervous Tissue, which ministers Life and warm Circulation to the whole" (*SR*, 172/216). Religious experience is the expansive force behind the entire Book, and it permeates all forms of society, raising them ultimately to a religious significance.

The religious keynote set in the earlier discussion of "The Everlasting Yea" is carried over into the first chapter of Book Three, in which George Fox with his perennial suit of leather escapes from oppression and night into perfect day. The mystic meaning is maintained in all the following chapters through "Natural Supernaturalism." The relationship of present man to his ancestors is called "a living, literal, *Communion of Saints*" (*SR*, 197/247), and the "Hero-Divinity" (*SR*, 201/252) is the godlike revealed in man—the "cornerstone of living-rock" (*SR*, 200/251), the foundation of the new church. Literature is the new religion, with its "voice of Prophecy" (*SR*, 201/252), "Church-*Homiletic*," and "*Liturgy*" (*SR*, 201/253). Man's history is a "perpetual Evangel" and "Immensity," "a temple" (*SR*, 202/253–54). Society achieves its spiritual rebirth in the death and resurrection of the phoenix.

In all of these instances the all-encompassing basic energy is natural but religious in intent. This expansive religious movement reaches its limits in the chapter on "Natural Supernaturalism," where the last two phantasms, space and time, are rent asunder. The Clothes Philosophy is complete with the disappearance of all clothes as the movement of spiritual vision which the book portrays is achieved. "In a word (Teufelsdröckh) has looked fixedly on Existence, till, one after the other, its earthly hulls and garnitures have all melted away; and now, to his rapt vision, the interior celestial Holy of Holies lies disclosed" (*SR*, 203/255). This is the ultimate in religious expansion. With the time-annihilating Fortunatus hat, one shoots "at will from the Fire-Crea-

tion of the World to its Fire-Consummation" (SR, 208/
261), achieving a total biblical vision from Genesis to
the Apocalypse, an encyclopedic sweep. Mystery is here
the pervasive force; man's life is a passage "through Mystery to Mystery" (SR, 212/267), and every event is a
miracle.

But once this exposition of the Clothes Philosophy has
achieved its fullest expansion, once the total living vision of man and the universe is attained, new problems
arise. Expansion no longer appears merely as expansion
but also as its opposite, contraction. The Fire-Creation
and the Fire-Destruction are indeed the most opposed
poles within the universe and the imagination, but
when they are yoked together in a single unitive vision,
when the process of time which keeps them as poles is
destroyed by the annihilation of time itself, and when
they are centered upon a self that simultaneously lives
in them, all expansive qualities seem to disappear. Fire-
Creation and Fire-Destruction collapse into identities; a
world without distinctions is created. Every action becomes miraculous; past, present, and future merge into
an "is" which becomes identical with "eternity"; and
the self lives beyond time in a mystic, undifferentiated,
almost fluid world of light and flames, with "heart set
flaming in the Light-sea of celestial wonder" (SR, 210/
264).

This process of contraction, with its possibilities of a
total self and its dangers of dissolution and collapse, is
traced even more fully in the development of the self,
Book Two's necessary complement to the unfolding of
the Clothes Philosophy. "Clothes" has already been
shown to be a relative term which only gradually ac-
quires the stability of the final state of symbolism. But
the self is an ever-present center, and even at the moments when it feels itself in dissolution or seeks its own

definition, it remains as that to which all experience is referred.

The self, indeed, opens to the most expansive possibilities of the universe, possibilities inconceivable in any mechanical or merely logical philosophy. But this expansive universe ultimately finds its meaning in terms of a central self that seeks its own stability. The picture of Teufelsdröckh meditatively seated above the "life-circulation" (*SR*, 15/20) of Weissnichtwo—with his windows open to all four corners of the earth, with his perch midway between the confusion of the life-flood below him and the stability of the eternal heavens above him—epitomizes the perspective with which the philosophical self views reality. The aim of the self is to bring the lowest, in all its complexity, multiplicity, and confusion, into relationship with the highest, the polestar, in its stability and eternity. If the quest is successful, self, universe, and eternity achieve a new interrelated meaning that is at once grand, total, and unified. The expansive complexity of vast complicated pictures of the life-circulation, then, is merely a preliminary to the central epistemological act in which the ME can confront a total vision of the NOT ME. Thus,

> The world, with its loud trafficking, retires into the distance; and, through the paper-hangings, and stone-walls, and thick-plied tissues of Commerce and Polity, and all the living and lifeless integuments (of Society and a Body), wherewith your Existence sits surrounded,—the sight reaches forth into the void Deep, and you are alone with the Universe, and silently commune with it, as one mysterious Presence with another. (*SR*, 41/53)

Since the Clothes Philosophy expands both to reveal the interrelationship of all things and ultimately to collapse

77

these relationships into a mystic but undifferentiated unity much like the "void Deep" that is also a "mysterious Presence," the self remains as a primary referential center in this perhaps otherwise open universe. The role of the self in discovering a center that will render ME and NOT ME is implicit from the beginning in the description of its activity.

> Many a deep glance, and often with unspeakable precision, has he (Teufelsdröckh) cast into mysterious Nature, and the still more mysterious Life of Man. Wonderful it is with what cutting words, now and then, he severs asunder the confusion; shears down, were it furlongs deep, into the true centre of the matter; and there not only hits the nail on the head, but with crushing force smites it home, and buries it. (SR, 23/30)

This quest for the self, while a correlate of the Clothes Philosophy and ultimately identifiable with it, offers a different development and new problems not so apparent in the unrolling of the Clothes Philosophy proper. Book Two contains negations which the forward-moving and positive expansion of the Clothes Philosophy could not treat. These are the problems of meaninglessness, emptiness, isolation, necessity, and evil. (Ultimately Book One will be seen to treat several of these problems in a more subtle way than Book Two.)

The opening chapters of Book Two, "Genesis" and "Idyllic," are designed to illustrate a world free from these problems, the world of the child. Here Teufelsdröckh's clothes are whole, a unified garment, a single piece of cloth (SR, 73/92). He is born under Libra, the Balance (SR, 66/83), and his world is a motionless world of heavenly, Eden-like harmony. He is aware of his heavenly origin; though he cannot recall his father, the mysterious stranger who left him with the Futterals,

he nevertheless feels close to him. His is a world in which nature is close to man: the flowers struggle through the windows; he eats out of doors and is friendly with the swine (*SR*, 74/92). It is also a world of order, with its methodic pile of garden tools (*SR*, 66/83), its recurrent mode of life. Moreover, it is a world with itself as a center—its linden tree under which the townsmen gather (*SR*, 72–73/91), its little brook that leads out into larger rivers and thence into the universe itself (*SR*, 72/91), its stagecoach that knits the town to the rest of the world (*SR*, 76/95).

This awareness of expansion and infinity, this possibility of "organic filaments," is somehow static, however. It is Entepfuhl (Duckpond) that stands in the middle of a country, of a world (*SR*, 76/95), and Entepfuhl and the self are identical. The world has a center, but it is merely a point. Teufelsdröckh's world is scarcely able to embrace the complexities of modern existence and is even unable to grow into an awareness of these complexities. Like Blake's world of innocence, it can be both life-fulfilling yet life-denying. In the world of the child, time, which can be villainous but which alone offers the possibilities of growth, does not exist.

> The young spirit has awakened out of Eternity, and knows not what we mean by Time; as yet Time is no fast-hurrying stream, but a sportful, sunlit ocean, years to the child are as ages . . . and in a motionless Universe, we taste, what afterwards in this quick-whirling Universe, is forever denied us, the balm of Rest. (*SR*, 72/90)

But soon, in the home, and with the approach of school, "the ring of Necessity, whereby we are all begirt" makes its appearance. Teufelsdröckh leaves his timeless child's world of Entepfuhl only to be confronted with images of brutality in his schoolmates (the

dog with the tin kettle tied to its tail) and the "hide-
bound pedants" of the Hinterschlag Gymnasium. The
gradual dominance of this ring of Necessity "till in after-
years it almost over-shadowed my whole canopy, and
threatened to engulf me in final night" (SR, 78/97), the
battle with this force and the victory over it, transforming it into a ring of duty, is the psychological process of
self-discovery chronicled in this Book. Unlike the confusing process of Wotton Reinfred, which failed to join
the problem of love with the problem of meaning, Book
Two of Sartor presents various strands of development
in which the self becomes isolated, empty, and despairing, but each of these strands finds its issue in the central problem of meaninglessness. The positive movement
of these developments foreshadows the final affirmation
of meaning in "The Everlasting Yea." The failure of
love is presented quite independently, with its own psychological rise and fall, but the outcome, unlike that of
Wotton, places the stress on false love and false friendship, the falsity being but another manifestation of necessity and contingency within the universe. All problems
are viewed as contributing to the problem of meaning:
Teufelsdröckh's extreme passivity and intellectual pride
that isolate him from his fellowman, his inability to
"get under way," his failure to find either inward or
outward capability, his loss of faith through the study of
skeptical writings, his overpowering by the monster
Utilitaria, and his betrayal and disappointment in love
and friendship. Little by little the self is left stranded,
isolated, and empty; soon it is completely without content. Teufelsdröckh lives in a parched world filled with
deserts, devils, and nightmare; this is the world of the
demonic, the world that desire rejects.[6] He is "every-

6. For the characteristics of this world, see Northrop Frye, *Anat-
omy of Criticism* (Princeton, 1957), pp. 147 ff.

where buffetted, foiled, and contemptuously cast out
. . . . A feeble unit in the middle of a threatening Infinitude" (*SR*, 132/163) .

It is out of the death of the soul, this dark night, that
rebirth becomes possible, and the center of this rebirth
is decisively the self. A return to the Eden-like Entepfuhl is contemplated for a moment as a solution, but
Teufelsdröckh, unlike many romantic predecessors, rejects it; he sees that this would be no solution, but an
escape or retreat, for it allows for no possibilities of
growth. Similarly—and equally unlike his antecedents—
Teufelsdröckh rejects both suicide and the writing of
Satanic poetry. Instead, he returns to the self and discovers that it is the protest of the ME which slays the Everlasting No, which eliminates the "hopeless Unrest" and
begins to create a "fixed center to revolve around" (*SR*,
136/169) . The possibility of a unitive self once again becomes apparent: "The fearful Unbelief is unbelief in
yourself" (*SR*, 132/163) .

It is this unbelief in the self which is conquered in
the first psychological stage of spiritual rebirth. The ultimate moral act that generates the Everlasting Yea—
self-annihilation—is an act of the self, however it may
appear to obliterate that self. It is still decisively the self
which forms the criterion of belief. "Feel it in thy heart,
and then say whether it is of God! This is Belief; all
else is Opinion" (*SR*, 155/194) . The self, then, in the
state of despair utilizes the very threat of meaninglessness and nonbeing to generate an affirmation of the
power of being. Without its implication, we are reminded of Schopenhauer's asceticism as a triumph of
self over nonmeaning. Carlyle's act, like Schopenhauer's,
rests on the twin subjective states of defiance and reverence (though Schopenhauer's features revulsion and disgust far more strongly) (*SR*, 163/205) , but Carlyle saves

81

the world rather than canceling it out; he redeems both self and world, "the skyey vault with its everlasting Luminaries" and "deep silent rock-foundations" (*SR*, 157/197).

It is true, of course, that chaos is transformed by this act into an organized world and an organized self, yet it is equally true in a deeper sense that darkness is maintained and with it the possibility of chaos. Teufelsdröckh himself always views the polarities of power as sharply divided between seraphic affirmation, order, and meaning and demonic denial, chaos, and nonmeaning. Throughout the book's course Love, Fantasy, and Revelation of Society are all endowed with these double directions, and each of these directions is ultimately grounded in the self. Teufelsdröckh, of course, sees himself as an agent of the godlike and constantly interprets himself in that light. The editor, however, with his constant references to Teufelsdröckh's angelico-diabolical qualities and his attempts to interpret one action in accord with the meaning of both poles, shows a skepticism which qualifies the affirmative pole of meaning and order stressed by Teufelsdröckh. At times Teufelsdröckh himself comes close to admitting the embodiment of darkness and nonmeaning within his vision; if he does not creatively use these qualities, he at least does not reject them.

> Ever, as before, does Madness remain a mysterious-terrific, altogether *infernal* boiling-up of the Nether Chaotic Deep, through this fair-painted vision of Creation, which swims thereon, which we name the Real . . . . In every the wisest Soul lies a whole world of internal Madness, an authentic Demon-Empire; out of which, indeed, his world of Wisdom has been creatively built together, and now rests there, as on its dark foundations does a habitable flowery Earth-rind. (*SR*, 207/260)

Such a statement recalls the central implications of "Characteristics": "Our being is made up of Light and Darkness, the Light resting on the Darkness, and balancing it; everywhere there is Dualism, Equipoise; a perpetual Contradiction dwells in us: 'where shall I place myself to escape from my own shadow?'" (*E, 3, 27*).

To different readers with differing backgrounds, the weight of these statements will vary. Some will see evasion and fear of further exploration, too easy a resolution, too simple a conquering of the darkness. Others will find a courageous admission of the problem of non-meaning. I am not myself without doubts about the evasive action in these remarks, but nevertheless it seems that what Carlyle is talking about bears a strong similarity to that kind of modern faith Paul Tillich has popularized in his *The Courage To Be*.

> The faith which makes the courage of despair possible is the acceptance of the power of being, even in the grip of nonbeing. Even in the despair about meaning being affirms itself through us. The act of accepting meaninglessness is in itself a meaningful act. It is an act of faith . . . . The faith which creates the courage to take (doubt and meaninglessness) into itself has no special content. It is simply faith, undirected, absolute . . . . There is the power of acceptance itself which is experienced . . . To accept this power of acceptance consciously is the religious answer of absolute faith, of a faith which has been deprived by doubt of any concrete content, which nevertheless is faith and the source of the most paradoxical manifestation of the courage to be . . . . The acceptance of such a situation as religiously valid has, however, the consequence that the concrete contents of ordinary faith must be subjected to criticism and transformation. The courage

to be in its radical form is a key to an idea of God which transcends both mysticism and the person-to-person encounter.[7]

Carlyle's faith, which absorbs doubt into its very content, issues in Tillich's terms from the deepest part of the self, where it is in contact with both being and non-being. Yet whether this is faith, especially a variant of Christian faith, remains open to question—and in Carlyle's case it is complicated by even stranger stresses. However much Carlyle pays lip service to Christianity as man's highest symbolic manifestation, there is ample evidence within *Sartor* that he regards its myth as totally outworn. The source of the new religious myth is simply the self, and it is this belief which Carlyle has emphasized in branding Teufelsdröckh's experience as paradigmatic, symbolical myth. Myth for Carlyle and the modern mind becomes a pattern that one creates out of the depths of the self rather than a pattern to which one submits oneself.

Carlyle openly uses traditional Christian theology as metaphor—and really only as metaphor. This approach allows him extraordinary flexibility in redefining terms as both natural and supernatural. His real protagonist is

7. Paul Tillich, *The Courage To Be* (New Haven, 1952), pp. 176–78. If we are willing to accept these ideas, we will find them illuminating in the controversy between John Sterling and Carlyle regarding belief in *Sartor*. (See the Appendix to Harrold's edition for the exchange.) Sterling focuses his critique on Teufelsdröckh's failure to believe in a personal God; this he feels is the source of the strain and, likewise, of the qualification and skepticism that so mark the style. Carlyle replies (p. 317) that Teufelsdröckh would lay his hand on his heart and express the solemnest denial; he takes refuge in a situation above the "personal" encounter, for he reduces the word "personal" to a kind of blasphemous naming of the unnameable. He commends Sterling for his belief in a personal God; though he (Carlyle) still accounts himself a Christian, he expresses contempt for any system, any creed.

84

not the traditional figure of Christ, but the independent self. It is this independent self which undergoes its own temptation in the wilderness (*SR*, 146/183–84), which plants the mustard seed for the new Church (*SR*, 159/200), which enunciates the new dogmas for the new society in Book Three. No overt mention is made of modeling this self upon the action of Christ; the model is the mythical biography of Book Two.

Within this self both the Ideal, the power of being, as well as the impediment, the threat of nonbeing, exist. Hence it is this self which alone must fashion the new myth for the society to be reborn in the phoenix death-birth. This heroic self will within the later works, through the studies of heroic models, fashion its role more fully and explore its frightening depths more thoroughly. "A Hierarch, therefore, and Pontiff of the World will we call him, the Poet and inspired Maker; who, Prometheus-like, can shape new Symbols, and bring new Fire from Heaven to fix it there" (*SR*, 179/225).

Thus, like the Clothes Philosophy, the self expands to take into itself the totality of experience. But also, and again like the Clothes Philosophy, the self paradoxically expands only to contract. By stressing energy, force, self-realization in action, the self becomes so aware of its own process of self-realization that any hold upon dogma, history, continuity is lost. "Nothing is completed, but ever completing" (*SR*, 197/247). All dogmas issue from it, but its highest dogmas are those that exploit the creative potential of each moment: duty, that which lies closest to hand, and hero-worship, reverence toward that man who is saying yes loudest to the process of self-realization. Christianity loses all historic validation as the self attempts to create a new philosophy of history by using Goethe's concept of alternate ages of faith and unbelief, systole and diastole, and symbolizes

this concept with the phoenix. But even this attempt at continuity and philosophy collapses into a single word like "death-birth" and into a single momentary process wherein "in that Fire-whirlwind, Creation and Destruction proceed together" (SR, 195/244).

In addition to the metaphysical ambiguities—the almost impossible task of reconciling philosophy, theory, and dogma, with immediacy, process, change, and action—further complications are abetted by Carlyle's fear of playing God, replacing him by the self, and by his need to transfer the qualities of God to the nature that had lost its meaning when deprived of his presence, thereby reaching the God who had disappeared through nature and not through the self. It is possible, of course, to find moments of Blakean insight which militate against this move. "Yes, truly, if Nature is one, and a living indivisible whole, much more is Mankind, the Image that reflects and creates Nature, without which Nature were not" (SR, 196/246–47). This reminder of Blake's Proverb of Hell, "Where man is not, nature is barren," is equally reminiscent, in words like "image" and "reflects," of Blake's indictment of Wordsworth for his fascination with the subject-object dichotomy, his use of mind mirroring nature and nature mirroring mind.

Despite these moments, however, the dominant vision of this last book of *Sartor* is not of a divine self redeeming nature but of a divine nature redeeming the self. The tone of the prophetic voice, the source of its own power, what Langbaum has called the subjective sense of the commitment over the dogma—these are not explored here. Inevitably, such a vision tends to cancel out the individual in its all-embracing mystery, and Carlyle frequently loses contact with the very reality and fact and actuality that he set out to redeem. Time becomes

an illusion, the final veil separating us from the All, Eternity, the redemption from time.

> Are we not Spirits, that are shaped into a body, into an Appearance; and that fade away into air and Invisibility? . . . Thus, like a God-created, fire-breathing Spirit-host, we emerge from the Inane; haste stormfully acrosss the astonished Earth; then plunge again into the Inane. But whence?—O Heaven, whither? Sense knows not; Faith knows not; only that it is through Mystery to Mystery, from God and to God. (*SR*, 211–12/264–66)

Nature is reenthroned as a Urizenic mystery, far more baleful than the utilitarian Newtonian universe of sense data, the hostile engine of the Everlasting No. Little wonder that the editor's final note of doubt about Teufelsdröckh does not seem to be the usual utilitarian misapprehension but a real enigma, Carlyle's own doubt about himself and his world. "How often already have we paused, uncertain whether the basis of this so enigmatic nature were really Stoicism and Despair, or Love and Hope only seared into the figure of these!" (*SR*, 235/294).

Furthermore, coupled with the metaphysical complications and the need to divinize nature instead of the self is the new feeling of even further aloneness in the seer himself. His vision, even his problem with the universe, is special. His intoxication with his vision, his special viewpoint on men, his own self-consciousness, all separate him from others. To see through social forms is somehow to be beyond them, to be alienated. Teufelsdröckh himself becomes curiously enigmatic. He has encountered the totality of the ME and the NOT ME in his travels, visits, and readings, but he still seems strangely contracted. He is in society but not of it. He

has laughed only once, and even there it was strangely analogous to that icy laugh of Zarathustra, unlike any laughter heard before by men, a bacchantic pessimism.

His philosophical perspective above Weissnichtwo, while allowing him to survey the totality of life, also bears potentialities that may exclude him from that life. Like Plotinus Plimlimmon, Melville's caricature of Emerson in *Pierre*, he sits behind his window surveying the universe, both able and unable to forge its meaning. Like Plimlimmon, though less intensely so, he is the "embodiment of the problematic." [8] There is much in Teufelsdröckh's character to substantiate the editor's frequent charges of an indifference apparently malign. In this totally expansive vision of reality that the self creates, both reality and self oddly seem to contract and once again plunge into nonmeaning from which they were to be rescued. Thus the editor eyes Teufelsdröckh askance; the world, which under the power of his expansive vision has become to Teufelsdröckh an object of infinite pity and concern, has also become to him nothing more than a meaningless toy.

> You look on him almost with a shudder, as on some incarnate Mephistopheles, to whom this great terrestrial and celestial Round, after all, were but some huge foolish Whirligig, where kings and beggars, and angels and demons, and stars and streetsweepings, were chaotically whirled, in which only children could take interest. (*SR*, 25/32)

The fullness of meaning paradoxically seems to lead to meaninglessness. Mechanistic philosophy resulted in the denial of meaning because it made no room for life; it isolated the individual until he was empty of any belief

8. Charles Feidelson, Jr., *Symbolism and American Literature* (Chicago, 1953), p. 204.

connected with living. But the expansive vital vision of
the universe and self could lead to an even more ambiguous universe than the one it attempted to eradicate,
and here the problems of meaninglessness, chaos, and
nonbeing are again raised. A universe which approximates that of absolute change is created, and the self
can find no stability. Teufelsdröckh's hum (*SR*, 24/32)
may indicate that he has linked the hum (*SR*, 16/22) of
the life-circulation with the celestial hum of the spheres
above him, but it may also point to a universe of ceaseless change whose only stability and meaning is its hum
of "Insanity and Inanity" (*SR*, 24/32).

With *Sartor Resartus* the prophet recognizes that he
can no longer merely preach the vitality of an organic
philosophy in opposition to empiricism or mechanism.
He must now face the challenges of that philosophy itself in its own view of nature and the self. *Sartor* marks
a transition point from what Lionel Trilling in "The
Fate of Pleasure" [9] has characterized as a dominant
pleasure principle behind artistic activity to one of
suffering and unpleasure as modes of self-discovery. The
problematic becomes as important as the prophetic.

Neither of these important strands in *Sartor Resartus*,
that of clothes and that of the self, can stand alone,
however. As they reach their fulfillment and present further problems, a form of dialectic supersedes narrative
or dramatic development, and this dialectic is the writing of *Sartor Resartus* itself. Here the relationship between editor and Teufelsdröckh and between the editor
and the Clothes Philosophy becomes crucially important, for within its perspective each of the two strands
achieves its fullest expression. Here too is the full development of the attempt to merge method with content

9. Lionel Trilling, "The Fate of Pleasure," *Romanticism Reconsidered*, English Institute Essays (New York, 1963).

sought in the early essays, and *Sartor Resartus* can now be seen as the flowering of "symbolism" as conscious method and theme.

With *Sartor,* Carlyle's conception of the work of art appears in an entirely new perspective. No longer does he as author confront the works of another author with hopes to expand his own vision of nature and self; no longer is the reader's attention directed to some subjective transformation outside the literary work. Instead, Carlyle focuses upon the literary work itself as the process of realization, the making of meaning. The old confrontation of the separate "reviewing voice" and "author studied" has disappeared; its basic configuration may still be present but is totally transformed. Not only has the reviewing voice emerged as a full bodied editor within the artistic framework, but the authors reviewed have been replaced with the literary character of Teufelsdröckh, who, unlike all the previous authors, has no historical existence outside the work of art. By absorbing the subjective and objective polarities into the art work, Carlyle calls attention to the work itself as the process of exploration and criticism. Both the editor and Teufelsdröckh represent attitudes and methods of Carlyle's mind, a possibility that the earlier essays pointed to but could not realize because the subjective and objective poles exercised constant threats upon the integrity of the book review as the process of forging meaning. The actual existence of an "author reviewed" collapsed the reviewer's concentration upon the supremacy of method. By shifting his artistic ground, making the book editor and Teufelsdröckh fully fictional, Carlyle circumvented the problems of his earlier essays.

Similarly, though the polarities of complexity and order were not totally dissolved, within the new framework both were fully seen as aspects of the self and nature. Teufelsdröckh and the editor represent double

stances of a single mind engaged in a single action—the making of meaning. Teufelsdröckh, in general, represents those forces of the mind habitually associated with the unconscious, intuition, imagination, and poetic creativity. Both his philosophy and autobiography approach the "noble complexity" of nature, but, like Richter's universe, "faith whispers" they are "not without a plan" (*SR*, 40/52). It is the task of the editor to reveal this plan; in general, he represents that part of the mind associated with reason, order, and logic. Here these two polarities of the mind and of being are given an equal distributive weight and engaged in a mutual and sustaining dialectic. If their conflict is not denied, neither is the hope that they can be combined into a new unitive picture of the universe. *Sartor Resartus* maintains both poles as continuous processes in experience.

The complexity of experience is psychologically primary (Teufelsdröckh's book and life come into the hands of the editor), but the ordering of that complexity by the editor is equally necessary for any real achievement. The two processes move through being, each now aiding and now criticizing the other, for both the editor and Teufelsdröckh represent partially conflicting but supplementary methods of reading the mystery of being. One tugs toward the world of number, logic, and total order; the other, toward the world of dream, nightmare, and disorder.[10] Yet *Sartor* is about a single action, its own writing, and within the fictional framework this is a task of both the editor and Teufelsdröckh.

As with any imaginative work, so long as some basics are credible the reader finds himself assenting to the fiction. Though the documents and the figure of Teufelsdröckh seem farfetched, the device of an editor writing a

10. Elizabeth Sewell, in *The Structure of Poetry* (London, 1951), sets up these movements and poles within language (see p. 50).

book is not. Thus the reader comes to believe that a Clothes Philosophy of ineffable complexity with some equally ineffable order exists ready-made behind the semiordered, semichaotic "selections" made by the editor, which is just as Carlyle wishes, though in actuality this is not the case. *Sartor Resartus* is not the ordered presentation of some philosophy Carlyle had on his writing desk before writing the book. Its unity is no preestablished harmony outside the book, even though it seeks to convince its readers of that very proposition, but the unity of the literary process itself. For that very reason Carlyle could regard the book as a way of embracing his encyclopedic array of philosophical ideas, propositions, allusions, epigrams, and quotations and giving to them the sense of a complete system. Beside the novelty of method, however, the wheels within wheels of the figures of Teufelsdröckh and the editor, the ideas themselves as a system tend to fade. The reader's interest is usurped by the making of meaning itself, an hourly advance both by Teufelsdröckh and the editor—and hence by the author. "Thus, too, in the sure expectation of these (autobiographical documents), we already see our task begun; and this our *Sartor Resartus,* which is properly a 'Life and Opinions of Herr Teufelsdröckh,' hourly advancing" (*SR,* 8/12).

In *Sartor Resartus* the double quest for meaning is really Carlyle's. Within the fictional framework it is Teufelsdröckh who has espoused this quest most fully, who has explored the complexity of existence and forged a meaning from that complexity. He has encountered and overpowered the darkness of life and the threat of chaos, and the autobiographical documents and the Clothes Philosophy are themselves the enigmatic reflection of his struggle with the riddle of life and the universe. It is the task of the editor to make some sense out of the chaos of autobiographical documents in the bags,

to articulate this philosophy in a more organized form, to make it public, and even to criticize it. But to perform those functions the editor must take Teufelsdröckh's journey with him.

This view of the editor is too often forgotten in the traditional picture of him as a kind of British dunce unable to understand the higher philosophy of Germany. Actually even this minor satirical function of the editor is double-edged. Negatively it serves as a weapon of satire against the typically omniscient yet uncomprehending British reviewer, but in a more positive manner it acts as a bridge between Germany and the English public; it can really be an image of the Carlyle who found these German authors difficult and had to struggle to understand them as he interpreted them to the public. But, most interestingly, the role of editor functions as a means of really qualifying Teufelsdröckh's philosophy: it both implements Carlyle's Voltaire-like bent of skepticism and incorporates that bent into the total vision. The editor can either reinforce the glory of Teufelsdröckh's philosophy by pointing to the sterility of its narrow opposite or reinforce the danger of Teufelsdröckh's philosophy by showing its leaning toward cant, its failure to conform to the world of common sense. This is a reminder of the opposition in *Wotton Reinfred* between Williams, the pleasant skeptic, and Dalbrook, the Coleridgean mystic. Each served as a partial ideal, and what was sought was a balance and reconciliation between the excesses of reason and imagination. In *Sartor Resartus,* by means of a fully developed editorial framework Carlyle can put brackets around the very material with which he is most concerned. The brackets even allow him a certain wildness and freedom, for they grant enough disassociation from the personality of Teufelsdröckh so that he can carry on through his bizarre character a more intense and expansive, almost

chaotic and mad, quest for unity and significance. Hence Carlyle is able to indulge in the "humouristico-satirical tendency of Teufelsdröckh, in whom underground humours and intricate sardonic rogueries, wheel within wheel, defy all reckoning" (*SR*, 161/202) and unrestrainedly to play to the full this "piebald, entangled, hyper-metaphorical style of writing, not to say of thinking" (*SR*, 233–34/293). Oddly enough, though at every point the brackets of the editor are qualifying, to some degree, that quest and style, subjecting them to a further more conscious and more rational interpretative method, the wheels nevertheless multiply again, at least from an auctorial rather than an editorial point of view. The editor can be as much a dissolving voice as he is an ordering or rational one. Not only does he break in with a new voice upon the more unified style and tone of Teufelsdröckh; he is obviously every bit as disorganized as his author, and his own leaping about only intensifies the sense of Teufelsdröckh's randomness. In a certain sense, perhaps, it can be said that he is even more disorganized than Teufelsdröckh, who usually shifts from high to low within a discourse, for his jumps from subject to subject convey a frightening sense of multiplicity and complexity.

Thus *Sartor Resartus* ultimately espouses the need for a unitive method that is not merely felt by Carlyle and his fictional characters but is demanded by the work's very conclusiveness, its own involvement as a product in space and time. According to the fiction—and Carlyle does create this belief in his reader—Teufelsdröckh's philosophy is a poem that expands symbolically into infinity itself; it is a "boundless, almost formless . . . Sea of Thought" (*SR*, 6/10). And the autobiographical documents (upon the promise of which the editor has undertaken his task in the belief that they will make clear the Clothes Philosophy), with their flow of unorganized

experience in zodiacal bags, provide an imbroglio, a "gaseous-chaotic Appendix to that aqueous-chaotic Volume" (*SR*, 62/79). Hence *Sartor Resartus,* like other symbolic works, is itself a "symbol of the tension between the infinity of symbolic aspiration and the conclusiveness which the objective work entails." [11]

Teufelsdröckh's philosophy cannot be completely formless, for if it fell into complete dissolution and meaninglessness, there would be no *Sartor Resartus.* Its glory is that it espouses a vision of infinity, grandness, and scope, while its danger is its threat to the self and meaning. Similarly, within the fiction the editor must make an act of faith in the order behind Teufelsdröckh's vision, for without this belief he could not pretend to discover or even create its order, selection, and coherence. The editor, in fostering the glory of Teufelsdröckh's philosophy, can only push it toward formlessness; he can only say that it is "almost formless" in its contents.[12]

This glory and this danger are present from the beginning in the editor's view of Teufelsdröckh and the Clothes Philosophy. Both are as enigmatic to the editor as the mysteries of the universe and the self are to Teufelsdröckh. The editor, of course, hopes to do justice to the complexity of the philosophy, but his principal concern is to order and organize it in his presentation. Yet, as I have pointed out, the processes are not discrete, for in unfolding the order, further enigmas are generated. Mulling over this "boundless . . . Sea of Thought,"

11. Feidelson, p. 73.

12. John Sterling in his letter to Carlyle, 29 May 1835, about *Sartor Resartus* spotted the reason behind this use of "almost." He noted (cf. Harrold's edition, p. 310) the use of Teufelsdröckh's "assertions, which seem to give the character of deliberateness and caution to the style. 'Almost' does more than yeoman's, *almost* slave's service in this way."

(*SR*, 6/10), the editor contemplates expounding the Clothes Philosophy and encounters a new difficulty:

> New the Volume on Clothes, read and again read, was in several points becoming lucid and lucent; the personality of its Author more and more surprising, but, in spite of all that memory and conjecture could do, more and more enigmatic. (*SR*, 7/11)

Within such enigmas which always remain, the editor recognizes the enduring possibilities of both glory and danger, heaven and hell, the "utmost depth" with "true orients" and "sea-wreck" (*SR*, 6/10), a "very Sun" with "black spots and troublesome nebulosities amid its effulgence" (*SR*, 21/28).

The reading process of the editor does not erase this problem of the enigmatic with its double possibilities. Like Teufelsdröckh, of course, the editor wages internecine war with the Devil (*SR*, 10/14) and strives to reach "the Elysian brightness" of the Clothes Philosophy, not its possible "reflex of Pandemonian lava," its "Asphodel meadows," not its "yellow-burning marl of a Hell-on-Earth" (*SR*, 55/70). His task, as he views it, is to reach the order he believes inherent in Teufelsdröckh's philosophy.

> Over such a universal medley of high and low, of hot, cold, moist, and dry, is he here struggling (by union of like with like, which is Method) to build a firm Bridge for British travellers . . . nor is there any supernatural force to do it with; but simply the Diligence and feeble thinking Faculty of an English Editor, endeavouring to evolve printed Creation out of a German printed and written Chaos, wherein, as he shoots to and fro in it, gathering, clutching, piercing the Why to the far-distant Wherefore,

his whole Faculty and Self are like to be swallowed up. (*SR*, 62–3/79–80)

But this initial hope of total order is scarcely fulfilled. At the conclusion of his task he recalls for the third time his function as bridgebuilder and weighs his success.

> No firm arch, over-spanning the Impassable with paved highway, could the Editor construct; only, as was said, some zigzag series of rafts floating tumultuously thereon. Alas, and the leaps from raft to raft, were too often of a breakneck character; the darkness, the nature of the elements, all was against us! (*SR*, 214–268)

Thus, while he is always striving for the possibilities of order, the meaning of meaning, the editor always reminds us, as Carlyle did in "Characteristics," that, however successful he may be in achieving that order, the possibility of disorder, the meaninglessness of meaning, also exists. This insistence is only partly the result of fear and doubt, for its advantages clearly outweigh its negative implications. It keeps alive the awareness of complexity and multiplicity in experience, it suggests the infinity of the Clothes Philosophy without having to render it, it argues for a union between the rigors of logic and the flow of experience, and it illustrates by its own semichaotic selective method the possibilities of such a union, thus providing the literary ordering of Teufelsdröckh's biography and philosophy that it seeks. But beyond all this it casts a haze of self-questioning over the writing of *Sartor Resartus* itself—a problematic aura that makes the book susceptible to diverse interpretations, in fact seems to make the book spawn such diversity. The editor through his own espousal of ambivalent viewpoints becomes as enigmatic as Teufels-

dröckh, and both of them partake of the larger self-
questioning of the author himself.

The editor's fear of chaos, disorder, and hell is even
more intensified in his portrayal of Teufelsdröckh.
Never does he allow Teufelsdröckh to appear without
exploiting his enigmatic character and its dual possibilities of heaven and hell. His eyes gleam with "an etherial
or else a diabolic fire" (SR, 12/16); "A wild tone pervades the whole utterance of the man, like its keynote
and regulator; now screwing itself aloft as into the Song
of Spirits, or else the shrill mockery of Fiends" (SR,
24/31). Even as late as in the supposed understanding of
Teufelsdröckh as "The Everlasting Yea," the editor insists upon this doubleness: "In Teufelsdröckh, there is
always the strangest Dualism: light dancing, with guitar-
music, will be going on in the forecourt, while by fits
from within comes the faint whimpering of woe and
wail" (SR, 149/186–87). Not only his appearance and
language, but his whole moral character seems equally
balanced between two contradictory interpretations.

> Under a like difficulty, in spite even of our personal
> intercourse, do we still lie with regard to the Profes-
> sor's moral feeling; Gleams of ethereal love burst
> forth from him, soft wailings of infinite pity; he
> could clasp the whole Universe into his bosom, and
> keep it warm; it seems as if under that rude exte-
> rior there dwelt a very seraph. Then again he is so
> sly and still, so imperturbably saturnine; shows
> such indifference, malign coolness towards all that
> men strive after; . . . that you look on him almost
> with a shudder, as on some incarnate Mephistophe-
> les, to whom this great terrestrial and celestial
> Round, after all, were but some huge foolish Whirl-
> igig, where kings and beggars, and angels and de-
> mons, and stars and street-sweepings, were chaotical-

ly whirled, in which only children could take interest. His look . . . is probably the gravest ever seen:
. . . the gravity as of some silent, high-encircled
mountain-pool, perhaps the crater of an extinct vol-
cano; into whose black deeps you fear to gaze: those
eyes, those lights that sparkle in it, may indeed be
reflexes of the heavenly Stars, but perhaps also
glances from the region of Nether Fire! (*SR*,
25/32)

Both demonic and apocalyptic poles appear in the Miltonic imagery, in the name Diogenes Teufelsdröckh
(the "Teufelsdröckh," "Devil's-dung," is never translated during the book), and in the conversion experience in the *Rue St. Thomas de l'Enfer*. The multiple
possibilities that emanate from these centers may imply
a union of opposites in tension or balance; a triumph of
the godlike over the ungodly, the apocalyptic imagination over the demonic one; or even an identification of
opposites.

This problematic rendering of the book's central
quest, this simultaneous espousal and questioning of the
search for unity and significance, sounds a new note in
literature. The nineteenth century threat of nonbeing
in its forms of emptiness and meaninglessness [13] extends
itself into the problem of literary method in *Sartor
Resartus*. The universe of the book bears, it is true, a
striking resemblance to the universe of a Romantic poet
like Wordsworth, but Carlyle constantly questions the
characteristics of that universe and pushes them to the
point of dissolution. Many of the Romantic poets had
also suffered a spiritual crisis not unlike Teufelsdröckh's, and some had come to rest in a Weltan-
schauung in which mind and things were seen in kin-

13. Tillich's delineation of the problem in *The Courage To Be*.

ship, belonging to and united by an infinite totality.[14] Carlyle certainly used this crisis and world view, but he also questioned it. As Charles Feidelson has pointed out, this Romantic typology was primarily a concern with content and not with method.

> Although the romantic was bent on expressing the complex mental content that escapes the net of logic, for the most part he did not challenge the essentially rationalistic metaphysics which left literature only two possibilities—expression and description. He was content to accept the greater elbow-room which idealism gave him within the traditional framework.[15]

By the time this typology had reached Carlyle, new difficulties had arisen. Not only did he see the conscious need to link method with vision, but he also realized that the infinite possibilities of an open and organic universe militated against the stability of meaning and of self and rendered the possibility of artistic form itself questionable. *Sartor Resartus* nevertheless conducts its quest for unity without eliminating these negative possibilities; in fact, it utilizes these very negative possibilities as sources of artistic value. In this respect, it closely resembles another book produced some years later by an admirer of *Sartor,* Melville's *Moby Dick* (1851).

Melville's and Carlyle's books are united not merely by a kind of surface chaos or experimentation with new forms; their similarity represents a basic literary typology for dealing with the problem of meaning. Ahab, the "ungodly-godlike" man conducts the principal quest through the complexity of existence, and in this respect

14. For an analysis of the typology of the Romantic world, see E. D. Hirsch, Jr., *Wordsworth and Schelling: A Typological Study of Romanticism* (New Haven, 1960), p. 63.

15. Feidelson, p. 56.

he parallels the action of Teufelsdröckh, the man of "angelico-diabolical" nature. But Teufelsdröckh forges meaning from that complexity, while Ahab is overpowered and destroyed by it. Ahab's monomaniacal focal point is the whale which gradually embraces the totality of meaning and the denial of meaning. Teufelsdröckh's milder monomania is already a creative product, the Clothes Philosophy, which, by a similar expansion, embraces and negates the totality of being. Surrounding these intense heroes of the quest is a critical consciousness that remains one remove from the "descent into the belly of the whale," but which nevertheless undertakes the quest at second hand, attempting to understand it. Ishmael and the editor are alike in this respect, but Ishmael represents a much more skeptical, free-floating consciousness, the bamboozled hero who is also the bamboozler artist. To be sure, the editor contains these potentialities, but they are not exploited. The emphasis is on the possibility of attaining an ordered and complex vision of the self, society, and nature. In their function of ordering material, both the editor and Ishmael agree, for technically and psychologically each provides the author with a way of organizing by a literary method what would otherwise be chaotic data of experience.

Despite the editor's intense movement toward order, it is interesting to see how often his negative criticism of Teufelsdröckh emphasizes the dangerous potentialities of disorder embedded in the contradictions of the Clothes Philosophy and the philosophical self. Teufelsdröckh, as we have already noted, feels that he has forged a "world of Wisdom" that rests as a "habitable flowery Earth-rind" on the "dark foundations" of the "Nether-Chaotic Deep," "an authentic Demon-Empire, a whole world of Internal Madness" (*SR*, 207/260). In this assertion of the godly over the ungodly, the "Diogenes" over the "Teufelsdröckh," nonbeing is not denied but is

absorbed and transcended. The editor, however, always makes an enigma even of this solution by casting his comments about Teufelsdröckh in strict "either-or" disjunctions. He cannot fathom to which realm, apocalyptic or demonic, Teufelsdröckh ultimately belongs. Some of this, of course, is mere joking, a light irony; the reader is expected to know which realm (the godly) applies. Much of the time, however, Carlyle's own skepticism and bewilderment show through. The incessant repetition of such a disjunction each time that Teufelsdröckh appears at least implies that the reader is not really expected to make a choice between the two realms, but to acknowledge that somehow Teufelsdröckh belongs to both, that somehow the two worlds are more closely related than he suspected, perhaps even identical.

This suspicion, which becomes the province of the later studies of the self in the titanic rebellious heroes, finds some support also in the implications of the total vision of the Clothes Philosophy. I have already mentioned that distinctions seem to dissolve, opposites to be gathered into a unitive apprehension, to become identities. The editor's insistence upon Teufelsdröckh's strange indifference is the psychological correlate of one potentiality of the Clothes Philosophy. The self seems to lose its connection with reality. Teufelsdröckh appears, from this negatively critical view, as a man removed from life, a visitor from the moon (SR, 22/29), a Melchizedek, the *Ewige Jude* (SR, 12–13/17). Surveying the life-circulation below him, he is somehow removed from it (SR, 17/23), and in the midst of the crowded tavern, *Zur Grünen Gans,* he seems curiously unaware of his audience; he sits behind a cloud of his own tobacco, and when he speaks, his phrases issue from a head "apparently not more interested in (his audience), not more conscious of them, than is the sculptured stone head of some public fountain, which through its brass mouth-

tube emits water to the worthy and the unworthy" (*SR,* 14–15/20). But it is actually in his very first presentation of Teufelsdröckh that the editor sees him as embodying most fully the opposites which collapse in the final vision. Here the editor explicitly indicates the ultimate outcome: the totality of organic motion becomes nonmotion; apprehension becomes nonapprehension, and self seems to lose all qualities that make it a self.

> In thy eyes too, deep under their shaggy brows, and looking out so still and dreamy, have we not noticed gleams of an ethereal or else a diabolic fire, and half-fancied that their stillness was but the rest of infinite motion, the *sleep* of a spinning top? (*SR,* 11–12/16)

Metaphysically, these may be the ultimate implications of *Sartor Resartus.* But they are only toyed with, never fully faced, and Carlyle refuses to go beyond them. Instead, he uses the excitement and mystery of the chapter "Natural Supernaturalism" as the real fulfillment of Teufelsdröckh's vision and the final step also for the reader of that vision before he returns to his own world, public and private, cleansed of his inward spiritual defects. From the height of this chapter, Carlyle releases Teufelsdröckh and the reader into the world of practical social realities. The chapter on "The Dandiacal Body" is designed as a new way of viewing the most pressingly urgent of contemporary social problems through the completed "optics" of the Clothes Philosophy, which reveals the relationship between the dandy, the product of a do-nothing aristocracy, and the pauper, the clothesless victim of the new industrial economy.

The reference to contemporary events is stronger here than at any prior point in the book. Such a stress aims to show the reader how the full vision of the Clothes

Philosophy should now be given grounding in immediate social realities, how it should be put into action and work. As at the end of "Signs of the Times" and "Characteristics," the voice of the social prophet emerges as the most clearly relevant, but in *Sartor,* unlike the earlier essays, the sense of a fatality engulfing society, ready to doom it, is kept alive and emphasized. The "upbeat" voice prevails only in the prophet's achievement of his complete inward vision; he now feels ready to confront society directly. But, correspondingly, his sense of the crisis facing society has actually deepened. England is about to be rent asunder by two whirlpools, or two electric charges, embodied in the picture of paupers and dandies. The celebration of society's regeneration in "Signs of the Times" and "Characteristics" has disappeared. If society is to purge itself, it will be through revolution, for Teufelsdröckh has, after a week of silence, been propelled back into the social dimension by the Parisian Three Days, the Revolution of 1830.

The final chapter of *Sartor* thus breaks the imaginative donnée of the book even more than the preceding one of "The Dandiacal Body." In an oblique manner, as at the end of the autobiographical documents of Book Two, it indicates that the book has been a hoax, a symbolic disguise for the life and thoughts of Thomas Carlyle. In these last pages Teufelsdröckh steps out of his Weissnichtwo tower and makes his appearance in London. Within the fiction he should properly still be in his tower—"In such environment . . . most likely does he still live and meditate" (*SR,* 20/27)—but here, in the last pages of the book, he is suddenly in London during the Paris Revolution of 1830. With this appearance of Teufelsdröckh Carlyle deliberately destroys his imaginative structure and fuses it with actuality. For Carlyle himself is shortly thereafter to leave Craigenputtock and turn to London, to become primarily a social prophet

and moral historian. "Our own private conjecture, now amounting almost to certainty, is that, safe-moored in some stillest obscurity, not to lie always still, Teufels-dröckh is actually in London" (*SR*, 237/297) .

With this announcement Carlyle declares that the imaginative exploration, the process of *Sartor*, is over; the vision is complete. To be sure, he still shows a tendency to turn back on his experience and ideas as crystallized in the book and use them for application to the present social situation. But though he always leans toward formulations and dogmas, these always remain— and I quote Langbaum again—"subordinate to the chooser." [16] It is the personality of the prophet that is released upon London and contemporary society.

In regard to the broader question of the modern tradition, it is instructive to place *Sartor* against two other autobiographical books that chart the history of rebellion, crisis, and spiritual rebirth. All three books are close kin, but the subtle differences among them will aid in the assessment of the emerging modernity of *Sartor*. The first is Wordsworth's autobiographical poem *The Prelude,* and the second is Nietzsche's *Thus Spoke Zarathustra.*

The similarities between *The Prelude* and *Sartor* have often been pointed out; in fact, *Sartor* has frequently been called a prose version of Wordsworth. Langbaum uses the two books almost interchangeably in *The Poetry of Experience* to illustrate the Romantic crisis. Both stress the harmonious relationship of the child with nature; both chart the effects of society and rationalism upon the poetic imagination and the ensuing crisis of identity, the drying up of feeling and life; both depict an emerging spiritual mission, a victory of the imagination by a redefinition of the value of the past, a return of man to his roots in nature and history,

16. Langbaum, *The Poetry of Experience,* p. 21.

and thereby a confirmation of himself in both present and future. Yet ultimately the differences between the two books are more weighty than the similarities. Wordsworth, it must be admitted, has more faith in the true thematic direction of his book, the development of the imagination, whereas Carlyle would like to enshrine his crisis as a kind of myth or paradigm for action, an anchor or principle to which he could always return in order to validate his mission to society. Wordsworth's crisis, while suggesting in its arrangement in *The Prelude* something analogous to the fall in *Paradise Lost,* is never the central concern of his poem. The narrative weight is, as Geoffrey Hartman has shown in his excellent study, "on this difficult process whereby the soul, having overcome itself through nature, must now overcome nature through nature." [17] But even this enshrinement in Carlyle is, as I have pointed out, minor. The real stress, like Wordsworth's, is on the forging of the vision, but Carlyle goes beyond Wordsworth, admitting to a certain skepticism, a feeling that the Romantic vision of a Wordsworth is too outmoded—too "mystical," Carlyle would say—to accommodate present social actuality.

Wordsworth, it is true, writes a process poem, but he is never so aware of this as Carlyle is in writing *Sartor.* His literary model remains the epic, particularly *Paradise Lost;* and he more than Carlyle fears the dissolution of literary structure and identity that a process poem might produce. Hartman has also shown how much he fears the full revelation of the imagination and has demonstrated that much of the poem is about the process of conquering this fear. Wordsworth also seems unworried by what appears to be a sharp dichotomy between his imaginative revelations as expe-

17. Geoffrey Hartman, *Wordsworth's Poetry, 1787–1814* (New Haven, 1964) , p. 221.

106

rience and his rather prosy, enlightenment analysis of them. The new Wordsworth of the "visionary" criticism noticeably omits this second Wordsworth. Carlyle shows a greater blending of form and content, image and idea. If his blendings are not so untroubled, it is because the problems are perceived more acutely.

It is in fact the anguish of the seer, of the triumphant visionary himself, that makes Carlyle more distinctly modern than Wordsworth. In "The Fate of Pleasure," Lionel Trilling, as mentioned earlier, has chronicled this transference from the principle of pleasure to that of pain and suffering as the very ground of modern creative activity. Carlyle is by no means Dostoyevsky, Trilling's other polarity to Wordsworth, for he is not really beaten; he has not gone underground. Like Wordsworth's seer, he has a strong social mission at the end of the book; but unlike Wordsworth's seer, he has not been purged of all pain, doubt, and skepticism. Despair may be the fundamental facet of his character— not the despair of the loss of belief produced through mechanism and utilitarianism, but a kind of humanistic pessimism akin to Schopenhauer, Nietzsche, and Dostoyevsky. His higher suffering is produced by greater insight; he endures the special pain of the man of genius who sees beyond others and who is afflicted with bringing that burden to others, the anguish of the man who must destroy, who finds it hard to love, but who must nevertheless ultimately save mankind. Carlyle is thus the first of a series of deeply troubled prophets. He seeks at once to return man to his sources, to the wellsprings of imagination, and to affirm the anguish of the new hero. It is this mixed voice, finding self-definition in unpleasure, that is heard in Carlyle's heirs—Nietzsche, D. H. Lawrence, and in our own time a figure such as Norman Mailer.

Sartor is actually far closer to Nietzsche's *Thus Spoke*

Zarathustra than to Wordsworth's *Prelude.* The sharp contrast between Carlyle's militant theism and Nietzsche's even more militant atheism should not blind us to deeper similarities, even stylistic ones. Like Carlyle, Nietzsche is marked by rebellion—in his case a total rebellion against all society and, in particular, Christianity. The resulting isolation, like that of Teufelsdröckh, is thus one of the central themes of the book. Nietzsche's seer is both exalted and plagued by this isolation.

> "When I am aloft, I always find myself alone. No one speaks to me, the frost of solitude makes me tremble. What do I want in the heights?
>
> "My contempt and my desire increase together; the higher I climb, the more do I despise him who climbs. What do I want in the heights?" [18]

He hovers between the need to save all society, his spiritual mission, and a contempt for all society issuing in the most radical rejection and loathing. More extreme in this regard than Carlyle, Nietzsche makes this disgust the foundation of his personal crisis, his loss of faith in man and the universe. More radical in his solutions, Nietzsche, at the end of the book, is still climbing higher, reaching for greater self-consciousness and self-perfection, rejecting his social role and even his former selves now incorporated in the higher men who have sought him out to join him.

> *"Pity! Pity for the Higher Man!"* he cried out, and his countenance was transformed into brass. "Very well! *That*—has had its time!"
>
> "My suffering and my pity—what of them. For do I aspire after *happiness?* I aspire after my *work!*
>
> "Very well! The lion has come, my children are

18. Friedrich Nietzsche, *Thus Spoke Zarathustra,* trans. and intro. by R. J. Hollingdale (Baltimore, Penguin Books, 1961), pp. 69–70.

near, Zarathustra has become ripe, my hour has come!

"This is *my* morning, *my* day begins: *rise up now, rise up, great noontide!*"

Thus spoke Zarathustra and left his cave, glowing and strong, like a morning sun emerging from behind dark mountains.[19]

So ends Nietzsche's book. But throughout it the need to enter society and to save it has been a perennial temptation that must be continually overcome. The affirmation of the end does not completely cancel that temptation out; there is an icy, lonely quality to Nietzsche's achievements of self; for a radical despair underlies them.

Nietzsche points up certain elements in *Sartor* that seemed implicitly understood by Carlyle but are not elaborated upon—probably for reasons of fear, especially of blasphemy or wanton destruction. *Zarathustra* focuses almost totally on the self, its crisis of withdrawal, its loathing, its need for a mission for both self and society, its lonely triumph in a joy that incorporates the contradictions of life within itself. Nietzsche openly, almost over-insistently, sings of this self-creation as the highest act; having killed God, he must replace God with the self. Philosophically, then, Nietzsche issues with a more elaborate and fully worked out belief in contradiction as the source of life and energy, as the fount of art and selfhood, and in tragedy as the source of joy itself, in which all the antinomies of life are not canceled out but accepted. Carlyle could not reach this position, even though it was implied by his aesthetic activity in writing *Sartor,* because he felt it necessary to replace God with nature and then redefine not the self, but nature, something outside the self, as God.

19. Ibid., p. 336.

Carlyle's conception of selfhood and his tone and voice throughout *Sartor* herald Nietzsche's, which finds its proper subject matter in this peculiar sort of self-celebration. Though Carlyle mutes this sense of selfhood, he will later explore it by analogues of the self in history, the heroes of the past, a method far less direct and dangerous for him. Carlyle's openly self-conscious sense of self-exploration and self-consciousness ends with *Sartor*, not to be reborn until the biography of Sterling and his *Reminiscences*—and then in a far different manner.

More importantly, the role of Zarathustra and his hyperbolic hortatory voice, uniting the roles of preacher and self-quester, point to an element of Teufelsdröckh which Carlyle may have felt but did not openly recognize. Carlyle tends to treat Teufelsdröckh's manner and voice with some irony, generally suggesting with the editor's accusations of mysticism and delusion a certain outmodedness or fakery in Teufelsdröckh's positions. The reader is never asked to invert this judgment completely by merely assuming that the editor is a dunce, that the voice is the voice of truth, which the British are unable to recognize, but he is invited to retain his skepticism. For Nietzsche such a voice is not really the voice of the past, but that of a future, a projection of selfhood that turns to the past and reabsorbs it in a special way, providing a model not only for society but for the present self writing the book. Carlyle's characterization of the events of Book Two as "symbolical myth" points in this direction, but Nietzsche, with more awareness of this problem, deftly manages a process book that combines all the problems of his present writing self with the future implications of a superman model, a heightened voice, and selfhood.

Nevertheless, it must be admitted that, like Carlyle, Nietzsche's projections tend to harden. If he himself

does not become the superman, he will always call himself the teacher of the superman. The process of rebirth assumes a similar paradigmatic cast, more reminiscent of Blake, perhaps, than Carlyle—camel, lion, child. And, unlike *Sartor*, the book's voices, those of the anguished Nietzsche and the equally anguished Zarathustra, are difficult to distinguish, often providing little of the self-criticism effected through the more distinguishable dual voices of *Sartor*.

Nietzsche understands his loathing far better than Carlyle, but he seems, when not writing about himself, oddly unaware that he is dealing with its most intimate aspects when he projects it in his indictments of those who say nay to life, those who want revenge, priests, and even his own "ape." Nietzsche's consciousness may be hypertrophied, but in some respects it is strangely limited. Despite the use of Zarathustra as a self-projection and his probing insight into the psychology of transference and all the other facets of depth psychology Freud tells us he heralded, he seems strangely unaware of the phenomenon of projection in himself and of his own psychological history as a conditioning factor. Large areas of self-awareness seem shut off to him by certain preconceptions, a fondness for dogmatizing, and certain psychological frameworks that have replaced religious ones. Carlyle's overt discussions of irony in relation to destruction and of humor to sport, love, and play point to problems of the self, as do Nietzsche's similar discussions of revenge, but Carlyle, if simpler, is really more aware and self-conscious in this regard than Nietzsche, and far more refreshing.

Nietzsche's connection of a world of chance with his own sportive creative play clarifies what is perhaps the most modern aspect of *Sartor*. Nietzsche, of course, deliberately and rebelliously, sometimes almost hysterical-

ly, celebrates the redemption of the world from the bondage of purpose by his restoration of all things to chance.

"Lord Chance"—he is the world's oldest nobility, which I have given back to all things; I have released them from servitude under purpose . . .

O sky above me, you pure, lofty sky! This is now your purity to me, that there is no eternal reason-spider and spider's web in you—

that you are to me a dance floor for divine chances, that you are to me a gods' table for divine dice and dicers! [20]

Such a concept acts as a check to the unitive implications of the will to power and a sense of world direction—or at least species direction—determining the self in the concept of the superman. By making the aesthetic moment supreme, he restores to each individual his own uniqueness, multiplicity, and freedom. Carlyle, needing order and belief, and especially purpose, will not risk spelling out the implications of his own peculiar and similar brand of aesthetic activity, but the discussion of humor in the essay on Richter certainly implies a similar view: what for Nietzsche would be will to power, and for Carlyle energy or the central fire of the universe, is here purged of its destructive streaks and given a direction in aesthetic activity, the creation and absorption of multiplicity itself, as sport, play, love. *Sartor*, principally in its method but often in its overt themes, toys with the possibilities of wheels within wheels, is fascinated with randomness, the shock of dislocation, and the excitement of forging new insights by linking the high with the low, allowing each to comment on the other, thereby filling both with new value. But Carlyle will never celebrate himself as the philosopher of

20. Ibid., p. 186.

chance. Nietzsche would regard such a failure as timorous, but Carlyle's reluctance at least manages to keep alive some interaction of terms. Nietzsche's need for rebellion and extremes seems pathological and often forces him quite unconsciously to be a victim of the terms he overturns, thinking in opposites of what he hates, and thus showing his failure to free himself from what he claims he is crushing. As a result, little interaction or dialectic or redefinition is really achieved. The problem of self-criticism and self-consciousness as a burden to the artistic mentality is never faced in *Zarathustra,* and the book itself threatens to dissolve into the very chaos feared by Carlyle. Even Thomas Mann, so great an admirer of Nietzsche, admits to being repelled by its unchecked and ungoverned ranting quality. And Walter Kaufmann in his classic study of Nietzsche gives it scant attention, no doubt because of a similar feeling.

Sartor Resartus in its literary method of making randomness and chance into art, its sporting aesthetic activity given full play in the wry humor of Book One, most closely resembles André Gide's *The Counterfeiters,* one of the cornerstones of the modern literary consciousness. This is not surprising, for I have already shown how certain structural features of *Sartor* could easily enter into a novel like *Moby Dick*. It does indicate, however, the large degree to which the modern novel has become in both theme and form an inquiry into the self and its relation to society.

Edouard, the hero of Gide's novel, resembles both Teufelsdröckh and the editor; in fact, he unites both personalities in a single figure. But even though he draws out the implications of *Sartor* in regard to its two voices, he does not obliterate the structural suggestions behind the division of these figures. As the central character of the novel, Edouard lacks Teufelsdröckh's sharp

113

prophetic manner but nevertheless embodies his basic characteristics and ambiguities; moralist, creative artist, and teacher, he is also bewildered by multiplicity, unsure of his identity, and hindered from creativity by too much thought and analysis. The "editor" side of Edouard appears in his role as novelist within the novel, for within the novel by Gide called *The Counterfeiters*, Edouard is himself a frustrated novelist trying to write a novel about the people and events, including himself and his problem of writing a novel, in the novel. As Teufelsdröckh and the editor fused with Carlyle's voice, both roles of Edouard finally appear as aspects of Gide; through the completed creative work, Edouard's project of writing *The Counterfeiters* seems redeemed of its impossibility, much as the Clothes Philosophy and Teufelsdröckh's vision is validated by the completion of *Sartor*. But the special kind of creativity of *The Counterfeiters*, its random literary form, embodies the jottings and haphazard events of Edouard's projected novel in much the same manner as the method of *Sartor* embodies the difficulties of method that Teufelsdröckh and the editor both encounter. Like Carlyle, Gide transforms the frustrations of his hero into a creative method and thereby succeeds in encompassing both his idealistic aims and his realistic difficulties.

Ultimately, there are more than two Edouards within the novel; the enclosed boxlike quality of *Sartor* is in *The Counterfeiters* endlessly reduplicated, with all the divisions between art and reality destroyed in the process. The reader's move from the real character Edouard in the novel to contemplation of the problems of a novel within the novel that will include both him and other characters the reader has already met inevitably induces a self-consciousness that propels him outward to the book he is reading. From Edouard's theories and notebook jottings within the novel the reader is led not only to the events of the novel but also to the notebooks

on the novel by Gide, printed as an appendage to the novel. The line between art and reality is destroyed; art becomes the play of the mind between different versions of perception, between reality and stylization, fact and ideality.

Like Teufelsdröckh, who leaps from utilitarian considerations of aprons to the vestures of the eternal, Edouard deals with counterfeiting from actual fake coins manufactured by a schoolboy gang to his own deliberate cultivation of masks, projects, and multiple identities—and ultimately, of course, to the writing of a book called *The Counterfeiters* that is faked in the sense that it is never delivered by him yet delivered by Gide himself. The symbolic, indeed duplicative, title of Gide's book can occasion a backward glance at both Carlyle's book and title. In fact, at one of Edouard's most frustrating moments, when he is explaining the new kind of novel he is attempting to write, *Sartor* is cited—only in a parenthetic manner, to be sure—as a model for his method.

> If he (Edouard) allowed his mind to follow its bent, it soon tumbled headlong into abstractions, where it was as comfortable as a fish in water. Ideas of exchange, of depreciation, of inflation, etc. gradually invaded his book (like the theory of clothes in Carlyle's *Sartor Resartus*) and usurped the place of the characters. As it was impossible for Edouard to speak of this, he kept silent in the most awkward manner, and his silence, which seemed like an admission of penury, began to make the other three very uncomfortable.[21]

Gide joins with Edouard's concerns and frustrations, suggesting that the method of *Sartor* belongs to his own completed novel as well as to Edouard's projected one of

21. André Gide, *The Counterfeiters* (New York, Modern Library, 1964), pp. 176–77.

the same name, and that both books, the written and the unwritten, are closely linked. Furthermore, the many extensions of the title *The Counterfeiters* may illuminate extensions of *Sartor Resartus* of which we may not have been aware. The tailor retailored may be not only the figure of Teufelsdröckh who has died spiritually and been reborn, but also the editor reworking the vision of Teufelsdröckh, and ultimately the author reuniting both of them in the principal creative act of "tailoring." Gide's title and structure point more explicitly than Carlyle's, but in the same manner, to a density of experience, best symbolized perhaps by metaphors of mirrors or endless tunnels (recall the editor's reference in *Sartor* to "wheels within wheels"). Like Carlyle, Gide points to a dimension of infinity and chance in reality that art can effectively symbolize in its sportive activity, its manner of linking things. At one and the same time, both infinity and unity, multiplicity and coherence, are embraced.

As Carlyle's book leaps wildly from perspective to perspective, from editor to Teufelsdröckh, and from real clothes to spiritual ones, from lofty considerations to silly ideas, from utilitarian ideals to transcendental notions, Gide's novel also deliberately cultivates discontinuity, suggesting the randomness yet relatedness of all life, its ultimate incoherence and yet its ultimate unity. Plots are left unfinished, characters disappear, styles change, yet from all this there emerges a sense of self-definition, a certain harmony. Rebellion for Gide is at the core of his novel; like Carlyle, he deliberately shatters traditional literary and social forms as impediments to self-development. But, unlike Carlyle, he locates self-fulfillment in a more momentary aesthetic "yes" than Carlyle would admit to, however much he points in this direction. The similarity of Gide's artistic solution to Carlyle's in *Sartor* indicates a similarity of

artistic priority as well. Edouard's words to La Pérouse could aptly serve as a keynote to the aesthetics of *Sartor,* especially to Book One: "Have you observed that the whole effect of modern music is to make bearable, and even agreeable, certain harmonies which we used to consider discords?" But, in a certain way, Carlyle is more programmatically like La Pérouse than like Edouard; he would prefer the "perfect and continuous chord . . . the mere expression of serenity." [22]

John Sterling caught the problems and tone of *Sartor* well when he wrote Carlyle about Teufelsdröckh: "He trusts (but with a boundless inward misgiving) that there is a principle of order which will reduce all confusion to shape and clearness." [23]

In the final analysis, *Sartor* preserves much of its life and appeal not because of its principle of order, but because of its dazzling aesthetic method, its new attempt at self-definition through dislocation, humor, and an approximation to chance wherein the aesthetic sport of the author approximates that quality of randomness in the universe. The bewildered editor and the wry and quaint Teufelsdröckh, with his occasionally demonic and mysterious turnings, his wheels within wheels, and his weird style, are still very modern figures. So too is a book which is about a book that for reasons of multiplicity within the self, confusion, and self-consciousness can scarcely be written; Gide's *Counterfeiters* and, more recently, Fellini's movie "8½" are ample testimony here.

With *Sartor* Carlyle brings to a close his early literature of self-exploration. Unlike Gide, he does not withdraw from his central character at the end of the book but collapses his hoax by revealing that he is both the editor and Teufelsdröckh and ultimately projects Teu-

22. Ibid., p. 151.

23. Letter of John Sterling to Carlyle, 29 May 1835. Cf. Harrold's edition of *SR,* p. 314.

felsdröckh as a sort of mythical superman into London society. As Nietzsche would play Zarathustra, Carlyle will now try to play Teufelsdröckh to an urban society in crisis. His focus shifts from self-investigation to social investigation, and his subject matter becomes history and social prophecy. The past is studied as an aid to understanding the deeper currents of a problematic present.

Carlyle's self-quest, like Nietzsche's, however, continues in an underground fashion. The quest into society and history is also a form of a deeper though oblique quest into the self. Both *Sartor* and *Zarathustra* focused on a widening and constantly progressing self; *The French Revolution* will turn more specifically downward and reveal aspects of the self that self-consciousness seemed unable to face. Carlyle continues an experimenter and a quester, a prophet, but a deeply problematic one.

PART TWO

LONDON—VARIETIES OF SOCIAL PROPHECY

❦ 3 ❧

THE FRENCH REVOLUTION:
CHANGE AND HISTORICAL
CONSCIOUSNESS

I think you a very good giant . . . pleasure and
peace not being strong enough for you, you choose to
suck pain also, & teach fever & famine to dance &
sing . . . . You have broken away from all books, &
written a mind.

Emerson,
Correspondence of Emerson and Carlyle

the world is wholly in such a newfangled humour; all
things working loose from their old fastenings, towards new issues and combinations.

Carlyle,
The French Revolution

The French Revolution: *A History* (1837) is Carlyle's
fullest attempt to come to grips with the totality of
man's historical existence. *Sartor Resartus* both studied
and discovered the new birth of the individual self from
the ruins of a psychological past grown outmoded; *The
French Revolution* widens this inquiry into a breakup
of the entire social fabric and a discovery of the implications of that breakup for both the new self and the new
society. Carlyle's focus shifts to a self that is primarily
embedded in history and to the inexorable drive of the
historical process as it moves, both in the Revolution
and in his own time, toward the realization of freedom,
the recognition of the rights and mights of each individual. For Carlyle, the first full and open social affirma-

121

tion of this true drive of history, its first step toward the emergence of new social ideals and institutions, is the French Revolution itself, when the twenty-five millions, beset by tyranny and oppression, ignored by their governing class, and dying of hunger, arose from their subterranean depths and, failing to find answers in outmoded institutions, destroyed the entire social fabric and began to reconstitute it according to their needs.

Thus, *The French Revolution,* unlike *Sartor,* directly confronts the destructive and demonic element in man and announces that in the expressions of this destruction man affirmed his fullest energies. The book presents a descent into hell, into the cauldron of fire and the madness of the nether self that *Sartor* affirmed as a part of man but did not fully explore. In accordance with the shift in focus toward history, historical existence, and man's energies in destroying and shaping institutions and ways of life, the transcendental and dualistic vocabulary of *Sartor,* already wavering there, recedes even further. Moreover, under the impact of the close scrutiny of men's actions, the sanction of nature as an ultimate source for such actions, so dominant at times in *Sartor,* now disappears. To be sure, the most significant actions of men are shown to be prompted by his most natural needs and instincts—hunger, self-preservation, relief from oppression, self-assertion, desperation, and terror—and Book One accounts for the origins of the Revolution in a proto-Marxist way by emphasizing economic needs and policies locked in a propelling dialectic. But nature herself never usurps priority over man's nature, as she threatened to do in "Characteristics" and *Sartor.* If there is still a threat of a black abyss beneath the earth rind and of the flux of an open universe, it lies primarily within the self and its passions, within Sansculottism and Rascality, not within external nature. Instead of a metaphysics and cosmol-

122

ogy, then, *The French Revolution* everywhere points to the more modern world of psychology, to individual and social passions complexly intertwined, and to the difficulty of historical understanding.

Such a shift in focus cannot be emphasized too strongly, for only through understanding it can the unique and modern achievement of Carlyle's work be appreciated. One may be tempted throughout the work to take the frequent theoretical interpretations of the Revolution as the final measure of the action and, since this theoretical material seems largely derived from *Sartor* and "Characteristics"—and does not even receive the exploratory treatment of these earlier works—to feel that *The French Revolution* breaks no new ground, is merely the illustration of a paradigm, the confirmation of a philosophy.

But to approach the work in this manner is to close off all its richness. Carlyle's theoretical material should not be seen as final, but merely as one facet of a wide-ranging voice, occasionally—and often quite unsuccessfully—attempting to fix the meaning of the Revolution in terms frequently derived from *Sartor* that prove all too inadequate. As *Sartor* used the materials of German thinkers without merely reproducing their philosophies or reducing its own scope, so *The French Revolution* uses the material of *Sartor* without reproducing that book.

Admittedly the blocks of theoretical material stand out; yet without being final, they are important in another way. The theoretical material seems to fall into three principal strands (though other divisions might be equally appropriate) which, if not paradigms for the actions, are at least centers of speculation around which the major themes, images, problems, and movements of the book can cluster and achieve increasing definition and interrelationship. One of these blocks seems dis-

tinctly minor in its relationship to the book's action (though, oddly enough, inverted as a positive impulse and rarely explored by Carlyle, it may be the driving energy behind the book). I am, of course, thinking of the frequent moralistic and usually shrill denunciations of Carlyle against quacks, hypocrites, sensualists, sinners, liars, unbelievers, and the like as the causes of the Revolution. To read the book according to these simplistic Puritan categories is to violate its basic vision. H. D. Traill, Carlyle's editor in the Centenary Edition and one of his sharpest aesthetic critics, has provided the irrefutable answer to such a reading:

> Carlyle, however, like many another preacher of his nationality, was far more charitable than his preachments. That is to say, he comes into far closer contact with the realities of life, and, in judging men's actions, approaches much nearer to that standard of the all-comprehending which is the all-forgiving when he descends from the pulpit. Once he has descended, the rich humanity of the man and his Shakespearian breadth of sympathy assert themselves; he forgets his Radical or Tory-Radical crotchets, his Puritan prejudices. . . . Once in the swing of his narrative, and his moralisings for the time abandoned, Carlyle does not find Quackery or look for it. (*FR, 1,* xvi)

Whenever Carlyle lapses into dogmatic denunciation, not only does the tone suddenly become shrill, but a totally new frame of reference comes to the fore. The simplicity of the causes gives evidence of a hasty desire for explanation and for finality—always the source of difficulty for the impulsive Carlyle—but the total absence of quacks, liars, and evil-doing hypocrites from the dramatic action of his work cancels out the validity of his own explanation of the Revolution.

The one aspect of this Puritanism which does make its presence felt throughout the book is positive, as I have indicated, and appears connected with the denunciations of quacks only insofar as it is frequently accompanied by the statement that a lie cannot be believed, that man's life must be founded on sincerities and realities. This phrase, in fact, is not so much a protest against liars, but a declaration of faith in the affirmative energies of the Revolution. Though Carlyle frequently laments that the Revolution can be only a destructive faith abolishing solecisms and not a constructive one, resting as it does on the "sensualism" and "rubbish" of Rousseau's atheistic gospel, he nevertheless treats Sansculottism and Patriotism as embodiments of an energetic faith that he would obviously associate with his own Puritanism. And once he has declared his Puritan reservations in regard to the origin of Sansculottism, he seems ready to abandon them. Mirabeau, for instance, is judged wanting, "without Decalogue, moral Code or Theorem of any fixed sort" but is nevertheless "A Reality . . . not a Sham" (*FR, 1,* 140), and by the time of his death, all reservations now forgotten, he appears as "a living Son of Nature, our general Mother." "The Morality by which he could be judged has not yet got uttered in the speech of men" (*FR, 2,* 145). And often Carlyle explicitly declares the positive faith of Sansculottism:

The age of Miracles has come back! "Behold the World-Phoenix in Fire-consummation and fire-creation . . . ". . . Whereby . . . shall one unspeakable blessing seem attainable. This, namely: that Man and his Life rest no more on hollowness and a Lie, but on solidity and some kind of Truth. . . . Truth of any kind breeds ever new and better truth. . . . Sansculottism will burn much; but

what is incombustible it will not burn. Fear not
Sansculottism; recognize it for what it is, the por-
tentous inevitable end of much, the miraculous beginning of much. One other thing thou mayest understand of it: that it too came from God. (*FR*, *1*,
213)

Carlyle, then, has it both ways: he utters his Puritan
denunciations in shrill pulpit oratory with all their narrow implications, and yet he somewhat covertly transfers
his faith to the faith of Sansculottism. The description
of his new faith remains obscure, clouded by the Puritanism or couched in the positive vocabulary of *Sartor*,
but this is because Carlyle feels uncomfortable with the
heritage of the Revolution, an upheaval which has resulted not in a new version of the stable social order of
feudal Christianity but the dislocated, relative, and
complex world of the modern spirit. Whatever his reservations, however, his utterance of belief in the direction
of modern history as inaugurated by the Revolution is
unequivocally affirmative in tone and religious in intent. I would further suggest that this belief is the driving impulse behind his book, the very thrust of the action itself, and the source for his conception of individual and social freedom (a statement which I think can
also be made about most of the works of his Puritan
successors, Ruskin and Shaw). Carlyle may not have the
false millennial hopes of the Revolutionaries, but he is
one with them in his hope for an era of freedom. He
explicitly describes the basic action of the Revolution
and of his book in religious terms and in a tone that
leaves no doubt about his own deep involvement:

Great meanwhile is the moment, when tidings of
Freedom reach us; when the long-enthralled soul,
from amid its chains and squalid stagnancy, arises,
were it still only in blindness and bewilderment,

126

and swears by Him that made it, that it will be
free! Free? Understand that well, it is the deep
commandment, dimmer or clearer, of our whole
being, to be *free.* Freedom is the one purport, wisely aimed at, or unwisely, of all man's struggles, toil-
ings and sufferings, in this Earth. Yes, supreme is
such a moment (if thou have known it) : first vision
as of a flame-girt Sinai, in this our waste Pilgrimage,
—which thenceforth wants not its pillar of cloud by
day, and pillar of fire by night! (*FR, 1,* 183–84)

As an impulse toward revolutionary belief and action,
then, Carlyle's Puritanism is extremely important, but
as overtly expressed in the frequent generalized denunciations, it is unquestionably minor.

The two other major blocks of theoretical material
that loom large in the text possess a more distinct verbal
relationship to the drama of the Revolution even
though they do not provide any final interpretation of
it. They offer not only focal points from which the action can be contemplated and evaluated but also central
images and metaphors for visualizing the march of freedom and giving it a literary and dramatic structure.
The two easily blend, and my categories are, of course,
not meant to be hard and fast. I simply find that behind
the generalizations two root metaphors, derived from
images of the world and the self in "Characteristics"
and *Sartor,* can be discerned. One of these is the image
of an abyss in man inhabited by the subterranean forces
of his unconscious and its wild energies and only thinly
covered over by a rind of habit, civilization, and social
institutions. The other is an organic vision depicting the
evolution of social ideals in history; as in *Sartor,* it easily accommodates itself to the metaphor of changing
vestures and validates such a change. Both metaphors
provide a means of endorsing the revolutionary action

127

yet recognizing all its threats and terrors, its destructive as well as its creative possibilities. Both link up with the inexorable march of freedom, but both also take account of the problematic nature of such a march by attributing to the revolutionary and modern era qualities of frenzied pent-up energies, wild action that verges on madness and anarchy, and institutional change that approaches individual and social chaos.

To Carlyle these central images offer an operational footing in a wild universe and indicate a direction in a vertiginous movement that the personages of the Revolution cannot attain. With their aid, he can chart both the significance and direction of the Revolution yet be at one with all the impulses of his actors. The metaphors provide structure, distance, and control, but also involvement and the heightening of every event with full revolutionary significance.

The metaphor of the subterranean self and its unconscious energies easily attaches to itself the theme of man's basic drive for freedom. The release of these energies, now legitimized by their instinctive demands but by no means purged of their mad and hellish qualities, becomes the basic action of the book.

> For ourselves, we answer that French Revolution means here the open violent Rebellion, and Victory, of disimprisoned Anarchy against corrupt worn-out Authority: how Anarchy breaks prison; bursts up from the infinite Deep, and rages uncontrollable, immeasurable, enveloping a world. (*FR, I,* 211)

As a source of the dramatic development, the centrality of the metaphor of unconscious energies and forces emerges most clearly in Book One, where Carlyle's structure is tightest. In a series of actions and reactions between the outmoded and powerless force of royalism

and the newly emergent power of the twenty-five millions, endowed with a strength grounded on hunger itself, it chronicles the rise of Sansculottism from the dim groanings of millions demanding bread and protesting oppression to their fierce uprising in mob actions against the Bastille and at Versailles where the "Menadic Women" petition their king and finally succeed in bringing him to Paris. Carlyle's choice of the actions and personalities he depicts is governed by the locus of unconscious energies: Louis XVI, believing he has the necessary force, is portrayed as empty and powerless in a sentimental mock-pastoral style, while Sansculottism, discovering it has natural powers, is pictured as an awkward and gamboling giant child in conflict with its king and soon to be his fierce destroyer.

Carlyle's mobs are his principal protagonists, for in their actions and instincts they are the primary manifestations of unconscious and natural forces that have been neglected by outmoded institutions. They are "instinct with life to its finger-ends" (*FR, 1,* 250), "original; emitted from the great everliving heart of Nature herself" (*FR, 2,* 49). Thus the two most important and memorable scenes of Book One are the storming of the Bastille and the Menadic Insurrection of Women; following close upon these are the procession of the king surrounded by "black deluges of Rascality" (*FR, 1,* 288) from Versailles to Paris and the Procession of the Estates-General. Through all three volumes, Carlyle portrays the actions of his mobs in elemental terms: they are seen as great tides of water overwhelming the old institutions, an ocean pressing round the diving bell of their king, huge fires erupting from beneath the earth and sweeping over it, great air gusts escaping through earth fissures and volcanoes, colossal electric charges reacting from group to group and galvanizing each other into furious action, and tornadoes and hurricanes. The

mythical analogues underscore this elemental sense and generally point to its fierceness and destructive capability: Enceladus under Trinacria, Menads, Megaeras, bacchantes. France is all one "Fountain-Ocean of Force, of power to *do*" (*FR, 2,* 103), all things in "continual movement, and action and reaction" (*FR, 2,* 103). Book One, furthermore, shows that these powers are released by the futile policies of Louis' parade of finance ministers, by unjust taxation, and by failure to meet the demands of the populace and to adjust to changing times. The actions of royalty are imaged in terms of elemental powerlessness: rapid, purposeless movement, windy gusts without direction, the airy nothingness of Montgolfier's balloon, the phony darkness of Mesmer, Cagliostro, and occultism, and the pasteboard pastoral nature of court life.

Yet, despite the power and depth of the elemental vocabulary, Carlyle's world is not elemental in the sense that men's actions find their ultimate sanction and source in nature's action; in *Sartor* Carlyle seemed to favor this view at times, but here the elements and myths are what they appear to be, metaphors giving depth, coherence, and power to his human actors and their actions. If man is lost in an unfamiliar universe and in actions that seem beyond his control, these actions are the results not of some participation in an overarching world-will that is impersonal but of individual and mob passions whipped up to a "transcendental" state, become, as Carlyle would say, "preternatural." Thus, Fear, Terror, Hunger, Oppression, Revenge, and especially Suspicion are frequently capitalized and become infused with the force of the original eruption of unconscious instincts. Individuals and groups participate in a sweeping force that is of their own making.

Another factor militating against a cosmic or elemental reading of the book is its distinctly human sense.

Not only are the preternatural passions released from the most pitiable of human situations, hunger and starvation and oppression, but even in the actions of mobs real human grievances are uppermost and distinct individuals make themselves felt. Furthermore, the three volumes contain a great many human stories, each told with sympathy and fullness that would fill many novels. Human beings are at the center of the drama, occasionally riding the whirlwind and sensing its direction but often merely moving with it without fully understanding it. Whatever their inadequacies, Carlyle can find a sympathetic voice for them simply because they are participants in a drama whose distinctly human forces have escaped both their control and full responsibility. One human force grown preternatural permeates both individuals and groups. Thus, the language of the book can cut across definitional levels and find a single force operative in all. "Brigands and Broglie, open Conflagration, preternatural Rumour are driving mad most hearts in France" (*FR, I,* 169). Individual and group, incident and state of mind are all sources of a single human attitude which will itself become the next link in the chain of action of the Revolution.

The final structural metaphor deals with change and organic growth. Much has already been said of change in the discussion of the violent disruption caused by the newly emerging forces, but the organic metaphor holds out the possibility of direction, some moment of flowering and fulfillment, a return to order and sanity in a nonrepressive civilization. It is this aspect of change, this belief in its potential good, that allows Carlyle to contemplate the violent change of the Revolution. Such a view, however, is not without its difficulties, as Book Three with its acceleration of deaths and disorder seems to suggest. *The French Revolution,* like *Sartor,* is threatened by a world of pure process and flux. Carlyle's

belief in organic development permits him to tolerate the most radical of changes, with all its attendant human horrors. His portrayal of action and reaction, even when its direction looks obscure, is a drama of progress and achievement—the validation of a society constructed upon the natural rights and mights of man.

Like *Sartor, The French Revolution* employs the organic metaphor as a background for hope of stability and direction, but it is difficult to detect its presence in the foreground of the book's action. Book One alone seems to promise the emergence of new social vestures and to mark off definite stages of development in Patriotism. In Books Two and Three, with their portrayal of the futilities of Constitutionalism, the internecine quarrels of Patriotism, and the Terror, what has flowered conforms to no traditional organic formulas. Throughout the three volumes, as in *Sartor,* the depiction of dislocation and upheaval, of man's bewilderment in a world from which all the old hierarchy and guideposts have disappeared, is striking. Change appears not so much as organic growth but as disruptive action begetting a new world that is basically characterized by the fluidity of change, the loss of social institutions, and a bewildering complex of multiple and ever-shifting points of view. The picture of Paris struck to fury and demanding arms on the eve of the destruction of the Bastille sets both the problematic tone of wonder, awe, and bewilderment and terror of the new.

What a Paris, when the darkness fell! A European metropolitan City hurled suddenly forth from its old combinations and arrangements; to crash tumultuously together, seeking new. Use and wont will now no longer direct any man; each man, with what of originality he has, must begin thinking; or following those that think. Seven hundred thousand

individuals, on the sudden, find all their old paths, old ways of acting and deciding, vanish from under their feet. And so there go they, with clangour and terror, they know not as yet whether running, swimming, or flying,—headlong into the New Era. (*FR, 1,* 178–79)

The sense of dislocation and bewilderment belongs not only to the people of Paris but also to the narrator. For Carlyle is also the man of the "new era," the heir of this original act of change and its dislocation of old institutions. His tone of awe and wonder—and even of acceptance—is not the narrow fright of the Revolutionists, however, but an extension of that fright to wider implications. Carlyle is distant in history from the Revolutionists, but only partially, for the new institutions promised by the Revolution have not yet come into being and the same sense of suddenly living without the legitimacy of the old individual and social sanctions still prevails.

Thus, the conclusion of the above description—dashes followed by a swift summing up ("—headlong into the New Era")—conveys no finality of resolution. A frequent technique in the narrative, this device points to Carlyle's superior view of the action, a view possible only with a separation in time. As always, however, the intended resolution is a highly qualified and ironic one, devoid of complete fulfillment in action or omniscience on Carlyle's part. The new era is itself characterized by all that goes before it, a bewilderment about direction and movement, the giddy sense of a headlong plunge. These qualities are as important as the element of finality contained in the words "new" and "era."

Carlyle's awareness of the testament of giant social change, of multiplicity and complexity in individuals and society, casts its spell over the three volumes. This

awareness more than any other factor contributes the problematic tone of the history, its strange mixture of hope and futility, wonder and bewilderment, excitement and pity. Far more than his reservations about the questions of belief and the madness of the unconscious energies, the problem of change tempers the enthusiasm of his commitments. Carlyle not only sees what a long battle awaits the Revolutionists; but also envisions his own role as their successor in the nineteenth century and man's similar pitiable plight under industrialism. It is the problem of change, in the Revolutionary past and in the world of the 1830s in England, which gives the book its peculiar urgency, wildness, and vibrancy, the manifestation of Carlyle's own deep involvement. For him the book was a private revolution, a "calcination" [1] as he later said, a descent into hell, the difficult measuring of the personal cost of change and of commitment to the new era.

The complexity of change makes Carlyle impatient with his own fixed theories about the Revolution. Disdaining any simple structure for his book, he utilizes a shifting "point of vision," which "seeking light from all possible sources . . . whithersoever vision or glimpse of vision can be had" may solve his problem in "some tolerably approximate way" (FR, 1, 214). As in Sartor, theories and fixed structure dissolve, to be replaced by randomness, prodigality, and variety. Now Carlyle is with one group of forces, now with another, throwing his readers suddenly against individuals pitted against other individuals, then just as suddenly against whole groups. At one moment he is within his characters, listening to their turbulent thoughts; at another he is watching them from a relatively changeless position, yet

1. Letter to Emerson, 13 Feb. 1837, *Correspondence of Emerson and Carlyle*, p. 159.

only emphasizing thereby the violent change of the Revolution. The sudden emphasis on ticking clocks that go about their normal task as the Bastille falls and on an empty Versailles underscores the thematic use of this device of focus. Characters who appear as patriots in Book One are led to the guillotine in Book Three, so that within the book the process of change is madly accelerated. And each procession of Louis through Paris is contrasted with its predecessor, the shortness of time between them carefully noted.

But nowhere is the problem of change so visible as in the marked peculiarities of the style. Whereas *Sartor* used the Clothes Philosophy to dislocate conventional vision and gain a flexibility of insight and a new way of approaching reality, *The French Revolution* relies far more strongly on its own special style. Narrative moments are rendered with a pell-mell haste, incident rolling upon incident all in the present tense. The exclamation points and question marks that dot the text create excitement and bewilderment in the immediacy of terrifying and complex situations. Sentences start, suddenly stop, or turn back on themselves, are contradicted, and frequently end with a Carlylean irony that underscores the limits of control and heightens the grim force of the Revolution. For instance, "Loménie has removed the evil, then? Not at all: not so much as the symptom of the evil; scarcely the *twelfth* part of the symptom, and exasperated the other eleven!" (*FR, 1,* 104) ; or, "Your Revolution, like jelly, sufficiently *boiled,* needs only to be poured into *shapes,* of Constitution, and 'consolidated' therein? Could it, indeed, contrive to *cool;* which last, however, is precisely the doubtful thing, or even the not doubtful!" (*FR, 1,* 234) . Action is subjected to a grimly ironic voice, questioned, and shown as limited and finally futile in the face of revolutionary power.

135

With further irony, the limited human action itself participates in a dialectic, goading the revolutionary powers onward.

As the sentences turn about and new qualities of voice are brought to bear on the material, the reader's own judgments are manipulated and he becomes a bewildered participant in and onlooker at a complex phenomenon. A single paragraph of the narrative may carry him from deep involvement to the most remote of detached viewpoints, from a single individual to a large group and thence to indifferent nature. In a tumultuous world, he is left without a resting place and no viewpoint is intended to be final. For instance, when Lafayette harangues a mob that insists on marching to Versailles and demanding bread, thus upsetting the slower workings of the new government, even the epic "Scipio-Americanus" bestowed on him provides no stability but is itself coated with irony.

> The great Scipio-Americanus can do nothing; not so much as escape. *"Morbleu, mon Général,"* cry the Grenadiers serrying their ranks as the white charger makes a motion that way, "you will not leave us, you will abide with us!" A perilous juncture: Mayor Bailly and the Municipals sit quaking within doors; my General is prisoner without; the Place de Grève, with its thirty-thousand Regulars, its whole irregular Saint-Antoine and Saint-Marceau, is one minatory mass of clear or rusty steel; all hearts set, with a moody fixedness, on one object. Moody, fixed are all hearts: tranquil is no heart,—if it be not that of the white charger, who paws there, with arched neck, composedly champing his bit, as if no World, with its Dynasties and Eras, were now rushing down. The drizzly day bends westward; the cry is still: "To Versailles!" (*FR, 1,* 258–59)

At other times, the action can suddenly turn into its opposite within the space of a single sentence. At the reception of Louison Chabray, who has petitioned the king on behalf of the Menadic women and has been assured that "grains shall circulate free as air . . . and nothing be left wrong which a Restorer of French Liberty can right" (*FR, 1,* 265), she gives the news with joy; then we are moved rapidly to the moment-by-moment workings of the mob:

> Good news these; but to wet Menads, all-too incredible! There seems no proof, then? *Words* of comfort,—they are words only; which will feed nothing. O miserable People, betrayed by Aristocrats, who corrupt thy very messengers! In his royal arms, Mademoiselle Louison? In his arms? Thou shameless minx, worthy of a name—that shall be nameless! Yes, thy skin is soft, ours is rough with hardship; and well wetted, waiting here in the rain. (*FR, 1,* 265–66)

The broken sentences express each moment of perception and the growth of doubt as it changes to anger and finally to violent antagonism, fury, and the assertion of power and genuine grievances. Louison is suddenly hauled off "to the lanterne," but just as suddenly saved by two bodyguards of royalty.

Yet the book as a whole is not, as I have repeatedly stressed, merely a chaotic whirlwind of endlessly reversing actions, for behind these scenes can be sensed an inevitability and power in the revolutionary forces and a growing assurance of victory in their conflicts with royalty. The declaration of freedom, the power of belief, and the trust in unconscious energies all act as a check to disintegration and flux and afford some stability as a central dynamic. Furthermore, the language of change is used not only to give the moment-by-moment turbu-

lence of the revolutionary drama, but also to come to grips with the very variety of the Revolution and thereby to afford some measure of control and some understanding of the problem of change itself.

Carlyle believes in the powers of the Revolution and their ultimate triumph and destiny, yet he knows that these powers are themselves clouded with the problems of change, the sense of complexity involved in living with the inheritance of the Revolution, its bequest of limitless freedom and awesome multiplicity. Carlyle's variety of viewpoint is intended both to ride the whirlwind and to be encyclopedic, to come to grips with the fullness of revolutionary action, to understand not only how each individual felt at the moment of action but also to provide as much of an assessment and judgment of that action as is possible and to relate it to the central dynamic. The elliptical nature of the style, its sheer density, and the irony and "partial" nature of the more auctorial voice point to this complex inheritance of change, to the immense difficulty of living close to individual passion as a guide without the easier categories and guideposts of the past. Change renders fact itself complex and makes doubly difficult man's attempt to detect its meaning and to embrace it in a realistic historical consciousness.

> And now . . . when History, ceasing to shriek, would try rather to include under her old Forms of speech or speculation this new amazing Thing; that so some accredited scientific Law of Nature might suffice for the unexpected Product of Nature, and History might get to speak of it articulately, and draw inferences and profit from it; in this new stage, History, we must say, babbles and flounders perhaps in a still painfuller manner. . . .

> But what if History were to admit, for once, that

all the Names and Theorems known to her fall short? That this grand Product of Nature was even grand, and new, in that it came not to range itself under old recorded Laws of Nature at all, but to disclose new ones? In that case, History, renouncing the pretension to *name* it at present, will *look* honestly at it, and name what she can of it! *(FR, 3, 203–04)*

Even the language of "Nature," with its "Laws," "Problems," and "Theorems," seems to disintegrate under the problem of change and the historically new, leaving Carlyle without a vocabulary. His overall view of the Revolution and its inheritance as a giant change in individual and social consciousness provides no resolution of problems, but only their full recognition.

The problem of change must be viewed in the context of Carlyle's literary intentions. He certainly intended to write an epic for the modern age, one that would be both ultimate and full in its recognition of man's deepest drives but would also be different from all previous epics, unresolved and problematic, like the process of history itself. The resemblance of *The French Revolution* to traditional epic is overt, and Carlyle underscores this quality by the frequency of his allusions to the epics of Homer, Virgil, Milton, and Dante and by his highly conscious imitation of their epic devices. It is part of his intention that all the traditional purposes of the old epic shall be subsumed into the new, and he appropriates and imitates epic devices to give to his drama the range, depth, scope, and importance of the great masterpieces.

The frequency of these devices is surprising, because in general *The French Revolution* gives a strong impression of artlessness and direct action, with little indication of literary imitation or the conscious epic manner

of Virgil or Milton. Yet there are a number of direct quotations from Homer and Dante in the original languages: geographical allusions to exotic places extend the range of the action much as they do in Milton (Louis' Acapulco ship, the Sahara sand waltz) ; many of the characters are given heroic epithets or phrases (the sea green, incorruptible Robespierre; brawny Titan Danton; Lafayette, the Hero of Two Worlds) ; the leaders are likened to gods or heroic figures from Greek mythology (Mirabeau as Hercules, Danton as Atlas) ; and their haranguing of the multitudes is often deliberately modeled and placed in the manner of the heroic speeches of *The Iliad* and *Paradise Lost.*

There is even the familiar tripartite world of epic with royalty and nobility acting the role of Olympian gods and Versailles as Mt. Ida overlooking the Troy town of Paris. Beneath human society are the Titans, Furies, Eumenides, bacchantes, Menads, Megaeras, and other figures of primitive myth; finally there is a spectral underworld, a kingdom of Dis with its watchdog of Erebus, and Book Three reenacts the traditional epic visit to the underworld: "O fuliginous confused Kingdom of Dis, with thy Tantalus-Ixion toils" (*FR,* 2, 242). Around the universe there is the traditional threat of chaos, of Cimmerian Night in the massed armies of Brunswick and the European powers; deep within there is the figure of Chaos and Old Night (*FR,* 2, 16) in the figure of sooty, blear-eyed Marat. Lastly, there is even "epical machinery" for a scientific age, preternatural states of mind that grip men and whirl them out of control and which Carlyle significantly—as though anticipating the Cambridge classicists—links to the role of godlike forces in the traditional epic.

May we not predict that a people, with such a width of Credulity and of Incredulity (the proper

union of which makes Suspicion, and indeed unreason generally) , will see Shapes enough of Immortals
fighting in its battle-ranks, and never want for
Epical Machinery? (FR, I, 127)

In even broader terms, the expansiveness and the very
subject matter of *The French Revolution* also seem
modeled on epic. What Thomas Greene says in his
chapter "The Norms of Epic" seems true of Carlyle's
work:

> The subject of all epic poetry might thus be said to
> be politics, but a politics not limited to society, a
> politics embracing the natural and fabulous worlds,
> embracing even the moral or spiritual worlds they
> sometimes shadow forth, and involving ultimately
> the divine. The implications expand to suggest, if
> not frankly to assert, a cosmic power struggle.[2]

Even though Carlyle uses these parallels and associations to reinforce the weight of his story, he is fundamentally interested in the enormous difference between
his book and all previous epics. The parallels exist fundamentally to point out that difference. For instance,
the epical machinery is intended to surpass its classical
counterpart in the sweeping power of its action. Suspicion is no longer an abstraction with a capital letter,
but a genuine force generated by men, seizing them and
pitching them into revolutionary terror. Carlyle makes
it clear that there is no room for supernatural action in
his epic of man and his history. For Carlyle and his age,
"True History is the only possible Epic," [3] and even the

2. Thomas M. Greene, *The Descent from Heaven: A Study of
Epic Continuity* (New Haven, 1963) , pp. 17–18.

3. Letter to John Stuart Mill, 28 Oct. 1833, *Letters of Thomas
Carlyle to John Stuart Mill, John Sterling, and Robert Browning,*
ed. Alexander Carlyle (London, 1923) , p. 80.

changing of the gods into metaphors and their attendant armies into human passions will not, Carlyle affirms, lessen its power. Instead, his universe unquestionably seems more of one piece than that of previous epics; from the lowest to the highest action, there is one human force, now appearing in individuals, now in giant masses of men. Carlyle's upper and nether worlds become a part of man's passions, and even when man seems to be the victim of forces beyond his control, he is still a participant in a distinctly human universe. With his preternatural machinery of passions and his metaphors of subterranean powers and Olympian gods, Carlyle achieves a universe that is modern in the implications of the rich interrelationships it manifests.

Not only do the devices and their uses differ from traditional epic; so also does Carlyle's fundamental purpose. His epic for moderns is also a heightened version of mock-epic, a true epic-in-reverse, in which the Titans war upon the Olympian gods and dethrone them forever. The Titanic forces of Patriotism have the real power, energy, and drive toward freedom, and the Olympian court of Louis is but a false mockery of that power: "It was the Titans warring with Olympus; and they, scarcely crediting it, have *conquered;* prodigy of prodigies; delirious—as it could not but be" (*FR, 1,* 197). Versailles may think it is still directing the country, but the gods within it are upon a "cloudy Ida" (*FR, 1,* 168). Carlyle pictures Louis' court in a language of soft surfaces, diffuse sentimentalism, and frivolous activity. Where real activities are concerned, an air of futile remedial measures—a parade of finance ministers —prevails without any attempt to answer new problems, reform existing institutions, or recognize the threat of revolution. Versailles is a playland, as Olympus sometimes is in *The Iliad,* but there is no Jove to give it any power when power is necessary. Carlyle calls its rule an

age of paper, underscoring both its spiritual insubstantiality and its poor economic policies. Its fittest emblem is Montgolfier's balloon, symbol of silly diversions, light-headedness, emptiness, and the possibility of a quick descent (*FR, 1,* 51). The real power is in the Titanic rising of the city of Paris: "Alas, it is no Montgolfier rising there today; but Drudgery, Rascality, and the Suburb that is rising!" (*FR, 1,* 128).

In the face of this uprising, the Olympian gods are ineffectual. Usher de Brézé, who displaces the Third Estate from its meeting hall by improvised construction work, is an ineffectual Mercury (*FR, 1,* 160), for the Third Estate meets in the tennis court of the king and utters the famous oath. De Broglie is an equally ineffectual Mars, since after he fails to deliver the whiff of grapeshot that will put the patriots down, the Bastille is soon conquered (*FR, 1,* 168). Carlyle's Olympian gods have no connection with nature or man's elemental powers or needs; it is the Titans, man in the mass, who carry for mankind the hope of freedom and the recognition of needs, even if violence and revolution are the necessary prelude to that end. Carlyle reverses the original victory of the Olympians over the Titans, not merely as an isolated metaphor but as a statement of the general significance of his epic structure: the inversion of all previous epics and the complete overturning of society, a grounding of society in its primitive basis of nature and fact, and the promise of a new social order that will recognize that grounding.

The ancient quality of the myth, its very pre-civilized "feel," enhances the sense of a return to a primitive ground that is ultimate and all-powerful. Carlyle wants his readers to feel that the Revolution, though an overturning of venerable Olympian institutions, is nevertheless a final and true destructive act. Like the Titans, it is filled with mad furies and strengths but also in touch

143

with the ultimate forces behind man and the universe. The myth of the Titans and the Olympians is used as a metaphor but, in the rich significance of its reversal, it permeates both the structure and content of the book.

Thus the new epic provides an overarching structure embracing the drive toward freedom and national ideals, the released force of unconscious energies, and a world in dislocation and transition. Like them, it is both ultimate and problematic.

The new epic, though an anti-epic, is marked by finality; at last, society has been returned to its foundations in nature, and the new society emerging promises to be consonant with man's economic and instinctual necessities. Homer, the very Father of Epics, is unseated, for the taking of the Bastille makes the taking of Troy town seem as "gossamer" (*FR, 1,* 210). The new epic appropriates the finality of archetypal and religious language: the Menads, petitioning for bread, are simply "Maternity" or "Judiths" and "Eve's Daughters" (*FR, 1,* 256); the taking of the Bastille, while diminishing the taking of Troy, is more like the miraculous overturning of the City of Jericho (*FR, 1,* 110); the Procession of the Estates-General is "the baptism day of Democracy" (*FR, 1,* 133); the Revolution has its own Night of Pentecost when it abolishes Feudalism and its privileges; the age of miracles returns; and the drive to freedom is like a Sinai vision. The strong use of such religious terms seems to suggest that for Carlyle the Revolution does not merely reincarnate ancient biblical goals, but actually establishes a new religion for a new era. If at first Carlyle associates some of these terms with Rousseau's gospel, as he does the Night of Pentecost (*FR, 1,* 219), the phrase soon leaps into an independence, when reiterated, that secures for it a biblical basis of comparison and ultimately the supersession of the original event.

The new epic overturns or overshadows all previous

144

epics not only in its finality and the truth of its social reversal but also by its problematic quality. The new epic powers working their way to victory threaten to go awry in their fierceness, for no simple and coherent social expression of them is available. Once unleashed, they threaten to blaze into madness.

> O mad Sansculottism, hast thou risen, in thy mad darkness, in thy soot and rags; unexpectedly, like an Enceladus, living-buried, from under his Trinacria? They that would make grass be eaten do now eat grass, in *this* manner? After long dumb-groaning generations, has the turn suddenly become thine? (*FR, 1,* 207)

Similarly, when Lafayette, who sides with the grievances of the Third Estate, tries to act as a force of moderatism, he is helpless. His traditionally epic appearance on a white charger and his epithet "Hero of Two Worlds" reflect an epic nostalgia that underscores his outmodedness.

> Hitherto, in all tempests, Lafayette, like some divine Sea-ruler, raises his serene head: the upper Aeolus blasts fly back to their caves, like foolish unbidden winds: the under sea-billows they had vexed into froth allay themselves. But if, as we often write, the *sub*marine Titanic Fire-powers came into play, the Ocean-bed from beneath being *burst?* If they hurled Poseidon Lafayette and his Constitution out of Space; and in the Titanic melly, sea were mixed with sky? (*FR, 2,* 135)

Carlyle's epic by its very subject matter and its reversal must accommodate itself to the threats of anarchy, chaos, destruction, and the end of Universal History. By choosing and then reversing the Titan myth, Carlyle seeks both a new finality and a new problematic.

Carlyle seems to draw on an analogy to Pope's *Dunciad* to reinforce these aspects. Like Pope, he acknowledges the terrible power of the threat and the inevitable strength embodied in the "dunces" as they blot out all learning and civilization, but, unlike Pope, he welcomes the overturning; his dunces are oppressed men, kept in ignorance and hunger, who are now asserting their natural might. The awkward gambolings of the giant Sansculottism bear not only a mock-epic quality when compared with Homer but also a strong resemblance to the comic and threatening picture of the dunces in Pope's mock-epic vision. Rascality pitched from the royal horses "amid peals of laughter" (*FR, 1,* 282) and a senate of Menadic women passing enactments reverse Homer and confirm the threat of the mock-epic *Dunciad*. "Thus they, chewing tough sausages, discussing the Penal Code, make night hideous" (*FR, 1,* 273).

Even his heroes possess none of the formal dignity associated with the high style of the traditional epic; they are rude, crude, filled with turbulent energy, not masters of the full scope of the action but only pitches of power in a whirlwind. In Book Three the reversal seems most frightening and complete: with the wild kingdom of Dis, the universal power, the nation is plunged into a saturnalia, a mad carmagnole dance, a Sahara waltz that seems destructive not only of the old order but of all order. A whole nation is stripped naked; Sansculottism seems to have become a term ready-made for the Clothes Philosopher as it acts out its logical destiny into nakedness.

Yet neither the work nor the world is ever completely out of control. A new epic voice comes to the fore to meet both the finality of the new powers and their unprecedented problems.

The "destructive wrath" of Sansculottism: this is what we speak, having unhappily no voice for sing-

ing. . . . Surely a great Phenomenon: nay it is a *transcendental* one, overstepping all rules and experience; the crowning Phenomenon of our Modern Time. (*FR, 1*, 212)

The voice cannot sing because the possibility of ancient epic has gone. All triumph is now tinged with a measure of futility and bewilderment, for the new social power is not yet realized. No single high style is possible, since the epic artist cannot be detached from his work when he is so deeply involved in the very historical forces set in motion by his actors. To judge these actors is difficult—except by outmoded Puritan categories—for truth is complex and relative in the world of historical fact and human passion. Stable moral and social categories dissolve, and there seems to be no single language, only a shifting vision, which can recognize with adequacy the mixed quality of the Revolution: "Transcendent things of all sorts, as in the general outburst of multitudinous Passion, are huddled together; the ludicrous, nay the ridiculous, with the horrible" (*FR, 1*, 282).

An epic of fact will of necessity be rough-edged like fact itself. The artist must "speak" to accommodate himself best to the variety of fact. Each event admits of many influences, perspectives, and interpretations; each person is a swarm of passions that can scarcely be disentangled. How then can any individual or single event be judged? The new artist will not preserve true epic distance, measuring his characters against fixed goals and standards, but, instead, will identify with the very thought processes of characters and the moment-by-moment action of the historical drama, judging as best he can, seeking what distance is possible, and remembering his trust in man's powers, his drive toward freedom, and the need for change and revolution. The new epic voice is not one of noble austerity but one of questioning and bewilderment; loyal to its trusts and not aban-

147

doning hope, it is nevertheless an ironic mixture of pity and futility.

More than anything else in the book, Carlyle's treatment of constitutional assemblies and feasts underscores this irony. As matters of traditional epic, important in the foundation of the new social order, they are in Carlyle signs of men's folly, their undue hopes of triumph, their overly early abandonment of the complexity of fact and the multiplicity of the new era. Carlyle has little use for the making of the Constitution, though inevitably it must provide a center of the drama since the major revolutionary actors are drawn to it. But for Carlyle it formulates paper theorems out of touch with the real mights of men; the real drama is in the countless complex influences bearing down upon each representative.

The famed gathering on the Champ de Mars with all Paris digging in preparation for the feast merits regard as a kind of symbolism, and Carlyle seems to welcome both the activity and the confounding of class distinctions (FR, 2, 57). Yet, though his language offers encouragement, it becomes clear that he is less than enthusiastic. The actual feast on the Champ de Mars is just another human theatricality, a paper celebration akin to the actions of nobility: "In comparison with unpremeditated outbursts of Nature, such as an Insurrection of Women, how foisonless, unedifying, undelightful; like small ale palled, like an effervescence that has effervesced!" (FR, 2, 49). His irony increases as he watches two hundred individuals in white albs with "Benjamin Franklin" rods and Talleyrand at their head trying to bring heaven's blessing on the new order; finally he treats with evident satiric relish the sudden rainstorm that droops the General's sash, the flags, the ostrich feathers of fashion and the goddess of Beauty herself (FR, 2, 64–65). Part of his attitude no doubt stems from his Puritan background, a fear of blasphemy and hatred of

148

ceremony and superstition; but the irony is more strongly justified contextually as a check on men who want finality without the attendant complexity and suffering. He soon goes on to treat, almost as a dialectical outgrowth of the Feast of Pikes, the rebellion at Nanci, "the unsightly *wrong-side* of that thrice glorious Feast of Pikes" (*FR*, 2, 100). The voice of irony is the voice of realism and admits no incident as final and totally affirmative. Far beyond his actors, Carlyle sees the complex interweavings of the Revolution in space and time.

Yet, however limited the revolutionary figures are, they are never treated with sharp satire or an irony that is merely destructive. A mild benevolent irony, tinged with pity, encompasses all human action. Anacharsis Clootz is, for instance, a ridiculous figure, trailed by representatives of all nations taking their oath to mankind, but ultimately he is more pathetic and silly than opportunistic, and he is certainly not malign. The author's voice clearly judges his folly, but its generality adds a note of pity and even self-reflection.

> Whereby at least we may judge of one thing; what a humour the once sniffing mocking City of Paris and Baron Clootz had got into; when such an exhibition could appear a propriety, next door to a sublimity . . . . But so it is; and truly as strange things may happen when a whole People goes mumming and miming. (*FR*, 2, 53)

Robespierre is also ironically treated as a narrow fanatic steeped in vinegar and self-righteousness, the very parody of the Puritan formalist, and his Feast of the Supreme Being is, by comparison with that of the Champ de Mars, futile and silly: a Mahomet Robespierre, "powdered to perfection," setting his torch to "Atheism and Company, which are but made of pasteboard steeped in turpentine" and watching his "Statue of Wis-

dom" arise by machinery "besmoked a little" (*FR, 3, 267*). Afterwards he is shown with his delusions of grandeur, nursing the hope of being the Christ of the Second Coming that an aged crone claims he is. Carlyle's judgment is succinct: "Mumbo is Mumbo, and Robespierre is his Prophet" (*FR, 3, 268*).

Yet Robespierre emerges neither as fool or villain; in Carlyle's fully rounded view he is both pathetic and threatening. Though he is the most fanatical and frightening figure in *The French Revolution,* Carlyle's voice, ironically placing him against actors and action, succeeds surprisingly in encompassing him with humanity.

Furthermore, by gently satirizing these feasts and triumphs as part of a mock-epic pattern, Carlyle draws attention to the true action of the Revolution and its complexity. As millennial hopes are shattered, more realistic ones, based on a conscious assessment of real powers, emerge. Carlyle's humor brings him back to reality and introduces that very flexibility and pity which he demanded of it in his essay on Richter. The sudden vision of the Goddess of Reason in her kitchen after her crowning in Notre Dame restores an essential humanity to the revolutionary scene and reinforces the true realism of the central drama.

> But there is one thing we should like almost better to understand than any other: what Reason herself thought of it all the while. What articulate words poor Mrs. Momoro, for example, uttered; when she had become ungoddessed again, and the Bibliopolist and she sat quiet at home, at supper? For he was an earnest man, Bookseller Momoro; and had notions of Agrarian Law. Mrs. Momoro, it is admitted, made one of the best Goddesses of Reason; though her teeth were a little defective. (*FR, 3, 229*)

Like his treatment of feasts and worshippers, Carlyle's handling of his heroes also reinforces the realistic and anti-epic nature of his narrative. Nowhere, in fact, does *The French Revolution* show such a distinct difference from traditional epic than in its refusal to offer a heroic focus for the political action. Though both Mirabeau and Danton, with their Titanic energies and grim, crude powers, seem to offer possibilities of a new and natural epic hero—and obviously prelude Carlyle's later fascination with heroes in *On Heroes* and the histories of Cromwell and Frederick—they never stand at the center of the action for more than a few pages. They exercise scarcely any real control over the action, achieve only a minimum of their objectives, and are finally thrown down, not by enemies, but by the very forces with which they are working.

Mirabeau alone seems to bear the closest resemblance to a figure of traditional epic heroism, but his trust in his own individual powers is precisely that which gives him a certain epic outmodedness, makes him fail to be really at one with the masses, and is ultimately the cause of his destruction. The forces set in motion by the Revolution are simply too powerful for one man's will. His attempt to meet with Marie Antoinette, who for Carlyle is royalty's most decisive and heroic figure, is fraught with epic possibilities; a new synthesis of powers seems to be emerging as the result of Mirabeau's heroic individual action. The scene is one of the most exciting and memorable in Book Two, promising a whole different history of France and of the world. But no single individual can shoulder such burdens in the new age; Mirabeau is exhausted by his efforts and dies.

The fierce wear and tear of such an existence has wasted out the giant oaken strength of Mirabeau. A fret and fever that keeps heart and brain on fire;

151

> excess of effort, of excitement; excess of all kinds: labor incessant, almost beyond credibility! (*FR*, 2, 139)

> This brother man, if not Epic for us, is Tragic; if not great, is large, large in his qualities, world-large in his destinies. (*FR*, 2, 147)

Mirabeau's attempt to save both monarchy and republic is later interpreted as a royalist plot and leads to his subsequent defamation and removal from the Pantheon of Heroes which ironically he was the first to inhabit. The meeting with Marie Antoinette which seemed so full of heroic daring and individual hopes now pales before the grim inevitability of the Revolution. Granted the power of the Revolution and royalty's tenacity in its refusal to change, one is left wondering what possible epic result could have issued from Mirabeau's action.

Danton has even fewer moments of greatness than Mirabeau, though he is described as a man of "wider gulp" and appears far more fierce in his energies. But his powerful voice, which mobilizes the citizens into their death-defiant plunge against the European powers, is no help when pitted against Robespierre's paltry accusations. Danton is destroyed by his own companions in the Revolution and is led to the guillotine. Furthermore, his generalized message *"to dare, to dare"* (*FR*, 3, 24) lacks the specificity, individuality, and concreteness of real heroic action. His demand is for a subordination of the individual to the headlong plunge of revolutionary action against European enemies—in short, to a kind of fanaticism. Carlyle's preface to the fiery activity of Book Three hovers over all the heroic actions it chronicles, depriving them of a sense of full individuation and giving them a collective dimension.

> For a man, once committed headlong to republican or any other Transcendentalism, and fighting and fanaticising amid a Nation of his like, becomes as it

were enveloped in an ambient atmosphere of Tran-
cendentalism and Delirium: his individual self is
lost in something that is not himself, but foreign
though inseparable from him . . . . It is a wonderful, tragical predicament . . . Volition bursts forth
involuntary-voluntary; rapt along; the movement of
free human minds becomes a raging tornado of fa-
talism, blind as the winds; and Mountain and Gironde, when they recover themselves, are alike as-
tounded to see *where* it has flung and dropt them.
(*FR, 3,* 121–22)

The real moments of individualism and heroism that
do occur, more tragic than epic, are the scaffold gestures
of bewildered figures, ranging from revolutionists to
royalty, and these provide the human drama of Book
Three. Marie Antoinette, Danton, Charlotte Corday,
King Louis, Madame Roland, and a host of others demonstrate the courage of equanimity, a refusal to despair,
and an assertion of their individual personalities at the
guillotine. Before forces that seem inevitable and beyond their control, they manage to keep their essential
selfhood inviolable. Robespierre's piercing scream as the
bandages are pulled from his wounded jaw contrasts
sharply with the equanimity of the other figures at the
guillotine, placing them in a heroic light and shedding
its own note of hysteria and horror over the previous actions of the Terror.

A world without heroes in control is an uncomfortable one—and one that Carlyle was unable to tolerate
for long—but this is the legacy of the Revolution. The
old carefully structured world, with its hierarchy of valuations, allowed for individual heroism of a high kind,
but in the new world, with its complexity of forces, the
threats to a minimal definition of personality are immense.

Book Three also underscores, more than the preced-

ing volumes, the final problematic nature of any epic realization. At the very moment when Sansculottism is locked in death-grips with the European powers and proving its innate strength ("There is an Unconquerable in man, when he stands on his Rights of Man" [FR, 3, 242]), it also releases its deepest difficulties. The second stage of the Revolution, once the king has been killed and some minimal gains have been made, is a stage of violence, terror, and fanaticism, disruptive of all possibilities of order and positive moral significance.

To believe in the drive of the Revolution, Carlyle must justify—or at least make some attempt to understand—the frightful actions of the Terror. He must deal with the butcherings of the Septemberers

a name of some note and lucency,—but lucency of the Nether-fire sort; very different from that of our Bastille Heroes, who shone, disputable by no Friend of Freedom, as in Heavenly light-radiance: to such phasis of the business have we advanced since then! (FR, 3, 41)

He must tell the story of massacres, drownings of humans in packed ships, fusilladings, the making of wigs from the dead, and finally the tanning of human skins. He must deal with the revolutionists' quarrels with themselves and their own group feuds, with Jacobinism turning against the Gironde, and, finally, with the Revolution devouring its own.

Granted these difficulties, Carlyle succeeds admirably. He avoids both the Scylla of voicing horror and outrage at the Terror and the equally dangerous Charybdis of excusing every action. He admits that the Terror was indeed terrible but sees that it cannot be shrieked away; "it is painful to look on; and yet which cannot, and indeed which should not, be forgotten" (FR, 3, 27). The Terror is at the heart of the Revolution, a testimony to

its ultimate power and a warning to future history—
especially to Carlyle's England—that no government
will be tolerated that does not recognize the needs of
millions who suffer from hunger and oppression.

> Yet our Life is not a Lie; yet our Hunger and Mis-
> ery is not a Lie! Behold we lift up, one and all, our
> Twenty-five million right hands; and take the
> Heavens, and the Earth and also the Pit of Tophet
> to witness, that either ye shall be abolished or else
> we shall be abolished!

> No inconsiderable Oath, truly; forming, as has
> been often said, the most remarkable transaction in
> these last thousand years. Wherefrom likewise there
> follow, and will follow, results. The fulfillment of
> the Oath; that is to say, the black desperate battle
> of Men against their whole Condition and Envi-
> ronment . . . : this is the Reign of Terror. Tran-
> scendental despair was the purport of it, though not
> consciously so. False hopes, of Fraternity, Political
> Millenium, and what not, we have always seen: but
> the unseen heart of the whole, the transcendental
> despair, was not false; neither has it been of no
> effect. Despair, pushed far enough, completes the
> circle, so to speak; and becomes a kind of genuine
> productive hope again. (*FR, 3, 205*)

The Terror must be measured by its circumstances, its
relation to revolutionary hopes, the psychology of the
people who lived through it, and its ultimate implications of hope for other ages. Carlyle abandons all rigorous moral categories and brings to the Terror a flexibility of judgment that places it in various lights without
abandoning its centrality in the Revolution.

His first act, as always, is to look and see rather than
to theorize and judge. The primary act of sympathy, the
realization that these were men fighting against an un-

just condition, makes much that might seem inhuman human.

> One thing therefore History will do: pity them all; for it went hard with them all. Not even the sea-green Incorruptible but shall have some pity, some human love, though it takes an effort. And now, so much one thoroughly attained, the rest will become easier. To the eye of equal brotherly pity, innumerable perversions dissipate themselves; exaggerations and execrations fall off, of their own accord. Standing wistfully on the safe shore, we will look, and see, what is of interest to us, what is adapted to us. (FR, 3, 120)

The pity will not only embrace Louis and Robespierre; but will also attempt to understand what it was like to live in fear, suspicion, and want. From the perspective of Carlyle's time, the killing of the king may seem a cruel and unnecessary act, but by making the situation of the revolutionists come alive with their fear, Carlyle places the act in a totally different light.

> But, on the whole, we will remark here that this business of Louis looks altogether different now, as seen over Seas at the distance of forty-four years, from what it looked then, in France, and struggling confused all round one . . . . For observe, always one most important element is surreptitiously (we not noticing it) withdrawn from the Past Time: the haggard element of Fear! Not *there* does Fear dwell, nor Uncertainty, nor Anxiety; but it dwells *here;* haunting us, tracking us; running like an accursed ground-discord through all the music-tones of our Existence;—making the Tense a mere Present one! Just so it is with this of Louis. Why smite the fallen? asks Magnanimity, out of danger

now . . . . So argues retrospective Magnanimity:
but Pusillanimity, present, prospective? Reader,
thou hast never lived, for months, under the rustle
of Prussian gallows-ropes; never wert thou portion of
a National Sahara-waltz, Twenty-five millions running distracted to fight Brunswick! . . . The
French Nation . . . has pulled down the most
dread Goliath, huge with the growth of ten centuries; and cannot believe, though his giant bulk,
covering acres, lies prostrate . . . that he will not
rise again, man devouring . . . . Terror has its scepticism; miraculous victory its rage of vengeance.
   (*FR, 3,* 81–82)

Carlyle's eye for the human drama, his psychological
sense, renders events that might seem cruel and inexplicable human, immediate, and real. His all-compre-
hensive viewpoint refuses to let him rest in a narrow interpretation of any event; the Terror is to be seen as an
intensification of the manifoldness of the modern
world.

Terror is as a sable ground, on which the most vari-
egated of scenes paints itself. In startling transi-
tions, in colours, all intensated, the sublime, the ludicrous, the horrible succeed one another; or rather,
in crowding tumult, accompany one another. (*FR,
3,* 206–07)

In keeping with this multiplicity, a sudden switch in
perspective can color incidents with a totally different
value: "That same fervour of Jacobinism, which inter-
nally fills France with hatreds, suspicions, scaffolds and
Reason-worship, does, on the Frontiers, show itself as a
glorious *Pro patria mori*" (*FR, 3,* 236) . The Terror at
home is only one side of a different kind of Terror on
the frontiers, action which Carlyle denominates "the
soul of the whole" (*FR, 3,* 230) .

157

In his final judgment on the Terror, Carlyle answers the historian Montgaillard with an irony that diminishes the horrors of the Terror in history and validates once again the aims and rights of Sansculottism.

It was the frightfulest thing ever born of Time? One of the frightfulest . . . . It is a horrible sum of human lives, M. l'Abbé:—some ten times as many shot rightly on a field of battle, and one might have had his Glorious Victory with *Te Deum*. It is not far from the two-hundredth part of what perished in the entire Seven-Years War. By which Seven-Years War, did not the great Fritz wrench Silesia from the great Theresa; and a Pompadour, stung by epigrams, satisfy herself that she could not be an Agnès Sorel? The head of man is a strange vacant sounding-shell, M. l'Abbé; and studies Cocker to small purpose . . . . There is no period to be met with, in which the general Twenty-five Millions of France suffered *less* than in this period which they name Reign of Terror! But it was not the Dumb Millions that suffered here; it was the Speaking Thousands, and Hundreds, and Units; who shrieked and published, and made the world ring with their wail. (*FR, 3,* 311–12)

Nevertheless, the Terror presents definite problems for Carlyle. Though a fundamental testimony of the depth and seriousness of the revolutionary instinct, its relationship to the legacy of Sansculottism is unclear. If Carlyle seems somewhat unappalled at the human cost of the Terror (there is, I feel, a sadomasochistic edge to his detailing of the noyadings), he is by no means so unflinching in the face of its anarchic implications. How the new social order emerges from ultimate Sansculottic disorder remains unclarified as Carlyle reverts to the

158

"mystery" language of body and soul to describe the epic legacy.

> And yet a meaning lay in it: Sansculottism verily was alive, a New-Birth of TIME; nay, it still lives, and is not dead but changed. The *soul* of it still lives; still works far and wide, through one bodily shape into another less amorphous, as is the way of cunning Time with his New-Births:—till, in some perfected shape, it embrace the whole circuit of the world! . . . But as for the body of Sansculottism, that is dead and buried,—and, one hopes, need not reappear, in primary amorphous shape, for another thousand years. (*FR, 3,* 311)

Both hope and social realization are present here, but the connection between historical fact (the death of the body of Sansculottism) and historical inheritance (the soul of Sansculottism) is nebulous. The soul-body dichotomy does not help in healing that split. And there is also fright at precisely that aspect of the Terror which creates the ambivalences of Book Three, its "primary amorphous shape."

Book Three, far more than the preceding volumes, is riddled with ambivalent feelings, ambiguities, and contradictions that do not and cannot fall within the scope of the "problematic" epic—the shifting viewpoint and the variety of voice that offered control of the new epic in Books One and Two. In the absence of the drama of patriots against crown, it suffers from a lack of focus and an absence of rigorous and mounting dialectic. Carlyle finds himself bewildered and without a central structure, and Book Three is especially marked by a desperation in its search for order. Nearly every circumstance that could provide a focus is soon hailed as a new center of order and a principle of organization for the revolutionary drama. Yet this desperation only intensifies Car-

lyle's feeling for the historical facts—that they are enveloped in madness, fanaticism, and chaos.

Apparently recoiling from the threat of such chaos, Carlyle loses some of his faith in the possibilities of his voice to engage such disruption. Though the Terror attests to the Revolution's fundamental might and right, he oddly weakens his case by associating the actual historical quelling of Sansculottism with its death. And though he labels this a death of the body only, he nevertheless thereby further harms his initial and overriding sense of existence as the process of historical existence. Such terms as "nether fire," "chaos," "anarchy," and "Tophet" gradually resume purely negative meanings, however positive their momentary intrusion into the surface of historical existence may be. Consequently, Sansculottism must die, anarchy like death must be self-devouring, and there must be a "Consummation of Sansculottism" (FR, 3, 243).

Carlyle's vision of the death of Sansculottism leaves little room for its continuity except as a moral warning to a later age. As we might expect, the historical method of the book is thus disrupted in the final pages with metaphysical—or at least metahistorical—discourses on the Gaelic and Teutonic fire that Sansculottism kindled, the figures chosen to represent that fire being drawn mainly from history prior to the French Revolution. A moralistic tone associated with Carlyle's harsh Puritanism also intrudes and even begins to dominate when the Gironde are rather suddenly accused of being strangers to the people, men of formulas, and lovers of luxury. Those qualities are again accentuated in the Republic of the Luxuries, with its Grecian dandies and Cabarus balls, that succeeds the Revolution. The historical narrative is by no means abandoned, but the warning to contemporary England seems to have the upper hand. The "Aristocracy of the Moneybag" that appears after

the demise of Sansculottism is obviously not merely a base historical successor to the revolutionary impulse but also and primarily an image of the present social situation: "It is the course through which all European Societies are, at this hour, travelling. Apparently a still baser sort of Aristocracy? An infinitely baser; the basest yet known" (*FR, 3,* 314–15). The new Republic of Mammon blots out the truth of Sansculottism's legacy at the very moment when some attempt at historical connection is being made; the legacy is reduced to a mere warning against contemporary shams, a cudgel with which Carlyle can threaten the money society of his own time.

Even within the actual historical narrative of Book Three there is a similar flight from disorder and complexity. The fear of chaos and madness generates a distrust of the capacities of the varied voice and prompts an occasional search for the finality of order at any price. Carlyle's very formulation of this order shows that it is a last-ditch measure, a desperate reaction to the disorder that he is chronicling. As if sickened by the mad whirl of the Terror, he welcomes the order of the army that will halt such chaos, but the subjunctive mood of his welcome underscores his hesitation.

> For Arrangement is indispensable to man; Arrangement, were it grounded only on that old primary Evangel of Force, with Sceptre in the shape of Hammer! Be there method, be there order, cry all men; were it that of the Drill-sergeant! (*FR, 3,* 288)

> Let there be Order, were it under the Soldier's Sword. (*FR, 3,* 316)

The army, however, offers other fascinations for Carlyle besides the assurance of order. He admires its force

so quickly put into operation, its structure of swift command and obedience, and its daring headlong plunge beyond all morality and personal consideration. The army is Carlyle's mob under a species of control. Early in Book Three he explains that in the shrieking confusion of a soldiery "and not elsewhere, lies the first germ of returning Order for France!" (FR, 3, 54). The army of millions hurling themselves against Brunswick later becomes the grand fact of the Revolution that history has overlooked (FR, 3, 230) and ultimately a justification for the Terror and a means for both affirming and controlling its wild force.

Carlyle has already laid a foundation for the importance of the army in the earlier volumes. Throughout the Revolution, he had always regarded it as the "very implement of rule and restraint, whereby all the rest was managed and held in order" (FR, 2, 73). And he will offer praise to anyone who maintains the soldier's code regardless of his side. Bouillé, a royalist officer, is the great recipient of Carlyle's admiration; in his heroic defiance of the insurrectionary troops on the staircase at Metz, he becomes an unforgettable symbol of power and the best of the royalists, fit to be mentioned as a possible ruler with Mirabeau. Similarly, since the worst and most unqualified evil is insurrection in the army (FR, 2, 73), Louis' greatest fault is his indecision and his worst action the order of cease-fire given to the Swiss Guard who are then destroyed in the Insurrection of August 10.

Fundamentally, the triumph of army order and the accompanying delight in the rush of military might must be seen with the triumph of the Mammon world as a blurring of the legacy of Sansculottism. Though Napoleon appears throughout the three volumes as a possible hero, his connection with the central drama remains peripheral. At the end of Book Three, however, he appears on the scene as the major actor, the successor

to Danton, and with the whiff of grapeshot that Broglie failed to deliver against the patriots at the beginning of the Revolution in Book One, he ends the Revolution and becomes, rather oddly, the inheritor of its power. As the chief figure of the new army sending its conflagration across the world in a series of kingdom-toppling shock waves, he ultimately joins with the tougher Teutonic fire "which no known thing will put out" (*FR, 3,* 297) and to which Carlyle is presumably heir.

> And even so it [the Gaelic fire] will blaze and run; scorching all things; and, from Cadiz to Archangel, mad Sansculottism, drilled now into Soldiership, led on by some "armed Soldier of Democracy" (say, that monosyllabic Artillery-Officer), will set its foot cruelly on the necks of its enemies; and its shouting and their shrieking shall fill the world!—Rash Coalised Kings, such a fire have ye kindled . . . it is begun, and will not end. (*FR, 3,* 297)

The center of Carlyle's history, the grievances of the masses, their human sense of oppression, seems to be forgotten. Destruction and a kind of delight in destruction now made orderly by the army usurp the focus. With the army Carlyle seems to indulge in feelings of sublimity and triumph over all obstacles; man is viewed under the impersonality of force and becomes a force of nature and history, impersonal and inexorable.

Ironically, the finality of the army and its structure of command and obedience point to a regression to the structure of the old order whose demise Carlyle has been so intensely urging. For, despite the rebellious quality of his book, scattered through it are frequent moments of nostalgia for the old order, especially for its hierarchy of authorities with its sense of degrees and the possibility of "transmitting and translating *gradually,* from degree to degree, the command of the one into the obedience of

the other; rendering command and obedience still possible" (*FR*, 2, 232). Such nostalgia is part of the theme of loss and contributes strongly to the mood of bafflement and bewilderment. For Carlyle the new era is characterized by negativity, what it has lost, just as easily as it is by positive affirmation. The severest censure is reserved for the nobles, who should have known what to surrender, what to hold, but instead emigrated and acted fatally on France (*FR*, 2, 232). The army then functions in part as a means of punishing them for abandoning France, in part as a reinstitution of the structure of command and obedience that they once constituted. Similarly, the yearning for epic heroes, for someone to command men—and Napoleon alone is seen as Danton's possible spiritual heir—is also a nostalgia for an older world and an older structure of existence that most of *The French Revolution* denies. Here then are the first signs of Carlyle's preoccupation with a philosophy of heroism in conjunction with army order, materials that will play an important role in his later writings. In *The French Revolution* such concerns are minor, and it is still possible to argue that the appearance of the army is a seal of victory set upon the rights and mights of Sansculottism and the guarantor of its spiritual continuance.

Basically *The French Revolution,* despite its blurrings and ambivalences, remains a strong evocation of rebellion, focusing on man's assertions of his rights against an outmoded and repressive order, and an equally strong statement of the difficulty of living in the new era. As a book of rebellion, it can be compared with two other famous works, Blake's *Marriage of Heaven and Hell* and Nietzsche's *Birth of Tragedy,* which it resembles in certain matters of theme, structure, imagery—and even ambivalence. Such a comparison will, I believe, illuminate all three books.

The *Marriage of Heaven and Hell,* engraved by Blake in 1793, is far closer to the revolutionary events than Carlyle's history but treats the Revolution less as subject matter than as a confirmation of the more generalized theories of the rebellious consciousness erupting against an evil social order that calls itself "heaven." (When in his earlier unfinished poem, *The French Revolution* [1791], Blake had attempted a narrative manner of events not unlike Carlyle's, he had encountered thematic problems that necessitated another kind of treatment and subject closer to the self.) It resembles Carlyle's work in two important respects: the endorsement of energy, rebellion, and "hell" as full life asserting themselves against weak oppressors who have behind them the sanction of traditional social institutions, and the vision of a hoped-for marriage, a new society that will not be repressive, that will be in touch with man's basic powers. The poem also shows something of the same odd mixture of genres and voice that Carlyle's work does—epic, lyric, gnomic, philosophic, satiric, polemic, prophetic, and ironic.

The heaven-hell dichotomy, present in a suggested inversion in *The French Revolution,* is treated far more radically by Blake, for whom the forces of the old order and those of the newly emergent energies are so polarized that he can actually satirically invert his terms, the traditional dualism of heaven and hell, angels and demons. He is so opposed to the forces of organized and orthodox religion as restrainers of life that he satirically acts out the role they would assign to him as a demon and writes in the *Marriage* a bible of hell, rising like Christ from the dead, uttering "gospel" truths, giving beatitudes in the famous "Proverbs of Hell" section, overpowering the "angel" in a temptation scene, and finally withstanding the leviathan of the Apocalypse in a climactic vision.

Carlyle, of course, is by no means the outright rebel

that Blake is, and Blake's satiric inversion, so deliberately flaunted as a corrective to the prevailing orthodoxy, would probably have struck him as shocking and outrageous. (I can find no evidence of Carlyle's reading Blake.) But his own use of the demonic element in man undergoes a shift in *The French Revolution* so that it is not unlike Blake's use in the *Marriage*. In its new spelling "daemonic," it even seems to suggest Greek and nonreligious associations, calling up the voice of genius behind poetry itself (much as Nietzsche was to use the term "daimon" to describe the sudden instinct of Socrates to write poems while imprisoned).[4] Thus, *The French Revolution* insists on the demonic, or the daemonic, as the most natural and fundamental instinct in man and ultimately the expression of his most "religious" impulse. Carlyle's highest praise for Charlotte Corday, a figure of true purpose in a confused France, is that she is "angelic-daemonic: like a Star!" *(FR, 3, 172)*.

Blake's terms, like Carlyle's, point beyond surfaces and Christian categories to a nature symbolism that makes a similar insistence: man, having lost touch with his roots, must be immersed in the cauldron of nature to recover his own nature and then defeat the threats of nature through the power of his own recovered nature. Both writers insist that the infinite element in man has been hidden by false forms, though Blake, more radical in tone than Carlyle, argues for the body as the source of energy and for cleansing the doors of perception, the senses, so that they may once again open man to infinity. But Carlyle also strips man down to his nakedness in the service of a similar cleansing and rebirth; he argues for a breakthrough of surfaces and an eradication of paper theorems and systems that are out of touch with nature, fact, and force. His mobs assert the fact of

4. See Nietzsche, *The Birth of Tragedy,* pp. 84, 90.

166

things as they really are: man is a natural creature linked to nature with his body, his digestive processes, his hunger. Filled with titanic energy, however, the mobs in their uprising reveal the concealed dimensions of man, the infinite expansion of his consciousness that is his unique property.

Both Blake and Carlyle see the world beneath the social surface as filled with repressed giants and titans. The mythical vision they share serves the same function for each. Blake writes:

> The Giants who formed this world into its sensual existence and now seem to live in it in chains, are in truth the causes of its life & the sources of all activity; but the chains are the cunning of weak and tame minds which have power to resist energy; according to the proverb, the weak in courage is strong in cunning.[5]

But Carlyle's world is far less polarized and far more problematic than Blake's; it is hard to imagine Louis and the nobility as evil and cunning however much they may plot to hold onto the old order. Louis' fundamental evil, if I may use that term, is his failure to perceive reality and act accordingly.

Most of the problems that commentators find difficult to explicate in the *Marriage* stem, I think, from this excessive polarization. If "heaven" is really evil and "hell" really good, why not merely an inversion, why a marriage of contraries at all? To this objection, Blake offers a voice of realism where the absoluteness of the inversions seems to be absent. Life is activity and conflict of forces; triumph is dependent on the energetic engaging and overcoming of obstacles. Blake's nonrebellious, nonsatiric voice points out: "Without Contraries

5. William Blake, *Selected Poetry and Prose,* ed. Northrop Frye (New York, Modern Library, 1953) , pp. 129–30.

is no progression. Attraction and Repulsion, Reason and Energy, Love and Hate, are necessary to Human Existence." [6] Like Carlyle, Blake also sees the danger of basing life on a single polarity. Recognizing the danger of man's instincts raging uncontrollably, he demands a nonrepressive order in touch with those instincts yet checking their excess. But so strongly has he espoused energy—both by his satiric inversion and fierce direct statements—that in his description of the Prolific and the Devourer, where the Devourer is allied to Reason and Order, he has difficulty conceiving of the Devourer as anything but repressive or a mere outer limit.

> Thus one portion of being is the Prolific, the other the Devouring: to the Devourer it seems as if the producer was in his chains; but it is not so, he only takes portions of existence and fancies that the whole.
>
> But the Prolific would cease to be Prolific unless the Devourer, as a sea, received the excess of his delights.[7]

Instead of a nonrepressive order, a marriage, Blake seems to argue exclusively for an awakening of energy in an eternal warfare between two classes of men that can never be reconciled. The revolutionary situation seems eternal: "These two classes of men are always upon earth, they should be enemies: whoever tires to reconcile them seeks to destroy existence./Religion is an endeavour to reconcile the two." [8] It is commonly stated that Blake argues for a dialectic of contraries, not of contradictories, but these affirmations in the *Marriage* make it difficult to envision that dialectic and that "marriage."

6. Ibid., p. 123.
7. Ibid., p. 130.
8. Ibid.

What readily predominates in Blake's work and ultimately distinguishes it from Carlyle's, however, is not
the philosophical theory but the fierce voice of protest
that generates (but overrides) the inversion, the satire,
the arrogance, the deliberate excess, and the very labeling of opposites that causes such confusion. He is the first
of the rebellious protest poets, still common in our own
day, for whom the existing social structure and morality
will always be a repressive force. To such poets the social order always appears at first stronger but then paradoxically weaker when compared with the inherent energies of their own poetic infinitude and affirmation of
natural values.

Toward the end of his book, Carlyle seems to be em-
broiled in some of the same confusions as Blake. Fearing
the excesses of his Prolific, he too seeks the finality of a
Devourer in the army. Left with the Cabarus balls at
the end of the Revolution, he seems to offer a theory of
history as an endless spiral of repression and revolt. Yet,
as I have shown, these problems do not touch the core of
his work, as they do in Blake's *Marriage*.

Carlyle also offers what might be called a "dialectic of
contraries," but here too he differs from Blake. Even
when his vocabulary approaches that of Blake, his picture of historical existence complicates the contraries, so
that, in the process of time, valuations shift into their
opposites (a process that was also explored by Blake in
his later visions). Blake's theory of contraries in the
Marriage pushes instead toward the opposition of final-
ities, an eternal situation scarcely varied by history.

Furthermore, Carlyle locates the contraries within
each individual as well as in history, much as Blake did
in his later poetry. The picture of both self and history
that emerges is even further complicated by the fact that
the contraries are not merely within the opposition of
classes but within the self. Carlyle thereby makes them

susceptible of a far less rigorous and more flexible treatment than in Blake's *Marriage*. Oppression exists, hope exists, and the violence of revolution is necessary; but the themes are now tinged with irony and acceptance rather than violent assertion.

> So, however, in this world of ours, which has both an indestructible hope in the Future, and an indestructible tendency to persevere as in the Past, must Innovation and Conservation wage their perpetual conflict, as they may and can. Wherein the "daemonic element," that lurks in all human things, *may* doubtless, some once in the thousand years, —get vent! But indeed may we not regret that such conflict,—which, after all, is but like that classical one of "hate-filled Amazons with heroic Youths" and will end in *embraces*,—should usually be so spasmodic? For Conservation, strengthened by that mightiest quality in us, our indolence, sits for long ages, not victorious only, which she should be; but tyrannical, incommunicative. She holds her adversary as if annihilated; such adversary lying, all the while, like some buried Enceladus; who, to gain the smallest freedom, has to stir a whole Trinacria with its Aetnas. (*FR, 1,* 39)

Carlyle eschews the finality of opposites, of all labeling, and even of rigorous moral judgment. The power of his vision is the power of his humanity, realism, and flexibility. Blake, while treating the same themes, delights in opposition, the use of philosophical and moral labels, and the drive toward ultimates. The power of his vision in the *Marriage* lies in an area that Carlyle shares, but to a lesser degree—in the power of the very fierceness of his individual protest and threats.

Nietzsche's *Birth of Tragedy* (1872) is closer than the *Marriage* to *The French Revolution* in its contempla-

tive and philosophic tone, which plays over the need for titanic assertion, but in its radical opposition to almost all of culture and history it is more closely allied to the radicalism of Blake. A bizarre first book, an anti-scholarly intuitive treatise of highly scholarly material by a skilled philologist in revolt, the *Birth of Tragedy* propounds the anti-civilized thesis that the greatness of Greek tragedy grew from the choric figure, a satyr god close to the Dionysiac forces of nature, who in this highest art was wedded to the Apollonian "epic" material associated with civilization and the Olympian gods. Nietzsche sees Greek tragedy as a restoration of the Titans to daylight, much as Carlyle sees the Revolution. Furthermore, the outcome of the conflict is, like the Revolution, a glorious reinstatement.

> The effects of the Dionysiac spirit struck the Apollonian Greeks as titanic and barbaric; yet they could not disguise from themselves the fact that they were essentially akin to those deposed Titans and heroes. They felt more than that: their whole existence, with its temperate beauty, rested upon a base of suffering and *knowledge* which had been hidden from them until the reinstatement of Dionysos uncovered it once more. And lo and behold! Apollo found it impossible to live without Dionysos.[9]

The "yoke of marriage,"[10] however, was short-lived; Socrates is the villain of the piece, propounding a lifeless reason, a dead form of Apollo that usurps control of the Western mind. Wagner—and presumably Nietzsche himself—are the first signs of a Dionysiac artist bringing about the new restoration.

Nietzsche's book is obviously not only a rather con-

9. Nietzsche, p. 34.
10. Ibid., p. 19.

fused and brilliant philosophical essay, but also a blast at culture, a titanic refusal that goes behind culture to its historical roots in nature only to prove that man's very roots with nature have been neglected. Like Carlyle's book, it is a look at instinctual man alive with energies and sharply contrasted to the weakness of a dead culture. Nietzsche's basic model is therefore much like Carlyle's, but his eye is on neither politics nor the complexity of history but on the role of art, particularly tragic art, as a justification for life, a perfect representation of its essence and a force that will reconcile man to his own suffering and to a terrifying and perhaps meaningless universe.

Carlyle has little to say about art, though the fact that he sees his history in relation to various literary models is rich in artistic implications. Nietzsche's speculations on tragic art and the tragic artist and his relationship to Apollo and Dionysos seem every bit as useful as Carlyle's own artistic implications, for they offer an interesting parallel to Carlyle's own concerns.

Nietzsche sees tragedy as a composition of two artistic genres—epic and lyric. The physiological and psychological bases of these genres when unmediated by art, are dream and intoxication, respectively. Such terms are obviously too clear-cut for Carlyle, and for Nietzsche himself they probably represent only the outline of an idea, the neatness of a philosophical and psychological solution to his problem. But the variety of states of which Nietzsche speaks, the similarity of genres, the manner in which he speaks of both, and the ultimate tragic fusion with a Dionysiac emphasis show how close he and Carlyle are in their basic considerations.

Nietzsche's discussion of the Apollonian state of dream and its artistic perfection in epic, where the philosophic eye regards life as an illusion and a comedy from which the self is removed, is obviously allied to

Carlyle's sense of his philosophical voice as an epic one playing over the material of *The French Revolution,* limiting and ordering it, making its rough edges smooth and tranquil, seeing it as essentially a comedy. Furthermore, Nietzsche's discussion of the Dionysiac state of intoxication and its artistic analogue, the lyric manner, that purges it of lust, cruelty, and sexual excess seems allied to Carlyle's participation with his mobs on the pages of his book and his aim to induce in the reader the sense of presence. "The 'I' thus sounds out of the depth of being." [11] For Nietzsche such a state approximates music, the Schopenhauerian world-will itself, not merely its image, and, by implication, an art like that of *The French Revolution,* where the density of style can be a barrier to understanding but once entered into carries the reader along on its own surge of intensity, rhythm, and imagery.

The merger of epic and lyric, of Homer and Dionysiac chorus, into tragedy with a Dionysiac emphasis shows a tragic concern in Nietzsche not unlike the one already noted in Carlyle. Nietzsche, however, stresses redemption through tragedy—a fusion with the original oneness, as he puts it in the youthful Schopenhauerian language that he is soon to discard. Carlyle denies neither the oneness nor the rapture of the fusion and the self-transformation implicit in it, but he does not seek redemption through art, not even a quasi-redemption from the temporal process. Carlyle's eye is on the present and the past and on historical existence itself; he speaks as one distanced in history from the Revolution and consequently aware of both the transports and the difficulties.

Nietzsche, of course, is primarily fascinated with the terror of the Titans, the unvarnished truth of instinct that they reveal to a surface of civilization. In this re-

11. Ibid., p. 38.

spect he is at one with Carlyle. His use of the Titan myth, however, is a historical one. He returns to the original users of the myth for his subject matter, and he sees it, presumably as they saw it in an unconscious manner, as an emblem of the relationship of personality and culture to nature. Thus he makes clear the link between Carlyle's use of nature images and his use of the Titan myth and underlines the ultimate nature of both.

In returning to Greek culture, Nietzsche succeeds in avoiding all Christian dualism and the difficulties of the angelic-demonic dichotomy; at the same time, he gives the impression of both undermining all of civilization and getting at its roots in the hope of recovering an authentic selfhood and culture once again. Implicit in such a drive behind history, however, is a repudiation —foreign to the later Nietzsche—of history itself and of most of culture. Both rejections are abetted by the metaphysical language of Schopenhauer which permeates the essay. Carlyle may risk a certain literary flavoring in the use of his Titan myth in connection with the modernity of the Revolution, but his gain in immediacy and historical consciousness is great.

Since his primary concern is the Revolution and its repercussions in history, not the philosophical principles behind it, Carlyle, in his own way, manages to have the best of both sides. Nietzsche, on the contrary, is more like Blake in his interest in the rebellious consciousness, an assertion of life and instinct that is primarily determined by philosophical and psychological attitudes rather than by the economic and historical conditions which Carlyle regards as primary. Since his rebellious role is both highly individual and total, he, like Blake, finds it difficult to conceive of his Apollo as anything other than a restrainer, and his philosophic desire for finality presents difficulties. In phrases startlingly like

those in the *Marriage* about the Prolific and Devouring, Nietzsche affirms that Apollo reminds one of the "holy, universal norms" but "threatens to freeze all form into Egyptian rigidity," to "prescribe its orbit to each particular wave," and thus "to inhibit the movement of the lake." [12] Carlyle's problems with the "marriage" and the order-disorder dichotomy are minor and merely theoretical compared to Nietzche's and Blake's, for the practice of his book leads not to them, but to a wider spectrum of viewpoints.

Nietzsche drives toward a resolution of contraries in art, Carlyle toward an understanding within history of the irresolution of life and the juncture of personality and history. His voice is consequently far less insistent than Nietzsche's, whose very singular manner thrusts itself boldly upon the material and dominates it. If part of the meaning of *The French Revolution* is that no single meaning or attitude can be drawn from it, the fighting voice of the author must necessarily recede in importance despite his commitments. Less philosophically ultimate and rebelliously intense than either Blake or Nietzsche, Carlyle is more objectively aware of the individuality and uniqueness of each dramatic moment. More bewildered than they at the conjunction of man's choice with the logic of history, his similar theme of rebellion against oppression is rendered with both more objectivity and greater irony.

In assessing the qualities that make *The French Revolution* different from Blake's and Nietzsche's works, it is useful to compare it with the philosophical novel of history which has flourished since the late nineteenth century. *The French Revolution* has obvious affinities with such books as *War and Peace, Nostromo,* and *A Passage to India.* Conrad's *Nostromo* (1904) affords the closest comparison in theme and method; ironically, it also

12. Ibid., p. 65.

rounds out an era of empire, which Carlyle's book might be said to inaugurate, while it points to the persistence of problems that Carlyle had both depicted and feared.

Like *The French Revolution*, *Nostromo* is epic and encyclopedic in scope. Presenting in its study of the revolutionary turmoil in the mythical South American kingdom of Costaguana a complexity of viewpoints toward imperialism, capitalism, colonialism, and revolution, it affords a similar sense of dual movements rarely in harmony. The inexorable thrust of history, a movement of man but often like nature out of his control, is opposed to the attempts of man at self-direction and the directing of politics and history. Nature, as in *The French Revolution*, is both massive and indifferent; it is best symbolized in the snow-covered mountain Higuerota that dwarfs the action as a gigantic and stable backdrop, inevitably emphasizing the precariousness, transitoriness, and futility of the action of the plain below it.

Nostromo is a far more somber and skeptical book than *The French Revolution*, undoubtedly because of its thematic center, the unfulfillment of the liberal heritage, and the more skeptical and pessimistic temperament of its author. *Nostromo* lacks Carlyle's sense of fieriness and his fierce use of nature and force, precisely those qualities which ally Carlyle with Nietzsche and Blake. Furthermore, Carlyle would have endorsed the imperialistic venture whose backbone Conrad is breaking in his protrayal of a very different kind of revolution, a mad eruption into what the Goulds and other idealists have conceived as a history of progress for Costaguana. Despite all these differences, however, both books are at one in their realistic assessment of man and history.

Nostromo has some of the same density and complexity of style and action as *The French Revolution*. In-

deed, for the first two hundred pages of a very long book, these qualities raise an almost insurmountable barrier to understanding. The implications, however, are clear: man lives in history, a process so complex and relentless, so capable of a variety of movements, so fraught with individual and social peril that it is difficult to discern the human figure within it. Yet, as both books show, history moves by man and, however much it resists or distorts his impulses, affords a ground in which man can affirm his spirit and transcend fate, chance, and the grim logic of mere events.

The silver in the town of Sulaco rather than the revolution provides a focal point about which a variation of viewpoints toward the revolution, imperialism, and capitalism can play. The shifting dance of attitudes toward the silver and the metal's transformation under the historical occurrences from an object for civilized progress to one of greedy debasement provides a variety of viewpoints much like that provided by Carlyle's epic eye. Around the silver cluster idealists, fanatics, rationalists, good-natured but unthinking men, and thieves. The complexity of viewpoint engendered, the human difficulty of achieving some solidity in a moving process, permits Conrad to attain the same tolerance and forgiveness that Carlyle achieves. Conrad's "villains," like Carlyle's, are more petty and pathetic than truly evil.

For Conrad these viewpoints, expecially the major ones—the guilt, hopelessness, and inferiority of Dr. Monygham, the instinctive trust of Nostromo, the idealistic liberalism of Giorgio Viola, the idealistic capitalism, later an obsession, of Charles Gould, the rationalistic skepticism of Decoud, and the noble charity of Emilia Gould—are all possibilities within the novelist himself and his book is a testing of them in dramatic conflict and within a microcosm that represents the process of history itself. Carlyle is more objective, of course,

177

and his history is real, but his identification with his figures and his own shifting viewpoint imply a conception of masks, of implicit viewpoints, that informs *The French Revolution* and was a fundamental concern and technique in the essays and *Sartor*. It is difficult, for instance, not to detect in Carlyle's satire of the Puritan formalist Robespierre an element of self-satire.

Like Carlyle, Conrad explores the futility of his various positions. The rigidity and finality of Charles Gould's idealism ironically betrays both the cause he espouses and his own humanity. He not only wants to accomplish too much single-handedly; he also fails to perceive his real involvement within time and history and within the larger capitalistic designs of Holroyd, his backer in America. A member not of a dying order but of a powerful one, Gould nevertheless has some of the blindness to historical reality that Louis manifests in *The French Revolution*. From another perspective, moreover, he reveals the same deficiency of historical perspective as Carlyle's revolutionary utopians.

All forms of idealism are suspect to Conrad, as they are to Carlyle, and this skepticism gives the two books a certain final tonal similarity. Emilia Gould's compassion is important and marvelous but, operating apart from the logic of material events, deprives her idealism of historical force and scope. Giorgio Viola's nineteenth-century liberalism and the reasoned hopes of Don José Avellanos are also rendered futile, much as Carlyle showed the hopes of his revolutionaries quashed. Utopianism remains a fiction, a matter of mind rather than history. The epic conceptions of self and society are as outmoded as they appear in *The French Revolution*. Nostromo's heroic individualism is sullied by his exploitations of the silver and his own swaggering heroics, the epithet "illustrious capataz de cargadores" is intended to have a hollow ring, and, posturing on his

charger, he reminds us of Carlyle's Lafayette, the Hero of Two Worlds.

But if Conrad refuses to endorse any static idealism, any fixed conception of self and society, he also, like Carlyle, refuses to fall victim to an endlessly ironic attitude, a skepticism that hinders all involvement in historical action. Decoud is his example of the relentlessly philosophical mind preying upon itself, corrupted by excessive civilization, and forced in solitude into self-destruction. He is ultimately defeated by the flux of vast and indifferent nature, from which man struggles to be distinct but upon which he must erect civilization. Believing in nothing and devoured by solitude, Decoud plunges into the Golfo Placido and is "swallowed up in the immense indifference of things." [13]

If the civilized man cannot provide an answer, neither can the natural man Nostromo, who is also corrupted by the silver. Like Carlyle again, Conrad sees man's subterranean nature as a brutalizing force awaiting him when the trappings of civilization are pulled off in revolution. During the frequent revolutions in Costaguana history relapses into "primeval club law" (as Carlyle would say): cheap dictators and opportunists take over with torture as their method; a bandit like Guzman Bento destroys the will and even the personality of a Dr. Monygham. Señor Hirsch, with his horrifying fear and terror, finally killed by the equally terrified commander Sotillo, provides with his killer an example of the will fallen victim to terror and fright. Both victor and victim are cheap and cowardly, but their terror is human and pathetic.

Conrad's universe is neither more nor less without hope than Carlyle's, however—despite the more somber and pessimistic tone of Conrad's work. There are no

13. Joseph Conrad, *Nostromo*, intro. by Robert Penn Warren (New York, Modern Library, 1951), p. 560.

philosophical ultimates, no utopias; neither is there any easy aesthetic coating to furnish truth.

Conrad's book, like Carlyle's, embodies both aesthetics and philosophy but refuses to rest in the finality of either. Three of its major figures perform a moral judgment upon themselves and in so doing not only reenter the human community but provide that human possibility for propelling history in new directions. Nostromo's repudiation of the silver is the prelude to the emergence of a newer, more hopeful vision of society with Marxist overtones, but it is not intended as final in any sense; true finality paradoxically lies in freeing the self from the finality of objects and concrete objectives. Nostromo's act is in sharp contrast to Gould's persistence in his obsession of civilizing Sulaco through his mine, an obsession which eventually succeeds merely in inaugurating a world of capitalistic tyranny, colonialism, and the promise of future revolution: "the time approaches when all that the Gould Concession stands for shall weigh as heavily upon the people as the barbarism, cruelty, and misrule of a few years back." [14]

This bleak vision is tempered by the fact that the society at the end of the book is in truth superior to that at the book's beginning. Ironically, it is Decoud's plan for the independence of Sulaco, a vision motivated by his real love for Antonia Avellanos, that survives the revolution. As Emilia Gould, Dr. Monygham, and Nostromo indicate in their major decisions, society's hopes are dependent upon the interplay of human wisdom and moral commitment. Robert Penn Warren in his introduction to *Nostromo* has stated the case brilliantly, and his remarks seem equally applicable to Carlyle.

Man must make his life somehow in the dialectical process of these terms (idea versus nature, morality

14. Ibid., p. 571.

versus action, utopianism versus secular logic), and in so far as he is to achieve redemption he must do so through an awareness of his condition that identifies him with the general human condition, not in abstraction, not in mere doctrine, but immediately. The victory is never won, the redemption must be continually re-earned. And as for history, there is no Fiddler's Green, at least not near and soon. History is a process fraught with risks, and the moral regeneration of society depends not upon shifts in mechanism but upon the moral regeneration of men. But nothing is to be hoped for, even in the most modest way, if men lose the vision of the time of concord, when "the light breaks on our black sky at last." [15]

Carlyle, unlike Conrad, only partially embodies the redemptive process in his revolutionary figures. Their utopianism and false philosophies from Rousseau and Voltaire seriously limit them, but their hopes are validly directed toward a time of concord, freedom, and release from oppression. This vision of an ultimate hope animates both books and is the source of the lofty human compassion which overarches the two works. The voice of the author who embraces his characters and their history is ironic but not ultimate. The process of engaging a variety of limited voices in the drama of history itself is the realistic and artistic way of learning the possibilities of selfhood and of maintaining the human direction of a hopeful history.

Carlyle did not go on to write philosophical novels of history, of course, for the urgency of the social crisis of his times compelled him to stress his prophetic role. But so long as he remained true to the problematic worlds of *The French Revolution* and *Sartor*, his works spoke

15. Ibid., p. xxxiii.

with a sense of realistic complexity and full humanity. When in the sometimes moving and occasionally fierce pamphlet "Chartism" (1839), he applied the truth of *The French Revolution* to immediate economic conditions in England, he found himself able to speak movingly of the worker's sense of oppression and feeling of neglect but less able to tolerate social upheaval or an economic breakthrough. The notion of guidance by an old order is a solution merely hinted at in *The French Revolution.* In *Past and Present,* however, treating the immediate social situation, he found a much more complicated clash of forces at work and explored them in a larger aesthetic framework which again engaged the full dimensions of his own voice. It is in this later book that he seeks the full flowering of a historical vision that will not be "utopian" but realistic, historical, and deeply transforming for every individual—a vision that is the proper fruit of the explorations of both *Sartor* and *The French Revolution.* *Past and Present* is thus the true continuation of the tradition of *The French Revolution,* not *On Heroes* and the later histories of Cromwell and Frederick the Great, which are expansions of that minor drive toward epic heroism, philosophical finality, and militarism which lay outside the more profound and realistic directions of the early history.

⋲§ 4 §⋺

PAST AND PRESENT:

APOCALYPSE AND FULL VISION

And did those feet in ancient time
Walk upon England's mountains green?
And was the holy Lamb of God
On England's pleasant pastures seen?

And did the Countenance Divine
Shine forth upon our clouded hills?
And was Jerusalem builded here
Among these dark Satanic Mills?

Bring me my Bow of burning gold:
Bring me my Arrows of desire:
Bring me my Spear: O clouds unfold!
Bring me my Chariot of fire.

I will not cease from Mental Fight,
Nor shall my Sword sleep in my hand
Till we have built Jerusalem
In England's green & pleasant Land.

Blake,
Preface to *Milton*

Although *Past and Present* (1843) is separated from *The French Revolution* (1837) by the lectures *On Heroes* (1840), I shall consider it here since in its revisions of the concepts of prophecy and apocalypse it is more close- ly allied to that prophetic and apocalyptic history. At first glance, *Past and Present* represents not merely a

183

new departure but an altogether different kind of book. It is no history, but a warning to England that what happened in France "can happen here." The prophetic voice clearly dominates the book, now satirizing and condemning, now excoriating sham and semblance and cant, now majestically and sublimely calling to witness the laws of God and the universe. To some extent the book shows a hardening of Carlyle's dualisms, a less exploratory manner than *The French Revolution*, but nevertheless, as it charts and heralds new literary directions, it remains fascinating in its own peculiarity of method and vision and in the problems it reveals. It may be seen as a unique link between the prophetic, radically Protestant, and biblical tradition of Bunyan, Milton, and Blake and the modern philosophical, economic, and social reformist tradition of Engels and Marx. *Past and Present* has a little of everything, and it is interesting to observe that authors as diverse as Engels and Emerson could find what they wanted in it and praise those findings highly in individual reviews.[1]

Though the concern of *Past and Present* with specific Victorian social policies may somewhat limit its interest for today's readers, the immediacy of a book which fosters such specific concerns should not be dismissed. Indeed, the main drive of the work is toward the fulfillment of vision that *The French Revolution* was unable to achieve. Carlyle wrote it in a more hurried fashion than was customary for his other works,[2] for he was

1. Emerson's review appeared in the *Dial* of July 1843 and is reprinted in *Works, 12,* 379–91. Engels also paraphrased *Past and Present* in his contribution "Die Lage England" in the *Deutschfranzösische Jahrbücher* (1844), pp. 171–72. For more information on this subject, see Peter Demetz, *Marx, Engels, and the Poets* (Chicago, 1967), esp. Chap. 2, "Economics and Intellect: Thomas Carlyle."

2. Grace J. Calder, in her study *The Writing of "Past and Present"* (New Haven, 1959), offers evidence that the book was

filled with shock and outrage at the condition of alienated and idle workers sitting banefully enchanted before
the St. Ives Workhouse. At the time he was somewhat
laboriously collecting material for his *Cromwell,* which
had not crystallized in form but was still projected as a
voluminous history of the Commonwealth and the Civil
Wars, presumably a book analogous in scope to *The
French Revolution.* His sudden perception of the workhouse as a particular emblem of the horrible condition
of England and its poor, when contrasted to the vast
industrial wealth and potential of the new society,
awakened him, as the Chartist uprisings had earlier, to a
sense of impending crisis and jolted him out of the evasion of society and the retreat into the past that the
work on *Cromwell* largely afforded. As he later said, as
long as *Past and Present* remained unwritten, his con-
science was reproached with a sense of duty failed; it
was a book that stood between him and *Cromwell.*[3]

As the historical and narrative structure of *The
French Revolution* disappeared in *Past and Present,* the
prophetic and apocalyptic came to the fore. To a certain
extent, Carlyle seems to have fallen back into the Puritan past and to have hardened religious truths almost
into their most traditional formulations, but that very
past gave him a strength to face the present that the
French Revolution could not provide. And in his direct
confrontation of the economic and social situation the
evasive action of digging up *Cromwell* sources was canceled. The past filled Carlyle with a solidity of voice, a
prophetic strength—dangerously left unquestioned, it is

---

composed over a period of five months and not during a "short
seven weeks" as tradition holds (p. 8). This is still a short period of
composition for Carlyle with a full-length book.

3. Quoted from his journals by James Anthony Froude, *Thomas
Carlyle: A History of His Life in London, 1834–1881* (2 vols. London, 1884, 1911), *1,* 318. My references are to the 1911 edition.

true—that launched the method and vision of *Past and Present* itself. The vision of darkness and the prophetic warnings of *The French Revolution* were deepened in a new way by the immediacy of Carlyle's warnings; the apocalyptic breakthrough of society and self now rested with the power of the prophet himself and his immediate relation to society, his own ability to shape the future by his visionary capacity.

In structure and method, and even in much of the content of its vision and the nuances of tone, *Past and Present* resembles that odd epic *Jerusalem,* a book obscure even today except to Blake devotees. And just as *Jerusalem* stands as full vision in relation to the fierce Orc-like and revolutionary writings of *The Marriage* and the early Blake, so *Past and Present* stands as full apocalyptic vision to Carlyle's earlier and occasionally rebellious *French Revolution.* Both *Jerusalem* and *Past and Present* move away from any narrative structure in favor of a prophetic and apocalyptic structure, and both books have been bewildering to readers because of their failure to conform to any expectations of a significant genre. Carlyle's has obviously been more accessible than Blake's, both because of its public subject matter and its easy resemblance to a social tract—which it is, but only in part. Strikingly similar in both books is the mixture of biblical language and the vision of the role of the prophet within the contemporary English landscape and history.

Both *Jerusalem* and *Past and Present* hearken back to the older tradition of the biblical prophetic books, particularly Ezekiel. Harold Bloom's apt description of the structure of each book of *Jerusalem* as a series of gradually sharpening antitheses between two contrary forces can be applied to *Past and Present* as well. Like the prophetic books of the Bible, both works are

poems of admonition delivered to a wavering people. The poems [of Ezekiel] are interspersed in
chronicles that deliberately mix history and vision,
the way events were and the way the prophet fears
they will turn out to be if they continue as they are
going, or hopes they will emerge if the people will
realize that they are at the turning, and can control
events by a change of spirit.[4]

This sense of a turning point, of a crisis and the call to
reform, is obviously all-important. In *Past and Present* it
deepens into greater horror of the imminence of chaos
and destruction and the greater need for affirmative vision and moral reform, a pattern which *Jerusalem* also
follows. Here Bloom's idea of the structure provided by
the contraries can be both central and fruitful. Blake's
epic seems obscure because it operates not with a narrative structure but with clashing, mythically designated
areas of consciousness in a reduced Albion, who is both
the hero as individual and England (and potentially total man as individual and restored society). But where
Blake uses areas of consciousness to conjure up a vision
of a problem that is basically individual, Carlyle primarily moves outward to survey dimensions of time, political institutions, and social groups that are at war
with one another and engaged in the dialectic of contraries. Such chapter titles as "Democracy" and "Aristoc-
racies" may seem prosaic and unmythical, but other
more symbolic titles—"The Sphinx," "Morrison's Pill,"
"Plugson of Undershot," and "Captains of Industry"—
suggest that Carlyle saw the whole book as a conflict of
vast social forces and that he grouped his material accordingly. As Albion is reduced to the nadir of vision by

4. Harold Bloom, *Blake's Apocalypse* (Garden City, 1963), pp.
366–67.

the conflict with his oppressive spectres, so too Carlyle reduces England through his own war of forces. His chapter headings point to centers of energy, forces, and symbolic nodes for understanding self and society. In their conflict, England, like Albion, is reduced to the brink of chaos, until by the very pressure of facing such a conflict it is reborn (like Albion again) apocalyptically in the vision of a total society with London, the home of deified man and labor, as an analogue to Golgonooza.

The differences between Blake and Carlyle are so obvious that they scarcely need stressing. Blake is far more subtle in his probing and difficult study of the prophet's relation to his visionary capacity and the construction of his total vision and is far more psychologically penetrating in his study of the construction of the total self and his knowledge of the pitfalls of solipsism, rigidity of doctrine, and egotistic pride. Blakeans would no doubt regard Carlyle as falling into these very pitfalls, and perhaps furthermore as merely regressive, concerned with nature and society at the expense of the individual, and unfree from the platitudes of traditional Christianity that shield him from insight. There may be, I think, some justification for such charges, and I shall deal later with the problems they present. They do not obliterate the positive similarities and even the advances that Carlyle makes upon Blake, however. What Carlyle loses in psychological subtlety, he gains in breadth and scope and a kind of tangibility of fact, social institutions, and character that can be found in Blake only through the protracted comments of a scriptural guide like Mr. Bloom. Carlyle's prose poem, his epic of Tools and the Man, of Work, as he calls it, marks an interesting link between a figure like Blake and a social revolutionary and theorist like Marx; it stands midway be-

tween visionary prophecy and social analysis with a prophetic goal.

Having absorbed large portions of Blake and the prophetic biblical heritage, Carlyle carries them into still new dimensions. He amplifies the historical dimensions of Blake, especially the odd mixture of biblical language and images with British history and place names, into a more realistic and social vision of apocalypse. In a sense, Carlyle takes Blake to the masses, for his forces are more often large social groups immediately recognizable to us and not unusual states of consciousness. In method he is more like Blake than Marx; in content, more like Marx.

Both these authors can also provide a clarifying context for Carlyle. Their vision of self-fulfilling labor, the joy of creativity itself, suggests that the fundamental drive of *Past and Present* need not be seen as a return to Christian platitudes of the Puritan past or as a march into fascism (and the later Carlyle) but can be understood as a forward move toward a new society that incorporates industrial progress and rescues labor by turning it into a source of individual self-fulfillment. Such a society also rescues man from his alienation by turning the world into an artifact, an objectification of human consciousness. Regressive elements are always present in Carlyle, and their origin and the problems they present will be considered later, but the main drive of his book is toward the aesthetic fulfillment of continuous creation, a universe of self-fulfilling labor, a heavenly Jerusalem that like Blake's is really an earthly London transformed into the image of a total and active man. As Blake's major poem works to attain this vision, so Carlyle's prose poem with its high symbolic density works to reach its own apocalyptic breakthrough. Both Blake and Carlyle use the potter's wheel of the prophets

189

to capture the process of their vision; as the wheel whirls, the perishable material flies off, leaving the true and the exact, the ordered artifact. Blake turns the Satanic wheels of the mills, of Locke and Newton, into the visionary wheels of Ezekiel's staggering insight, and Carlyle whirls the potter's wheel until the perishable material flies off and the final utopia of the last section is glimpsed.

When I return to these analogous books later—more particularly to Marx's *Economic and Philosophic Manuscripts of 1844*—I shall suggest in more detail how they can clarify the problems of *Past and Present* and how they can help to place Carlyle in literary history and distinguish his unique achievement. For the present, my analysis, in more or less purely Carlylean terms, of the book's central images and themes will take note of the symbolic density of the book, its quality as a prose poem, and the way in which it intends itself as both a self-contained artifact and a document of social analysis. This dimension points to one of the central confusions in all the later Carlyle.

Book First, "Proem," establishes the double movements of the severance which society manifests and which are to be explored more fully through the study of the past in Book Second, "The Ancient Monk," through the study of the present in Book Third, "The Modern Worker," and through the study of the future in Book Fourth, "Horoscope." What frightens the "picturesque Tourist" (*PP*, 2) in front of the St. Ives Workhouse is the testimony of a negative process in society that is completely opposed to all that makes society meaningful. Society may be a process of union, order, growth, and light, as Carlyle images it, but the idle workers testify to a process of estrangement and alienation, isolation, chaos, decay, and darkness. Such a sight would not be so frightening if Carlyle were still certain

that nature allowed but one process, the process of total social affirmation. But here he discovers that negativity is not simply an interference with the positive process of the universe but is itself another *process*—a vicious and powerful force which, despite its characteristics of isolation and severance, contains a paradoxical power of union and a measure of strength that can totally overthrow the positive process. The soul of the world may be just, God may still dwell in the center of the world-whirlwind (*PP*, 8), and God's law may at last assert itself when both nature and men's patience are exhausted by this evil process; but this giant movement of "universal Social Gangrene" may lead to an unexampled chaos before Fact and Nature act. The heaviest may reach the center ultimately (*PP*, 12), but a "fatal paralysis spreading inwards . . . towards the heart itself" (*PP*, 6) can cause the total disruption of civilization before Universal Law rights the balance.

Carlyle's symbols for the embodiments of this negative process of destruction and disorder are always in motion, but that motion suggests their lack of substance, their formlessness and meaninglessness, at the same time as it reveals their power. For the sources of his vision here, Carlyle draws once again on the double imagery of Pope's *Dunciad,* alluding to his source in a key phrase, "pudding and praise" (*PP*, 136; cf. *Dunciad,* I.54). Thus Carlyle's dunces, like Pope's, form in their very formlessness a united threat to life itself; like the mock-epic figures of *The French Revolution,* they are leading English society into chaos, but they act in a far more heartless and sinister manner. Carlyle does not give his villains particular names (though he does almost all of his heroes), thereby suggesting not only the loss of their individuality but also the power of the united type. His final antithetical figures are Friend Prudence, the Quaker, and Blank, an individual who has lost his identity,

191

however successful he has been materialistically. His names, masterpieces of caricature, point backward to Bunyan and to his contemporary Dickens but are less traditionally moral than Bunyan's, more animal-like and filled with outrage and contempt than those of Dickens: Sir Jabesh Windbag, Pandarus Dogdraught, Viscount Mealymouth, Plugson of Undershot, Bobus Higgins. Like the *Dunciad's* movement of "flying lead," of emptiness combined with complete dullness (*Dunciad*, I.181–85), the negative process of *Past and Present* is equally formidable and equally meaningless. Often Carlyle fixes on forms deprived of significance and human value. "The great Hat seven-feet high, which now perambulates London streets" (*PP*, 141) is a symbol of unsuccessful success, public display without accompanying public worth, bigness without content.

Other images center on accelerated motion which, lacking in content and any stabilizing principle, leads only to Chaos, Emptiness, and the abyss—that is, to total annihilation of society and the loss of selfhood as well. Of central importance here are the spinning dervish, the nomad, the chattering Dead Sea apes (once men who rejected Moses), sliding scales, Bucaniers, and the heaping up of such futile remedial measures as Poor Laws and Election Franchises. The victims of this process, those who demand work, who want to be ordered and led, are also drawn into the whirlpool. True social union disappears, replaced by "Poor-law Prisons" and men "shut in by narrow walls . . . pent up, as in a kind of horrid enchantment; glad to be imprisoned and enchanted, that they may not perish starved" (*PP*, 2). Permanence of relationship vanishes; men are alienated (and Carlyle is again one of the first to use this word in its more modern sense) and estranged from one another and themselves. "Human faces gloom discordantly, disloyally on one another" (*PP*, 5). Idle dilettantism takes

no interest in leading the workers or providing them with food from the land; the aristocracy of old has proved useless. And among the workers, marriage loses its significance of permanence. Even family ties disintegrate; at the Stockport Assizes a case is revealed wherein a family has murdered their starving son in order to acquire money from his "insurance" (i.e. burial money) (*PP*, 4). A poor Irish widow is dismissed by Scottish charitable associations who disclaim any connection with her, but she "proves her sisterhood" by dying of typhus fever and infecting seventeen other people (*PP*, 149).

Carlyle sees all these examples of isolation and decay as emblems of a great process. "Such instances are like the highest mountain apex emerged into view; under which lies a whole mountain region and land, not yet emerged" (*PP*, 4). They are examples of a fatal paralysis spreading inward, a universal social gangrene, an elephantine leprosy that has brought society to the brink of chaos, where it now reels and whirls. All evidence of human relationship tends to vanish; hearts, the organs of individual and social vitality, are set against one another as mankind retreats further and further under his thick integuments.

Fortunately, Carlyle knows he can see another process, one which is sanctioned by nature; the study of the past and the voice of the prophet in touch with that past cancels any doubt he might have. Unlike Pope, who effected a condemnation of his dunces by embodying them in mock-epic and measuring them against a true but implied ideal, Carlyle explicitly delineates the ideal process. For once again he is an explorer: his ideal is no ready-made series of propositions, no Morrison's pill, paper-theorem, or magic word, but a giant human struggle, beginning in each individual and finally reaching out into all society and into Heaven itself. The very

efflorescence of this process throughout the book is the condemnation of the antithetical movement. It is with this positive process of true social fulfillment that Carlyle is centrally concerned.

Primarily this is a movement of the self. The voice of "Fact, speaking once more, in miraculous thunder-voice, from out of the centre of the world" requires a "hearing few" (PP, 29) who must go down within themselves, "descend into . . . thy inner man" (PP, 26) and develop the traces of a soul discovered there. This interrelationship of eternity addressing man and man coming more and more to live in tune with the universe and being suffused in its mysterious spiritual dimension makes Past and Present a religious book with a distinct typology. Much of its imagery, as has already been shown, is drawn from the Bible, especially the Hebrew prophets, and utilizes many of its methods, such as direct address and terms like "friends," "brothers," and "thou," which seem to be closely connected with Calvinist pulpit oratory. But such devices alone do not make it a religious book. The vision of society in Past and Present is religious because it is an exploration of the way of salvation and deliverance, of apocalypse and of ultimate triumph over worldly limitations, and of the way of incorporation within a spiritual and universal body that stands as the eschatological goal toward which each individual struggles.

This organic process by which the self reawakens its full possibilities and those of society is rooted in a central triad of images that provides the psychological basis for this reawakening. Two of these are physical organs —eye and heart. Each has the tangibility, the firm rooting in fact and matter, that Carlyle needs as a basis, but each is also surrounded with overtones of spirit, suggestions of some ineffable quality. The heart embodies notes of both centrality and diffusion, organization and

organic expansion, rooted fact and vitality. The eye as a physical organ seems even less tangible, though it lacks the traditional overtones of the heart; in its purest state of full awakening, it provides a clarity and depth, a focus but with openness, into the mysterious realms of the spirit. The third image is the medium of transfer—light, equally material and equally spiritual, shaped, yet diffuse and expanding. These three images underlie the entire process of ordered expansion and fulfillment; connecting themselves now with one aspect of the universe, now with another, together they build toward a total universal vision in which all reality is seen as participating in a single organic rhythm.

The process of reawakening begins by opening eyes darkened by the acrid divisiveness of the present social situation. It is an immediate transfer to a different dimension of experience, enabling one to distinguish between sham and substance. Galvanic glazed eyes or opaque shut owl eyes become noble pure eyes open to Heaven's light. When the inner man is awakened, inner reality can then be seen. This is the fundamental experience of radical Protestantism.

> Seek through this Universe; if with other than owl's eyes, thou wilt find nothing nourished there, nothing kept in life, but what has the right to nourishment and life. The rest, look at it with other than owl's eyes, is not living; is all dying, all as good as dead! . . . Jesting Pilate had not the smallest chance to ascertain what was Truth. He could not have known it, had a god shown it to him. Thick serene opacity, thicker than amaurosis, veiled those smiling eyes of his to Truth; the inner *retina* of them was gone paralytic, dead. He looked at Truth; and discerned her not, there where she stood. (*PP*, 13–14)

The origin of this reawakening is primarily the self, but the process is not purely subjective. The heart of man has its correlative in the universal heart of nature, and the light that man irradiates in his spiritual renewal is quite simply the divine light behind the universe. Carlyle's emphasis is always on the man who sees the light and unfolds it organically in real fact. He talks of God's revelation, His coming to man, but his real interest is in man's movement toward a redefined divinity.

> Reform, like Charity, O Bobus, must begin at home. Once well at home, how will it radiate outwards, irrepressible, into all that we touch and handle, speak and work; kindling ever new light, by incalculable contagion, spreading in geometric ratio, far and wide. . . . Infallibly: for light spreads; all human souls, never so bedarkened, love light; light once kindled spreads, till all is luminous;—till the cry *"Arrest* your knaves and dastards" rises imperative from millions of hearts, and rings and reigns from sea to sea. (*PP*, 35–36)

Carlyle's characters, in description and incident, fulfill this process. For example, Abbot Samson's "clear eyes" were always "flashing into you" (*PP*, 70), and the clear vision in his heart brought clear vision in his head (*PP*, 96). His eyesight, his spiritual discernment, is in fact almost godlike; Carlyle compares his making of order, his kindling of light, to the creation itself: "The clear-beaming eyesight of Abbot Samson, steadfast, severe, all penetrating,—it is like *Fiat lux* in that inorganic waste whirlpool; penetrates gradually to all nooks, and of the chaos makes a *kosmos* or ordered world!" (*PP*, 91–92).

Similarly, the irresistible power of light conveyed by the eyes is perhaps most clearly indicated in the story of

St. Anselm who is about to be ambushed by a vengeful
Burgundian duke.

> Old Anselm . . . a man of rough ways, in whom
> the 'Inner Lightbeam' shone very fitfully . . . . The
> fire eyes of his Burgundian Grace meet these clear
> eye-glances, convey them swift to his heart: he be-
> thinks him that probably this feeble, fearless, hoary
> figure has in it something of the Most High God;
> that probably he shall be damned if he meddle with
> it . . . He plunges, the rough savage, from his war-
> horse, down to his knees; embraces the feet of old
> Anselm. (*PP,* 247–48)

This process of diffusing light, though inevitable and
ultimately the law of Nature, is not an easy one, however. For Nature is a Sphinx and contains her secret of
light-ordering deep within her. It is only to the "laborer," the man who struggles incessantly and unyield-
ingly, that she awards the mission of diffusing light. Nature is dual and, though the diffusion of light is her ultimate goal, man can either conquer her or be conquered by her.

> Nature, like the Sphinx, is of womanly celestial
> loveliness and tenderness; the face and bosom of a
> goddess, but ending in claws and the body of a
> lioness. There is in her a celestial beauty,—which
> means celestial order, pliancy to wisdom; but there
> is also a darkness, a ferocity, fatality, which are in-
> fernal. She is a goddess, but one not yet disimpris-
> oned; one still half-imprisoned,—the articulate,
> lovely, still encased in the articulate, chaotic. (*PP,*
> 7)

Once again the emphasis is thrown onto the heroic self,
the Promethean man who by his own activity discovers

Nature's Law and God's Light. We have a loadstar in the heavens to follow by which our ship may reach the "Heroic Promised Lands" (*PP*, 37), but we must plough through "cloud-tempests and roaring billows" and often will be sunk in the trough of the sea where the loadstar, though still shining, is no longer visible. Columbus must fight against waste oceans, winds, and howling monsters to discover the deep secret of the universe, the silence of himself which Carlyle equates with the silence of God (*PP*, 109–200). He is a wrestler who must conquer nature by finally subduing her in a somewhat sexual "embrace" of affection and control so that he may discover her living heart. Thus Labor becomes the chief means whereby man discovers the mystery of the universe and the mystery of himself, the way in which he realizes the sacred order upon earth. Man's deepest vital rhythms are awakened and shaped in labor, and with this shaping of the self, the vital rhythms of the universe are approximated and the universe itself is shaped into an artistic product.

> Man, Son of Earth, and of Heaven, lies there not, in the innermost heart of thee, a Spirit of Active Method, a Force for Work;—and burns like a painfully-smouldering fire, giving thee no rest till thou unfold it, till thou write it down in beneficent Facts around thee! What is immethodic, waste, thou shalt make methodic, regulated, arable; obedient and productive to thee. (*PP,* 201)

I shall return to this subject of labor several times more in this chapter, but it is important here to establish its function in the reawakening of the new self, its role as the restorer of light and discoverer of the vital heartbeat behind the universe and the self.

By struggle, then, the hero enters the order of full personal salvation and also inaugurates the unfolding of

social salvation on earth. Edmund provides a good example of this process. Even death cannot subdue him, for, in standing by the order of light, God's eternal law, he transcends death and achieves even greater victory for himself and his loyal subjects. By his death, the imagery of sight (eyes), feeling (heart), and light begins to unfold with lasting results.

> Landlord Edmund was *seen* and *felt* by all men to have done verily a man's part in this life-pilgrimage of his; and benedictions, and *outflowing love* and *admiration* from the *universal heart,* were his meed . . . . They raised his slain and martyred body; washed its wounds with *fast-flowing universal* tears; tears of endless *pity,* and yet of a sacred *joy* and *triumph* . . . . The beautifulest kind of thing: like a sky all *flashing diamonds and prismatic radiance;* all weeping, yet shone on by the everlasting *Sun:*—and *this* is not a sky, it is a Soul and living Face! (*PP*, 54; italics mine except the last)

This expansion is not merely personal, for he is canonized a saint of Heaven. But Carlyle's interest focuses not even on that fact, but on the social realities attained by the "overflowing heart" he has enkindled in his followers. The results are expansive, initially in space. The movement from loculus to shrine, from shrine to temple, from temple to monastery and town is no undirected or formless extension. Though "stately masonries, long drawn arches, cloisters" and "sounding aisles" are all expansive, they are nevertheless buttressed and begirdled far and wide, i.e. given a form of organization. In time too the action reaches out to embrace the whole "Spirit of the Time," but this also is ordered, for "the Spirit of the Time" has "visibly taken body, and crystallized itself here" (*PP*, 56) .

Nevertheless, personal fulfillment, if not of such last-

ing value or extensive scope as social fulfillment, is more intense, more immediate, and more transcendent. Here Abbot Samson provides the best example. While Book Second is largely concerned with his efforts to "educe organic method out of lazily fermenting wreck" (*PP*, 90) and his struggle to establish a true social order informed with real religious spirit, "the culminating moment of Abbot Samson's life" (*PP*, 119) is not primarily a social act but a religious one—the gazing upon the radiant and effulgent body of the martyr St. Edmund. In that incident the imagery of light and dark receives its fullest extension and attains new expressions and meanings.

Carlyle faithfully translates Jocelin's chronicle and then comments on the scene.

> What a scene; shining luminous effulgent, as the lamps of St. Edmund do, through the dark Night; John of Dice, with vestrymen, clambering on the roof to look through; the Convent all asleep, and the Earth all asleep,—and since then, Seven Centuries of Time mostly gone to sleep! (*PP*, 123)

Then he explicitly identifies the reverence paid to Edmund's body with the setting itself. "Oh, all mystery, all pity, all mute *awe* and wonder; *Super*naturalism brought home to the very dullest; Eternity laid open, and the nether Darkness and the upper Light-Kingdoms, do conjoin there, or exist nowhere!" (*PP*, 124). Here, not only do Edmund, Samson, the viewers, and the universe all merge into a mysterious unity, but Darkness itself, purged of its traditional evil associations by the intensity and climactic quality of the experience, can be reaffirmed once more as a necessary element of the total vision, one which contributes to the depth of mystery which that total vision manifests.

Present here is an intensity of silence in which eternity is glimpsed. This becomes clearer in the analogous

experience of the Chinese and the reminiscence of Goethe's two great silences, "Stars silent rest o'er us/Graves under us silent" (*PP,* 228) .

> (The Chinese) visit yearly the Tombs of their Fathers; each man the Tomb of his Father and his Mother; alone there, in silence, with what of "worship" or of other thought there may be, pauses solemnly each man; the divine Skies all silent over him; the divine Graves, and this divinest Grave, all silent under him; the pulsings of his own soul, if he have any soul, alone audible. (*PP,* 235)

Carlyle hopes that in the description of such a situation the meaning of the two great silences and that of the pulsings of the human heart, the life rhythm, will become resolved in unity. Death and life, this world and eternity, are all linked and blended into each other. The human religious experience here obviously borders on mysticism, a term often wrongly applied to too much of Carlyle. In Pauline terms, the religious situation moves from one where God is seen through a glass darkly to the pleroma where God is all in all, where man is fully a part of the mystery and inseparable from it. Carlyle's religious terms here may be more psychological and naturalistic than Paul's, but they decidedly embody his structure and significance and are, in fact, quite traditional.

But these are only glimpses of transcendence and eternity, however bright their clarity and intensity (*PP,* 235) . They are moments in time though somehow outside it. St. Edmund's loculus must have the veils reverently replaced, John of Dice and his vestrymen must slide down from the roof, the Convent must wholly awaken to matins, and the normal flow of life must resume (*PP,* 124) .

This movement of rise and fall, of pitch and decline,

is the rhythm not only of the experience of characters within the book, but also of *Past and Present* itself. Though the book may aim constantly toward a world of pure vision, it must also struggle, like all literature, with the internecine darkness. This struggle appears most clearly in the attempt to edit Jocelin's manuscript, the battle to discern the light of its meaning.

> Through the thin watery gossip of our Jocelin, we do get some glimpses of that deep-buried Time; discern veritably, though in a fitful intermittent manner, these antique figures and their life-method, face to face! Beautifully, in our earnest loving glance, the old centuries melt from opaque to partially translucent, transparent here and there; and the void black Night, one finds, is but the summing-up of innumerable peopled luminous *Days*. (*PP*, 49–50)

The struggle extends into the present, where it is the attempt of the prophet to discover the spark of light that exists beneath the mud, the Egyptian darkness, of the present social situation. In this respect, then, Carlyle's positive emblems are points of pitch, since they illuminate a vast area of social experience. Furthermore, since they reveal the one inner law of the universe, they can be applied theoretically to innumerable social situations and shed further light upon them.

Thus, the very attempt to interrelate metaphors that permeates *Past and Present* and makes of it a prose poem is the literary struggle to envision society's true direction and its possibility of reaching a point of intensity equivalent to Abbot Samson's. Carlyle's struggle is relieved by a series of strong visionary points throughout the book, all of which are effected through a conflict of contraries, a facing up to the abyss of the present, and which finally generate the apocalyptic vision of la-

bor in Book Fourth, "Horoscope." From this fully realized goal, there is no return into the flow of ordinary experience, for labor and struggle themselves have been directed, redefined, and heroized. There is only a strong forward movement of fully animated labor under the Captains of Industry (though, to be sure, the confusion of how metaphorical or literal these captains are to be persists).

It would be false, of course, to deny the traditional criticism of *Past and Present*: that it maintains a divided allegiance, a nostalgia for the ordered religious life of the Middle Ages, a wish to retreat to the seventeenth-century world of Cromwell, to the old dialect, and an equally idealistic and often imperialistic faith in British industrialism, progress, and labor. But such criticisms usually ignore the fact that Carlyle himself was well aware of his own divided allegiance and was making every effort to join the two situations in a unitary vision that would be both religious and industrial. The charges not only ignore the fascination of the fusion but never leap beyond this objection to see what underlying potentialities of vision are revealed.

Carlyle is always certain that there is only one meaningful process behind the universe, and while that process may appear traditionally religious, it is actually labor. Carlyle is careful to portray not religion as labor, but labor as religion. Everywhere he takes precautions to guard labor from any imputations of transitoriness, preserving its status as the one enduring principle behind the universe. The energy by means of which man will realize the new society, his most full activity, determines the real aesthetic drive of the book.

Early in Book First Carlyle shows himself eager to halt any criticism of industry as such. Only in its lack of organization is it held at fault; its own soul has accelerated beyond humanity's power to adjust to it.

> The world, with its Wealth of Nations, Supply-and-demand and suchlike, has of late days been terribly inattentive to that question of work and wages. We will not say, the poor world has retrograded even here: we will say rather, the world has been rushing on with such fiery animation to get work and ever more work done, it has had no time to think of dividing the wages; and has merely left them to be scrambled for by the Law of the Stronger, Law of Supply-and-demand, Law of Laissez-faire, and other idle Laws and Un-laws. (*PP*, 21)

Similarly, at the beginning of Book Second, "The Ancient Monk," Carlyle clearly states what his central concern throughout will be. "The Gospel of Richard Arkwright once promulgated, no Monk of the old sort is any longer possible in this world" (*PP*, 43). The glory of the Middle Ages was not its religious forms (for Carlyle detests the mediating institutions of Catholicism that stand between man and God) but its sense of wholeness, purpose, and order. If modern theologians bent on returning to primitive Christianity find in these ages the beginnings of secular elements in Christian culture, Carlyle will focus on precisely these elements and call them religious.

> No one will accuse our Lord Abbot of wanting worldly wisdom, due interest in worldly things . . . . Nay rather it might seem . . . as if he had his eye all but exclusively directed on terrestrial matters, and was much too secular for a devout man. But this too, if we examine it, was right. For it is *in* the world that a man, devout or other, has his life to lead, his work waiting to be done. The basis of Abbot Samson's, we shall discover, was truly religion after all. . . . Not a talking theory, that; no, a silent practice. (*PP*, 115)

204

The glory of the Middle Ages is its unitive sense, the feeling each man had of being connected with another. "Gurth, born thrall of Cedric," Carlyle notes in referring to Scott's *Ivanhoe*, "it is like, got cuffs as often as pork-parings, if he misdemeaned himself; but Gurth did belong to Cedric; no human creature then went about connected with nobody" (*PP*, 245). "Gurth was hired for life to Cedric, and Cedric to Gurth" (*PP*, 278). But Democracy and the new industrial society with its vastness have obviously made this brass-collar method of binding outmoded and impossible. The problem of the new spiritual epoch is to find "nobler and cunninger" methods of binding (*PP*, 251). The glory of the new age is not democracy, however, but its industrial animation, its potential for work that makes the Middle Ages appear paltry by comparison. "Gurth could only tend pigs; this one will build cities, conquer waste worlds" (*PP*, 251).

Carlyle forthrightly casts his vote for the new spiritual epoch over the old. The moment of transfer is unequivocal.

It was as if King Redbeard unconsciously, addressing Anselm, Becket, and the others, had said: "Right Reverend, your Theory of the Universe is indisputable by man or devil. To the core of our heart we feel that this divine thing, which you call Mother Church, does fill the whole world hitherto known, and is and shall be our salvation and all our desire. And yet—and yet—Behold, though it is an unspoken secret, the world is *wider* than any of us think, Right Reverend! Behold, there are yet other immeasurable Sacrednesses in this that you call Heathenism, Secularity! On the whole, I, in an obscure but most rooted manner, feel that I cannot comply with you. Western Thibet and perpetual

205

mass-chanting,—No. I am, so to speak, in the family-way; with child, of I know not what,—certainly of something far different from this! I have—*Per os Dei,* I have Manchester Cotton-trades, Bromwicham Iron-trades, American Commonwealths, Indian Empires, Steam Mechanisms, and Shakespeare Dramas, in my belly; and cannot do it, Right Reverend!" . . . We will now quit this of the hard, organic, but limited Feudal Ages; and glance timidly into the immense Industrial Ages; as yet all inorganic, and in a quite pulpy condition, requiring desperately to harden themselves into some organism. *(PP,* 248–49)

Never before has Carlyle been so explicit in describing his faith in the new spiritual epoch of industrial progress. At last, it seems, he has discovered beneath the process of the universe a principle of continuity which was both firmly rooted in fact and yet mystic and spiritual enough for him, deeply connected with both the universe and man, historical and yet transcending history. And Carlyle finds immediate confirmation of his principle in the great industrial expansion of England. If men were merely to awaken to their truly human role in this gigantic process, the possibilities for society would be infinite. A utopia in which man would be restored to his full humanity and society to one body in its self-fulfilling activity could be just over the horizon.

Work, then, is supremely tactile yet supremely spiritual for Carlyle. It is the religious basis behind all existence. "Work? The quantity of done and forgotten work that lies silent under my feet in this world, and escorts and attends me, and supports and keeps me alive, wheresoever I walk or stand, whatsoever I think or do, gives rise to reflections!" *(PP,* 133) . Work is of man, but Carlyle labels it "the one God's voice we have heard in

these two atheistic centuries" (*PP,* 169). It is religious because nature has endorsed it; she has not condemned it as she has the Church of Warburton and Hurd or the Anti-Church of Paine and Hume (*PP,* 167). In work man finds his own fulfillment and that of nature. By striking into the land, he discovers his own roots, which are also a part of the world center. Work is fundamentally energy, the full power through which the self is restored to nature's vitality and is thus restored and reintegrated. Salvation becomes possible in this new religion by a descent into the self effected through work (and quite often merely a work regarded as painful Calvinistic duty and suffering rather than self-fulfillment). Only by sacrificing oneself to the process of the universe does one gain all. "Thou must descend to the *Mothers,* to the *Manes,* and Hercules-like long suffer and labour there, wouldst thou emerge with victory into the sunlight" (*PP,* 205).

Carlyle most often sees work as a struggle of great postlapsarian pain, though at times, in a more Blakean and Marxian manner, it is the spontaneous outpouring of the individual. Both views find confirmation in the typology of Christian experience, of initiation into a mystery, but with several striking differences: work is often treated as an end in itself, the process of work being its own goal; the savior is no longer Christ, but man himself; and the ultimate incorporation is not in any transcendent supernatural order but in the order of the natural process itself. In Carlyle's new religion, man becomes Promethean and the nation assumes Titanic power. Man is his own maker, perfecting himself through work and thereby redeeming society. Moreover, like the Hebrew God, he creates ex nihilo.

I tell thee, they had not a hammer to begin with; and yet Wren built St. Paul's; not an articulated

syllable; and yet there have come English Litera-
tures. . . . Arachne started with forefinger and
thumb, and had not even distaff; yet thou seest
Manchester, and Cotton Cloth, which will shelter
naked backs, at twopence an ell. (*PP,* 133)

Effecting salvation through work also means instilling
order with continued organic movement into the self
and society. As in Marx, the cash nexus is replaced by a
permanence of contract, the sliding scale of profit-and-
loss by a true center of gravity. The whirling dervish
and the nomad give way to the controlled artistic movement of the potter's wheel. Images of mud, slime, ooze,
swamps, and tumultuous oceans are transformed into
those of productive nourishing lands and tilled meadows. Dissolution is replaced by resolution. The green
garden of the restored England of Carlyle's apocalypse is
the direct issue of his artistic concept of work.

Salvation means even more than the replacement of
disorder by order, however. It is not only the construction of "the garden," the world restored, but also of the
Heavenly Jerusalem, the world of industry fulfilled; in
this case it is London which functions as a trade center
and home for all the world but primarily—in a rather
imperialistic manner, to be sure—as an "All Saxon-
Home, rendezvous of all the 'Children of the Harz-
Rock!' " (*PP,* 268). Lest this vision appear unreligious,
Carlyle casts apocalyptic language about it, language
which fortunately also saves it from being merely imperialistic by assimilating it to the artistic and social fulfillment of work.

"Work is Worship": yes, in a highly considerable
sense,—which, in the present state of all "worship,"
who is there that can unfold! He that understands
it well, understands the Prophecy of the whole Future; the last Evangel, which has included all oth-

ers. *Its* cathedral the Dome of Immensity,—hast thou seen it? coped with the star-galaxies; paved with the green mosaic of land and ocean; and for altar, verily, the Star-throne of the Eternal! Its litany and psalmody the noble acts, the heroic work and suffering, and true heart-utterance of all the Valiant of the Sons of Men. (*PP,* 233)

Humanity, then, moves through labor in an ever-expanding spiral, and the full order toward which it grows abandons traditional religious expression as a mode of thought proper only to a lower and narrower circle on the spiral. Cathedrals, altars, liturgies, and gospels are all replaced by this last evangel of labor made sacred.

Under the intoxicating pressure of this vision, Carlyle becomes glowingly optimistic. All the evils of the present social situation become the mere dust of controversy soon to be cast off by the "increase of velocity, an ever-deepening, ever-widening sweep of momentum" (*PP,* 182) in the true universal process. Underneath all the present darkness exists the spark of light which must inevitably expand into a light flood. John Bull is nine-tenths nonsense, but only in his spoken speech as it is articulated in Puseyism, Methodism, or laissez-faire philosophy. In his unspoken sense, the real manifestation of his power, he is Promethean. With his complete vision Carlyle can now bore underground beneath semblance.

His unspoken sense, his inner silent feeling of what is true, what does agree with fact, what is doable and not doable,—this seeks its fellow in the world. A terrible worker; irresistible against marshes, mountains, impediments, disorder, incivilization; everywhere vanquishing disorder, leaving it behind him as method and order. (*PP,* 161–62)

209

Even the unjust, Mammon-worshipping Plugson of Undershot contains in his depths not merely the possibilities but also the promise of real "religious" fulfillment. "Thou are hitherto a Bucanier, as it was written and prescribed for thee by an evil world: but in that grim brow, in that indomitable heart which *can* conquer Cotton, do there not perhaps lie other ten-times nobler conquests?" (*PP*, 195).

Carlyle's enthusiasm for his vision once again leads him into an ambivalent attitude toward force. He would like to mobilize mankind along the model of the army not merely to halt dissolution as Napoleon did in *The French Revolution* but to accelerate the coming of the new order. This glorification of force easily leads to an enthusiasm for pure militarism—as the battle scenes of *Cromwell* and *Frederick* and the bald demands and bullying of the *Latter-Day Pamphlets* testify—but in *Past and Present* the army serves primarily as a model, a guide to the implementation of force and its organization; it points to the metaphor of a noble chivalry of workers and to captains of industry. Almost alone in the present social situation, the army exists as a fact for Carlyle and not a shadow (*PP*, 261). In fact, this might be his only enduring link with Cromwell's world, for he seems to ask the Cromwellian question: could it not serve as a model for nobler ends than mere killing of man's fellowman?

> O Heavens, if we saw an army ninety-thousand strong, maintained and fully equipt, in continual real action and battle against Human Starvation, against Chaos, Necessity, Stupidity, and our real "natural enemies," what a business it were! Fighting and molesting not "the French," . . . but fighting and incessantly spearing down and destroying Falsehood, Nescience, Delusion, Disorder, and the Devil and his Angels! (*PP*, 263)

210

In the new spiritual social world, the state would maintain an army directing emigration and education for the salvation of the outer and inner man. Such requests for the expansion of governmental power mark Carlyle as a socialist.

The greatest moving force will not be state reform, however, but self-reform. However much he may distrust the individual, Carlyle is and remains an individualist. Education and emigration are only the preliminary conditions of making light possible. Friend Prudence, the Quaker manufacturer, is still the noblest type of the new order; in the combination of religious radical and industrialist, real ties between Master Worker and workers are recognized and human factory conditions are accomplished. Friend Prudence's personal power is deeper than any force the negative process can manifest. The mountain apex that was emerging so threateningly at the beginning of the book (*PP*, 4) is now replaced by the emergence of the real process of nature. Prudence is a Quaker because he must have no vested interest in any of the corrupt institutional forms of religion but must base his force on the "inner light."

> Can the sagacious reader descry here, as it were the outmost inconsiderable rock-ledge of a universal rock-foundation, deep once more as the Centre of the World, emerging so, in the experience of this good Quaker, through the Stygian mud-vortexes and general Mother of Dead Dogs, whereon, for the present, all swags and insecurely hovers, as if ready to be swallowed? (*PP*, 280)

Nevertheless, the new Heaven and the new spiritual fulfillment, however expansive Carlyle's images may claim them to be, are completely of this world.

> Chaos is dark, deep as Hell; let light be, and there is instead a green flowery World. Oh, it is great,

and there is no other greatness. To make some nook of God's Creation, a little fruitfuller, better, more worthy of God; to make some human hearts a little wiser, manfuller, happier,—more blessed, less accursed! It is work for a God. Sooty Hell of mutiny and savagery and despair can, by man's energy, be made a kind of Heaven; cleared of its soot, of its mutiny, of its need to mutiny; the everlasting arch of Heaven's azure overspanning *it* too, and its cunning mechanisms and tall chimney-steeples, as a birth of Heaven; God and all men looking on it well pleased. (*PP,* 298)

The traditional religious imagery does not disguise the fact that it is man the laborer who is his own redeemer and that it is the order of this world which is the final religious order. Quite correctly, then, it is man the laborer who becomes the new God in his own energetic self-fulfillment of activity. When the traditional religious language is pared away, the hortatory and inspiring rhetoric of socialist and communist visionaries remains.

Unstained by wasteful deformities, by wasted tears or heart's-blood of men, or any defacement of the Pit, noble fruitful Labour, growing ever nobler, will come forth,—the grand sole miracle of Man; whereby Man has risen from the low places of this Earth, very literally, into divine Heavens. Ploughers, Spinners, Builders; Prophets, Poets, Kings; Brindleys and Goethes, Odins and Arkwrights; all martyrs, and noble men, and gods are of one grand Host; immeasurable; marching ever forward since the beginnings of the World. The enormous, all-conquering, flame-crowned Host, noble every soldier in it; sacred, and alone noble. (*PP,* 298)

As poet and prophet, then, Carlyle, struggling with darkness, is also absorbed into the mystical order of labor. Not the fullness of God but the fullness of man is the goal of the new religious movement. As forger of this vision and its spokesman, Carlyle is not merely one among many heroic laborers helping to build the new spiritual order; instead, he occupies a position above that of the average worker and even above that of the prophet and exhorter of men warning them of their evils and lifting them to truth. His voice and method speak for this special role even if self-consciously he will not claim it. For if man is saved by his own self-activity in labor, it is man and not God's grace that is the forger of the new redemptive process.

Similarly, Carlyle as prophet and seer is no longer like the Hebrew prophets, listening to the voice of God and attempting to make it heard by moral exordiums. Carlyle's scope is far grander, far more cosmic than their modest role in effecting salvation. His is the voice not only of the prophets, but, like Blake's, also of the New Testament Apocalypse. The visionary voice becomes a central element in the new religion. More and more Carlyle testifies not so much to God's truth but to an order of his own insight and forging. Like Brindley, Wren, and Arkwright, he too is a maker and a member of the new army; but his position is even grander than theirs, for he is the maker of makers: It is through his vision that the new order comes into full consciousness.

Consequently, comparisons that liken Carlyle to the Hebrew prophets stop short of a central insight, the fundamental difference between his role and that of prophets. It is true that he employs their language: the strong awareness of God's condemning voice behind the degeneracy of the times, the harsh and stern urge to reform a people who have wandered away from God, the promise of destruction if such reform is not carried out.

But such a superficial comparison touches only the reforming aspect of the book, the attempt to alter the negative process of present society, leaving unnoticed the different religious nature of the positive process, the making of the new order.

Here a comparison with St. Paul, even more than with St. John of Revelations, seems appropriate, for Carlyle boldly uses, though with most important differences, the language of Christian mystery. Unlike Blake, however, he does not try to redefine Christian material within the terms of his own humanism; instead, he struggles to keep his view of labor and his vision of Christianity parallel and to make both apocalypses into one. This rearguard saving action, of course, ultimately gives the book its strange aura of divided allegiance and is the source of so many of its confusions and pitfalls. Carlyle lacks Blake's courage for real redefinition of his own role and that of Jesus as deified man; at the other extreme, he would regard Marx's atheism and hatred of Christianity, his need to assert man's independence of external forces, as blasphemous. In his vision of energy, activity, labor, and selfhood, he moves in their direction, as I have shown, but a reading of St. Paul's *Epistle to the Ephesians* will reveal how much of a traditionalist Carlyle is, how closely he weighs his insights by Christian touchstones and makes them conform to Pauline typology, and how, oddly enough, the clinging to these assertions not only shuts off many aspects of exploration but allows him to indulge his worst impulses without questioning them. For whatever he would say, he could attribute to scriptural and eternal truth; and as his sense of strength in scripture hardened, so too did the truths. *Past and Present* already shows signs of the harsh philosophy that "might makes right"—argued earlier with subtlety and real redefinition in "Chartism" —and reveals that Carlyle would like to be the drill sergeant of the future.

214

The resemblances to St. Paul are very close. Paul, for instance, is strongly aware of a new spiritual order in which each must work to achieve salvation until God is "all in all" (1:23). The method of admittance into this new religious order is also parallel to Carlyle's in its basic imagery; the metaphor of light and dark permeates the epistle. Man's understanding has been "darkened" because of the "blindness" of his "heart" (4:18), but now man must awaken to the light and "walk as children of light" (5:8), reproving the unfruitful works of darkness (5:11). Light is the symbol of inner rebirth for both Carlyle and St. Paul. Both also talk about the movement of rising from death in a symbolic fashion (5:14), the strengthening of the *inner* man (3:16), the birth of the new self with the casting off of the old man (4:22), and the renewal of the spirit of the mind (4:23).

The qualities of the old irreligious world and of the new religious world are also exactly parallel. For St. Paul, as for Carlyle, the old world is without form, without permanence, and without ordered growth and direction. "That we henceforth be no more children, tossed to and fro, and carried about with every wind of doctrine, by the sleight of men" (4:14). Man is to be reborn, to be incorporated in an ordered process of growth, the effects of which will transcend the self and embrace all mankind.

> But speaking the truth in love, may grow up into him in all things, which is the head, even Christ: From whom the whole body fitly joined together and compacted by that which every joint supplieth, according to the effectual working in the measure of every part, maketh increase of the body unto the edifying of itself in love. (4:15–16)

Even the particular applications of this religious vision are similar. Carlyle's insistence on the maintenance of

hierarchy and the need for obedience to leaders finds precedent and confirmation in St. Paul's injunction: "Servants, be obedient to them that are your masters . . . . And ye masters, do the same things unto them, forbearing threatening; knowing that your Master also is in heaven" (6:5–9). And St. Paul's final call to the Christian to enter life as a battle with the "shield of faith," the "helmet of salvation," and "the sword of the Spirit" (6:16–17) achieves a parallel in Carlyle's address to labor to become a "new chivalry" similar to the noble Christian chivalry of the Middle Ages for which the Pauline image also provided a cornerstone.

The central difference between Carlyle's use of this typology and St. Paul's has already been shown: in Carlyle's religious structure, man the laborer replaces Christ as redeemer and the new heavenly Jerusalem is no longer the completed Body of Christ but an apotheosis of the very process of labor itself. Thus, process becomes goal, a theme which has been sounded as early as *Schiller*. Nevertheless, still another analogy, though with a most startling difference, can be investigated: if man replaces Christ as savior in the new redemptive process, Carlyle, as author of the process, might be expected to occupy a position grander than St. Paul's in scope and more godlike in tone. As the maker of the new religious vision of man, he will assume a most prominent role in it; in a special sense, he becomes the principal savior. Unlike St. Paul whose attitude toward the mission of the revelation of God's design is one of supreme humility—"Whereof I was made a minister, according to the gift of the grace of God given unto me by the effectual working of his power. Unto me, who am less than the least of all saints, is this grace given, that I should preach among the Gentiles the unsearchable riches of Christ" (3:7–8)—he manifests an attitude of exultation closely approaching divine consciousness itself. And it is this role that gives the book its peculiar tone.

Carlyle's eye embraces all of world history with a sense of cosmic affirmation and assertion. He regularly condemns present moral situations as anomalies by invoking the entire cosmic process as his witness. "Brother, I say there is not, was not, nor will ever be, in the wide circle of Nature, any Pill or Religion of that character" *(PP,* 228). As prophet and visionary, he maintains a special, sanctifying contact with "Eternity."

> Brother, this Planet, I find, is but an inconsiderable sand-grain in the continents of Being; this Planet's poor temporary interests, thy interests and my interests there, when I look fixedly into that Eternal Light-Sea and Flame-Sea with *its* Eternal interests, dwindle literally into Nothing; my speech of it is— silence for the while. *(PP,* 226)

Such declarations not only assert the priority of spirit and "eternity" over matter and time but also, and far more strongly, point to the titanic priority of Carlyle himself over all men. By canceling his more self-conscious presence from this voice, he fails to notice the tone of smug self-righteousness, to see any of the horrible self-destruction or the temptations to might and power that Blake had already explored in the Orc cycle and represented again in the pains of Albion in *Jerusalem.*

As forger of the new religion, Carlyle stands above all other religions and surveys them. Historically they lie in sequence before him, and he supersedes them.

> Rituals, Liturgies, Credos, Sinai Thunder; I know more or less the history of these; the rise, progress, decline, and fall of these. Can thunder from all the thirty-two azimuths, repeated daily for centuries of years, make God's Laws more god-like to me? Brother, No. Perhaps I am grown to be a man now; and do not need the thunder and the terror any

217

longer! Perhaps I am above being frightened; perhaps it is not Fear but Reverence alone, that shall
now lead me! (*PP*, 230)

Carlyle does not need the thunder because he has taken
it over himself. Thus he becomes the God of his new religious world, the author of the new Bible, issuing the
new and ultimate evangel of work (*PP*, 196, 232). He is
the new Christ delivering new beatitudes: "I am for
permanence in all things, at the earliest possible moment, and to the latest possible, Blessed is he that con-
tinueth where he is" (*PP*, 280). (Note both the conservatism and the need for haste, possibly force, in the
above.) As surveyor of universal history, he is also aware
of its future, for he knows the lines of its development.
He claims to be able to read the Apocalypses (*PP*, 255)
and anticipates with great certainty "light *in* the Human Chaos" (*PP*, 270). The word "will," with its tone
of absolute prediction, dominates all the visionary material, from prognostication about industry to the picture
of the New Jerusalem itself. For example, Plugson cries
out: "Let me have elbow-room, throat-room, and I *will*
not fail! No I *will* spin yet, and conquer like a giant!"
(*PP*, 208; italics mine). The wishful will of the opening
book—"It will be a blessed time; and many 'things' will
become doable" (*PP*, 24) —is transformed into the more
strongly assertive and powerfully certain will of the final
visions: "It will be a priceless time" (*PP*, 185); "There
will again *be* a King in Israel; a system of Order and
Government" (*PP*, 250).

Carlyle never explicitly draws out the full implications of his stance, of course, for he sees himself as a traditionalist fighting against chaotic evil, not as a god.
Nor does he claim to be the new King of Israel, a role
that he ostensibly sees as belonging to the new leader,
the new aristocrat of the middle class, the noble master

worker. The new aristocracy is already heralded by the Duke of Weimar in Germany and Ashley, the Earl of Shaftesbury, but even those real heroes are members of an older order, whose place will gradually be taken by the middle-class captains of industry. Yet Carlyle's exultant vision of the new hero at the close of his book shows, at least covertly, that he considers himself in the most immediate relation to the new hero. The picture of the new hero, of the suffering Christ, and of the new man of letters (i.e. Carlyle) becomes thoroughly confused. The link between the figures may be obscure on the surface, but one can see that in the master worker Carlyle is projecting a more active version of himself, much as he was to treat his heroes of the past in his later histories.

Carlyle first portrays the new visionary hero whose "place is with the stars." The new hero is with men but above them, outside them, much like the alienated Teufelsdröckh of *Sartor*.

He walks among men; loves men, with inexpressible soft pity,—as they *cannot* love him: but his soul dwells in solitude, in the uttermost parts of Creation. In green oases by the palm-tree wells, he rests a space; but anon he has to journey forward, escorted by the Terrors and the Splendours, the Archdemons and the Archangels, All Heaven, all Pandemonium are his escort. The stars keenglancing, from the Immensities, send tidings to him; the graves silent with their dead, from the Eternities. Deep calls for him unto Deep. . . . He eludes thee (O world) like a Spirit. . . . He is above thee, like a god. (*PP*, 291)

In this transformed Calvinistic vision of the new "elect of the world," the fit inhabitants of the new heavenly Jerusalem, Carlyle is both the lonely one just man in

219

the tradition of Milton and also god. But then, as if to check himself from drawing this very conclusion, he suddenly turns his attention to the "man of genius," apparently a synonym for the new hero and for himself. Here the highest figure is not the new hero striding god-like over his fellowman, but Christ with his crown of thorns—a reversion of the idea of labor and fulfillment to pain and suffering rather than as power and energy. "The Highest Man of Genius, knowest thou him; God-like and a God to this hour? His crown a Crown of Thorns?" (*PP*, 292). Finally, with a description of genius as "the inspired gift of God," "the clearer presence of God Most High in a man," Carlyle turns to his hopes for the future genius of the man of letters, presumably the genius that was in his mind anyway. "I conclude that the Men of Letters too may become a 'Chivalry,' an actual instead of a virtual Priesthood, with result immeasurable,—so soon as there is nobleness in themselves for that" (*PP*, 293). Under the disguise of "men" instead of "man," Carlyle is actually putting on his armor.

Overt links connecting these three groups of heroes are sought in vain. Is the man of genius a divine figure of the past (Christ) or of the future (the new elect)? And what precisely does the sudden intrusion of the man of letters (Carlyle) mean? But Carlyle, obviously identifying himself with the new hero, is somehow suggesting that that figure is modeled on the sufferings of the Christ of the past and, at the same time, claiming that he, the man of letters, is both the new Christ and the new elect.

The multidirectional quality which is dominant throughout *Past and Present* produces a constant danger of overreading or of oversimplifying it along one political party line. The book contains many elements that can be realized in varying and often contradictory direc-

tions. Although *Past and Present* suggests the moral reform of capitalism itself as a central line of reform, other proposals point to different goals. The application of the typology of religious experience to the process of labor, the sympathy with the poor, the deification of the laborer, the final embodiment of society as a this-worldly heaven, and even the cooperative sharing in industry (*PP*, 282) are elements which communist visionaries could appropriate, but the elements of socialism and fascism which the book also contains cannot be overlooked. The worship of the hero, the approval of forcible methods to attain his goals, and the use of the army as a model of government all suggest fascistic developments, while the demands for greater state control, especially of emigration and education, point to socialistic reforms. *Past and Present* points only vaguely and upon special occasions to specific remedial measures or programs. It does not present a system, for Carlyle's occasional systematic bent, like Blake's and Marx's, is aimed to deliver man from bondage to systems. Its primary goal is a cleansing of vision, a restoration of selfhood by opening the doors of perception.

The writings of Carlyle, Blake, and Marx have similar structures and similar effects upon the reader, however much they may differ in depicting and placing their vision or denoting its application and emphasis. As Blake helped in locating the central drive of Carlyle's book—the warfare of a host of limiting contraries and the final breakthrough into an apocalyptic vision of wholeness, the warfare of energetic contraries—Marx will help to clarify certain difficulties connected especially with the industrial, social, and economic problems of *Past and Present*. Just as Nietzsche's *Birth of Tragedy* provided a quasi-philosophical illumination of themes in *The French Revolution,* so Marx's early and more humanistic writings, *The Economic and Philosophic*

Manuscripts of 1844,[5] can offer an interesting means of assessing how far Carlyle has traveled from Blake and what peculiar problems he has encountered in that journey.

Marx's book, like Nietzsche's, is obviously more philosophical than its counterpart in Carlyle, but it is hardly one of the paper theorems against which Carlyle protests. Marx is basically expressing a pseudophilosophy, an inverted Hegelianism which is less essential to the real drive of his vision than helpful methodically as a tool in establishing relationships between terms. Like Carlyle (and Blake), he assails all abstractions and systems as unreal and limiting, failures to deal with reality and fact. He, like Carlyle, proclaims, "We proceed from an *actual* economic fact" (p. 69), and that fact is the same, though it is not given in Carlyle's particularity. Carlyle begins with the idle workers, estranged and alienated from their work, their fellowmen, nature, and themselves, before the St. Ives Workhouse; Marx, with the condition of "estranged labor," an economic state which is every bit as psychological as it is social. As he searches out the reasons why the worker feels outside his work, removed from the object of his work and from his own basic nature, Marx, like Carlyle, seems to be driving behind the false relationships set up between the worker and manager, the worker and his product, the manager and his money. Like Carlyle, he sees society as splitting apart in an ever-widening series of rifts, all launched by the initial dislocation of true human relationships, protests against the cash nexus, the use of labor as merely a means to success, is fascinated with the possibilities of increased production, and argues for a fairer distribution of economic wealth. Finally, again fundamentally like Carlyle, he argues for a return to

5. References subsequently in the text are to the English language edition published in Moscow in 1961.

true human relationships of spontaneity, trust, and fulfillment in work.

However "philosophic" the manuscripts may appear, there is always, as in Carlyle, the voice of the outraged revolutionary, muffled as he tries to gain some philosophical perspective, but struggling for a solution, aiming to secure release from bondage. Marx's fascination with polarities and inversions, the overturning of categories, including his own great overturning of Hegelianism from the abstraction he felt it was to economic fact, testifies to a revolutionary impulse, a desire to shake the categories up into greater conflict and ultimately to drive behind them into fact for an apocalypse in which man is actually freed from any categories. Behind every general principle there is the outrage at horror. It is found, for instance, behind Marx's attempt to break through the whole concept of political economy as it traditionally stands.

Political economy conceals the estrangement inherent in the nature of labour by not considering the direct relationship between the worker (labour) and production. It is true that labour produces for the rich wonderful things—but for the worker it produces privation. It produces palaces—but for the worker hovels. It produces beauty—but for the worker deformity. (p. 71)

Thus, Marx's work is as determined as Carlyle's by prophetic denunciation of the limited man, the man reduced to an animal, whether through poverty or wealth. Marx's poor are as bewildered as Carlyle's enchanted men at the workhouse, and his wealthy are determined only by success, wealth, and cash—the accumulation of Chactaw Indian heads, as Carlyle would say. Like Carlyle too, Marx sees the arena of struggle as both individual and social, but even more than Carlyle he stresses

the social: man's alienation from himself, society, and nature proceeds from his alienation from his work. Through a skillful manipulation of his terms, Marx never loses sight of the peculiarly individual nature of this problem, its deeply disturbing emotional implications, what it really feels like to be alienated. By locating the evil in private property itself, he carries his accusations much further than Carlyle; his state of transcendence offers a similar breakthrough of great extremity, the abolition of private property through communism and the overturning of the foundations of political economy itself. But at this stage Marx's utopia, like Carlyle's, is not yet reified: communism is an ultimate social goal, but it is primarily a psychological situation of restored selfhood, joy and spontaneity in work, love and trust in human relationships. In this early variety of communism, Marx proposes a return to nature, a restoration of man to his real roots, and the development of the total man. He envisions labor as primarily an aesthetic activity, with man as the artist working up inorganic nature, as he puts it, and giving it his imprint in order to form (as in Blake and Carlyle) the city of man and art. "Labour and man as the subject are the point of departure as well as the result of the movement" (p. 103); "What is to be avoided above all is the re-establishing of 'Society' as an abstraction vis-à-vis the individual" (p. 105).

Marx clarifies and deepens a belief implicit in Carlyle: that the individual process manifests the social process and vice versa. His philosophical terms for relationships enable him to develop a sense of dynamics, of charges of meaning going from pole to pole, from individual to individual, and from individual to society—or, correspondingly, the failure of these charges, an atomizing or isolating of individuals from one another and of individuals from themselves and society, Carlyle's

negative process. He is thus able to superimpose several levels of significance upon one another and to observe their mutual interaction: communism is naturalism is humanism; the individual is society; economics is aesthetic activity; and even history, so long a history of repression, can be truly a part of nature once it is returned to its roots. Blake achieves much the same density by means of his giant mythical forms and through the figure of Albion, fallen England and fallen man, and Carlyle attains a similar depth through the interplay of giant social forces and individual types.

More than Blake and Carlyle, Marx provides a sense of evolution at once a historical, economic, and social process and a dynamic movement of the mind, a psychological development. Within each individual the historical process is recapitulated. Marx's philosophical approach demonstrates that once the primary relationship of worker to his work and the manager was perverted, the whole growth of man as a species and individual was stunted. The present condition, as in both Blake and Carlyle, is the result of a fall from some primal truth and it covers the sweep of history, but it recurs whether one is aware of it or not in each individual.

Like Blake and Carlyle, Marx aims, through an understanding of the "key to the return," i.e. man's relation to man, for the restoration of total man. Man will be restored to himself "as a *social* (i.e. human) being—a return become conscious, and accomplished within the entire wealth of previous development" (p. 102). Marx's language here obviously derives from Hegel, but it is more psychological, aesthetic, and even industrial than metaphysical. He shows much the same fascination with industry and accelerated production as Carlyle does; through an increase in goods and with work that is spontaneous and self-fulfilling, both the self and the city of labor can expand. What has been accomplished

225

"through industry, even though in an estranged form, is true anthropological nature" and hence not to be denied but *aufgeheben,* assimilated. This is the same as Carlyle's view of English labor as the silent, enduring reality beneath sham; Marx too can both condemn Plugson of Undershot and praise him and urge him onward.

In Blakean terms that would have offended the more puritan Carlyle, but which I have already pointed out were implicit in his idea of fact, Marx argues for a "sensuous appropriation for and by man of the human essence," though not "in the sense of direct, one-sided gratification—merely in the sense of possessing or having" (p. 106). The end of society is to produce the full individual: "the *rich* man *profoundly endowed with all the senses*" (p. 109). And this is a progressive vision, wherein nature and history will be at one: "The *forming* of the five senses is a labour of the entire history of the world down to the present" (p. 108); "Need or enjoyment" will lose "their *egotistical* nature, and nature . . . its mere *utility* by use becoming *human* use" (p. 107). Instead of relationships of estrangement, need, use, and the cash nexus, the aesthetic relationships of trust, love, and humanity are used to present activity that is spontaneous, energetic, independent, and self-generating.

All of these points are helpful not only in charting the direction of *Past and Present* as prophecy and apocalypse, but also in discovering the confusions that impede Carlyle's central direction. In their apocalyptic insistence on getting behind conventions and systems of political economy, Carlyle's protests against all theories and theorists, radicals or Tories, conservatives or utilitarians aim in the same direction as Marx's. Moreover, his unrelenting appeals to fact, God's law, nature, the eternal core of the universe, and the like, which often

make him appear a mere Puritan prophet, are perhaps less platitudinous than they seem; they may harbor a similar drive to get beyond systems and capitalistic history as ordinarily understood. Their traditional tone may not be merely regressive but may imply a futuristic impulse, a desire to restore man to nature beyond history and systems, a nature that is at once original and progressive. If Carlyle's goals are not so apocalyptic as Marx's analyses, they at least express the yearning for an apocalypse.

Marx also shows that the ideas of the restored man, the universe as a garden and as laboring activity, arise from the vision of labor as man's essential nature rather than from any religious reform that Carlyle may wish to inculcate. Carlyle, however, as we have noted, is ambivalent in his view of labor: he is often content to see it in the Christian and Calvinistic view of struggle, pain, duty, and anguish in a post-lapsarian world. He frequently pushes it back to the Garden of Eden, but usually only after Adam and Eve have fallen. This more stoic approach, with its Christian conventions, often yields to the fascination with labor as self-fulfilling activity, the sheer excitement of industrial progress, of the full and complete vision. By this point in his career, Carlyle's distrust of the imagination and art is more severe than that of the early Marx, however, and he is even more reluctant to admit the aesthetic character of his picture of restored humanity. As the social chaos worsens around him, art seems, in his Puritan view, to be a superfluity, a luxury, even an immorality.

Carlyle's apocalyptic drive is also hindered by his view of the feudal order of nature as the primal truth from which man has fallen. Marx goes beyond the limits of Carlyle's vision, which favors feudalism because it suggests a realm of order and nature, the Middle Ages because Gurth knew to whom he belonged even if he

was only a serf, and his own peasant childhood for the security of place it provided in nature and society. Often Carlyle thinks only in these terms, seeking more cunning methods of binding as if he were attempting to bring feudalism over in its totality into the industrial age. His demand for a new aristocracy and his metaphorical plea for a drill sergeant to establish order both have feudal attitudes as their source and consequently clash against the main drive of *Past and Present*.

Connected with this idea of binding and aristocracy is another notion, the most reactionary idea of the book: Carlyle's opposition to democracy and to extending the franchise. Even this has a positive as well as a negative side, however, as in Nietzsche, for both thinkers—and Marx would probably agree too—see democracy as an extension of the present chaos, a lowering of society, one more paper theorem, and, worst of all, an intensification of the present atomism of man and his social isolation from his fellowman. Carlyle and Nietzsche both fear the death of aristocracy, the self-fulfilled individual, the noblest man. But behind their hero worship there is a strong negative, even a pathological streak, which intensifies in the later writings of each. For both, the opposition to democracy and the gradual worship of the strong and mighty hero is, I believe, a deliberate desire to affront society at its most basic level. Neither Nietzsche nor Carlyle could be heroic in the sense he conceived, so their glorification of past ages and heroes and of the past of a race functioned as a compensation, an acting out of roles unavailable to them or to society. As society swirled in more turmoil, gradually being lowered by democracy as they saw it, both Carlyle and Nietzsche augmented their ideas of heroism so that they became more shocking and cruel. The added strength of their heroes and their chosen race or periods of history gave the writers an increased sense of power which they, un-

heeded by society, felt they would have lacked otherwise.

Carlyle's ideas reveal a strong conservative streak—and often a prelude to a fascistic one—but frequently he quite frankly labels his conservatism as such, though he clearly sees its conflict with the intensity of his appeal to reform. Even after the primacy of labor and activity as a self-transforming principle has been granted, however, some of the conservative ideas have the possibility of breakthrough implicit in them. "Liberty requires new definitions" is conceived as a protest against extending the franchise, but it is also a yearning for some really original definition of liberty, one that will free man from the atomism of democracy itself. Similarly, the organizing of the masses by the drill sergeant is often not an actual suggestion (as it will become in the *Latter-Day Pamphlets,* a sad reversal from the days of *Schiller,* where the drill sergeant of the Stuttgart school impeded Schiller's organic growth and rooted it out), but merely a metaphor designed to point toward the glittering possibility of transforming the world by work. Carlyle's armies are meant not for killing, but for fighting against stupidity and chaos and for shivering mountains asunder. "Not as a bewildered bewildering mob; but as a firm regimented mass, with real captains over them, will these men march any more" (*PP,* 275). The intoxication with the power of work and its possibilities for transforming the earth and man is every bit as strong as the implied militarism in containing the chaos of a fragmented society. All of these statements probably have an origin that is quite complex; a variety of motivations, both reactionary and progressive, lies behind them. Carlyle yearns for a stable order, fears social chaos, and must call for a new compulsion to prevent the nether madness of the self from raging uncontrollably: "Leave me not to walk over precipices" (*PP,* 213).

He also responds to the biblical desire to force the judgment day, to unvest the forces of God, to rout the forces of destruction once and for all, to marshall the masses for Armageddon, all of which the drill sergeant will hasten. And, finally, he is positively fascinated with the energies of man released through new labor. But always, despite his faith in the power of the individual, he distrusts the individual and his imaginative freedom.

It is this distrust of the aesthetic activity of his own writing and vision, of the art that he despises but by which he lives, that drives Carlyle into extremes and confusion. He obliterates his own prophetic role and mission from the book because it would presumably court an intrusion upon the role of God. But, paradoxically, he himself appears far more godlike, presumptuous, and egotistic than either Blake or Marx. Blake, more aware than Carlyle of the pitfalls of egotism, pride, and solipsism that awaited the visionary in his lonely working out of his vision, knew the temptation to play the Urizenic deity he was seeking to rout but in the Orc cycle and *Jerusalem* exposed these pitfalls and temptations and overcame them. Carlyle—almost like the figure in Blake's "A Poison Tree"—suppresses them and thus his hidden arrogance strikes us all the more fully.

At bottom, Carlyle is not certain whether his book is an artifact or a social program, visionary literature or self-help manual. His distrust of art, imagination, and aesthetic fulfillment leads him to advocate for its existence as a social tract in his attempts at the end to ground his utopia in real fact, with its beginning in real contemporary figures, to reify what was metaphorical in either the present or the future rather than primarily within the individual, to establish real captains of industry, and to project his vision into real time and outward upon society rather than within the individual.

Yet the basis of *Past and Present* calls for inner crisis and breakthrough and founds the new society on a positive self-transforming vision of labor in an industrial society.

A similar confusion pervades the book's most radical suggestions. Taken literally, they, like Nietzsche's statements about the need for war in *Zarathustra*, are horrifyingly fascistic, and Carlyle's literalization of such notions whenever he opts for the actual realization of this vision, without the mediation of the aesthetic vision as prior, makes them seem filled with the lust for power. I shall cite only two of the most remarkable instances of this wobbling between metaphor and fact. From his picture of the soldier whom he finds as the one enduring thing from the centuries past, presumably a legacy from Cromwell's days, Carlyle concludes that he must be the most real. In its suggestions of "whatever is, is right" and "might makes right" and "the strongest will prevail and is right," the picture is frightening: "But he of the red coat, I say, is a success and no failure! He will veritably, if he gets orders, draw out a long sword and kill me. No mistake there. He is a fact and not a shadow" (*PP*, 261) . But soon the soldier is purged of his horror as he is absorbed into the new laboring society and is converted into a metaphor for the warfare of contraries, the building of Jerusalem. Even though the literal meaning is clouded and disappears, a sense of its power and fact continues into the vision.

> The Soldier is perhaps one of the most difficult things to realize; but Governments, had they not realized him, could not have existed: accordingly he is here. O Heavens, if we saw an army ninety-thousand strong, maintained and fully equipt, in continual real action and battle against Human Starvation, against Chaos, Necessity, Stupidity, and

231

our real "natural enemies," what a business were it!
(*PP*, 263)

Similarly, in a confusing description of the battlefield
the idea of the soldier and the fight slide from metaphor
to literal realization and back to metaphor again.

> Man is created to fight; he is perhaps best of all de-
> finable as a born soldier; his life "a battle and a
> march," under the right General. It is forever indis-
> pensable for a man to fight: now with Necessity,
> with Barrenness, Scarcity . . . —now also with the
> hallucinations of his poor fellow Men. . . . All
> fighting . . . is the dusty conflict of strengths . . .
> —of Mights which do in the long-run, and forever
> will in this just Universe in the long-run mean
> Rights . . . . So will and must God's Justice and
> this only . . . ultimately prosper in all controver-
> sies and enterprises and battles whatsoever . . . .
> Blessed divine Influence, traceable even in the hor-
> ror of Battlefields and garments rolled in blood:
> how it ennobles even the Battlefield; and, in place
> of a Chactaw Massacre, makes it a Field of Honour!
> A Battlefield too is great. Considered well, it is a
> kind of Quintessence of Labour; Labour distilled
> into its utmost concentration; the significance of
> years of it compressed into an hour. (*PP*, 190–91)

Internal and external battles are blended here, and the
battle against the delusions of one's fellowmen, Carlyle's
literary battle, is equated to a real war. Any image of
self-perfection through the strife of contraries is muted
in favor of a purely aggressive and militaristic will to
power that claims to be the voice of God.

The final section of the book, however, clearly gains
its power not by assertions of militaristic might but by
the transformed voice of the prophet, especially in the

pressures it brings to the confrontation of the conflicting forces of society and the sense it conveys that in this apocalypse it has come into full vision. Yet Carlyle seems just as self-consciously absent as ever; the prophet has not grown with his book because he has been in possession of the unchanging truth from the beginning. The transformations are projected as the result of changes in other men and institutions, yet it seems impossible to deny that the completion of the book is an aesthetic one, the result of Carlyle's earlier contemplation and analysis of the various conflicting forces. The work's aesthetic quality is nowhere so heightened as in the last section, where, with great symbolic density, all of the earlier phrases, catchwords, slogans, symbols, parables, and images recur in a pell-mell fashion and are absorbed by the final vision of society, transformed, and resolved. Nowhere does the book—or, for that matter, any of Carlyle's writings—so strongly point to its own personal linguistic world, the work of Carlyle's own personal vision. If one opened the book first to these pages, its very words would be a mystery. Here the book itself may be said to affirm its strong internal drive as an artifact, but Carlyle tugs against that drive by reifying his metaphors and insistently looking to a very real future which he wishes he could hasten.

Both Blake and Marx seem to avoid this problem by keeping inner and outer planes in constant mutual interaction. Marx, who deals more carefully with social problems, works in such a manner that the sense of social conflicts he shares with Carlyle can be seen as constantly internalized as well as externalized. By guarding against the sheer objectification of those conflicts and the horrors of war and social dissolution they entail, he wards off a gap between vision and reality and a corresponding psychological gap, a potential for schizophrenia in the prophet. Nietzsche ultimately succumbs to

that gap, and Carlyle felt a predilection toward it. Nietzsche, with Blake, fights off the inhumanity of the prophet battling under the banner of a Urizenic deity, certainly the major temptation throughout *Past and Present,* by his trust in man, his humanity, his claims for man's independence and self-divinity, and his belief in man's ultimate power for remaking himself and society *in perpetuum.* Carlyle, more fearful of disorder, ultimately sanctions far more disorder by his irrational invocation of force and power in God's name; the self-transforming quality of labor then becomes a savage struggle against enemies, ultimately the pure pursuit of power alone in a demonic and hostile universe that refuses to go the way its prophet charts.

Since Marx ultimately abandoned his own interests in the transformation of the self in favor of pure economic reform, it may seem that Blake alone escaped these problems of the relation of the reborn self to the reborn society. But this does not seem to be the case either, since for most of us, Blake remains a private mythology, Northrop Frye and Harold Bloom notwithstanding. That mythology may convey a strong sense of the imagination's ability to unfetter man from a hostile universe, and its picture of man as his own tormentor may be convincing, but it is ultimately weak in its handling of those external and hostile pressures of the real world that present such multiple difficulties to the unifying power of the imagination and to the integrity of the self. Carlyle's move toward a prophecy that embodies closer social analysis seems to me to be the correct one; it represents the need for the prophet, whether his inner vision is fulfilled as Blake's is or his own transformations are undefined as Carlyle's are, to come into contact with all the very real social, economic, and political forces, in all their complexity and multiplicity, that mold our contemporary society. Blake may make godlike radicals

of his readers, but he may leave them far more solipsistic than he was. Carlyle and Marx at least offer ways of bringing this vision to society itself, and their failure to solve this difficult problem of the relationship of the inner man to the outer, of inner harmony to public complexity and possible public harmony, is not their responsibility; their work is still going on, and most of us find ourselves involved in some form of compromise that is not a yielding but a quiet and careful quest. Carlyle will ultimately turn toward what I regard as a more realistic assessment of the role of selfhood in the modern world, but not until he has explored the futility of the heroic strain, indeed not until he has played it out fully. For the moment, he is split, finding the fulfillment of vision in either the past of his heroes or in an objectified future. He is taking a long look at the abyss of the present and raging against it.

✒️ 5 ✒️

HUNTING FOR HEROES:
THE FLIGHT FROM REALITY

HERO-WORSHIP: EVERLASTING ADAMANT
OR SOLACING FACT?

Great men, like great ages, are explosives in which a
tremendous force is stored up . . . . Great men are
necessary, the age in which they appear is accidental.

Carlyle: a man of strong words and attitudes, a rhetor
from *need,* constantly lured by the craving for a strong
faith and the feeling of his incapacity for it . . . .
Carlyle drugs something in himself with the fortis-
simo of his veneration of men of strong faith and with
his rage against the less simple-minded: he *requires*
noise. A constant passionate dishonesty against himself—that is his *proprium;* in this respect he is and
remains interesting. Of course, in England he is admired precisely for his honesty.

Nietzsche,
Twilight of the Idols

Carlyle first revealed the major motif of his retreat in
the most public of settings, the lecture hall. The lectures
on heroes, the only ones he bothered to write out after-
ward from his notes, delivered in 1840, were the last of
his annual popular series. But the public setting was
more a matter of formality than any actual impulse to
meet society directly. Carlyle had undertaken the first
series of lectures in 1837 when, badly in need of money,

he had been approached by Harriet Martineau and some American admirers of *Sartor* who suggested that he deliver some talks on his specialty, the history of German literature. With *Sartor* still unpublished in book form in England and with his fame from *The French Revolution* still unattained, mixed feelings of hope and terror gave way to necessity.[1] Carlyle never fully conquered his stage fright, but the lectures had been successful and had amply aided his income. By 1840 Carlyle had accepted lecturing so much in the course of things that no unusual significance can be predicated for the public presentation of the theme of heroes and a history of hero-worship. That Carlyle admired the series sufficiently to write it out in book form is significant, however; two other sets of lectures dealing with the history of literature obviously no longer imaginatively interested him after he had whipped up subjects from his past into lecture form, and the material on the French Revolution also was of the past.

Heroes represented the new bent of Carlyle's mind, but the more low-pitched and less creative method of the lecture platform did not offer an arena for his typical methods. Hence the common arrangement of a progressive historical theme in all four series of lectures may suggest not so much an inquiry into historical method as merely a convenient way of spacing out several lectures in a series. That formal arrangement may, however, give certain ideas more weight than Carlyle intended and grant more significance to his confusions than they deserve. Any interpretation of *Heroes* must therefore be surrounded with certain caveats—not least of which should be a warning that their form is perhaps

1. For information on the various sets of lectures, see Froude, *Life in London, 1,* 105 ff., 170–71. The second series, *Lectures on the History of Literature* (Apr. to July 1838), is available in notes by J. Reay Greene (New York, 1892).

rather artificially imposed and stultifying, that it leads to certain distortions rather unwillingly intended, and that it in fact fetters the freedom Carlyle normally achieved in his other writings and forces him to play the philosopher over the explorer.

Unfortunately, because the lectures contain such clear-cut philosophical statements of themes, they now form a basis for most studies of Carlyle by philosophers, literary critics, and intellectual historians and, snipped up into minor anthology pieces, constitute (beyond a few set pieces from *Sartor* and *The French Revolution*) for most educated readers their total image of Carlyle. The problem, as Eric Bentley notes in *A Century of Hero Worship*, is that Carlyle's study of heroism from Odin to Napoleon "is an expression of (his) mental confusion and one of his least convincing works." [2] Almost any thesis can be supported by recourse to this work, and each, it must be admitted, is to some degree true. Interpretations of Carlyle thus range across a wide and exceedingly varied spectrum: at one end, he is condemned as a precursor of fascism and racism, a worshipper of instinct, emotion, and irrationalism (H. J. C. Grierson's *Carlyle and Hitler*, Pieter Geyl's *Debates with Historians*), toward the middle, he emerges not entirely absolved of these faults, but at least not fully culpable (Bentley's *A Century of Hero Worship*, Ernst Cassirer's *The Myth of the State*); and at the other extreme, more positive interpretations praise him as a seeker after religious and social truth. (Basil Willey's *Nineteenth Century Studies*, Emory Neff's *Carlyle* and *Carlyle and Mill* [3]). All these studies are of inestimable value in

2. Eric Bentley, *A Century of Hero Worship* (rev. ed. Boston, 1957), p. 34.

3. The works referred to are H. J. C. Grierson, *Carlyle and Hitler* (Cambridge, 1933); Pieter Geyl, *Debates with Historians* (New York, 1958); Ernst Cassirer, *The Myth of the State* (New Haven, 1946;

charting the presuppositions and implications of his beliefs, yet each is conducted from the viewpoint of the intellectual historian, with Carlyle regarded either as a representative of some larger intellectual development (e.g. *A Century of Hero Worship, The Myth of the State*) or as a philosopher who reached his apex—of influence at least—in the lectures on heroes, certainly the most systematic of his works, for better or worse.

For my purposes, the focus must be shifted away from the more common center of investigation and the work studied in alliance with the problems of the imagination which I have been examining. Even if *Heroes* is a failure as both art and philosophy, it still offers a novel attempt by Carlyle to face the recurrent problems of order and disorder, heart and head, spirit and matter, process and form, permanence and change. Its confusion is a mirror of new confusions in Carlyle's approach to social problems, a study of the techniques of evasion that culminate in *Cromwell* and *Frederick*. To thread my way through this labyrinth, I shall first investigate the ostensible program of the book, then examine some of the problems that program generates, and, finally, attempt to show how the artistic and formal defects of the book are linked to its philosophical ambiguity and to Carlyle's evasive action.

What Carlyle is really concerned with in *Heroes* is theoretical support for his belief in the hero. Spreading his lectures out over history permits him to describe an inner spiritual unity behind history, which allows for substantial continuity and permanence but also for living evolution and progression. The hero and history are perfect mates: what better solution than that which dis-

Garden City, 1955); Basil Willey, *Nineteenth Century Studies* (London, 1949); Emory Neff, *Carlyle and Mill* (New York, 1924) and *Carlyle* (New York, 1932).

covers both unity and continuity in the hero and the divine substance to which he bears witness and with which he is in special contact? what more ingenious solution than that which finds man's spiritual progress in the movement from the hero as god to the hero as king? By postulating a theory of changing vestures of the hero, Carlyle, in the manner of Teufelsdröckh, can satisfy the demands of the new spokesmen of scientific relativism; yet, at the same time, by postulating a substantial spirit to which the hero bears witness, he can, also like Teufelsdröckh, attest to a spiritual truth which endures and cannot be defeated by a scientific age.

The first hero, Odin, the hero as divinity (significantly, Christ or a Hebrew prophet is absent), sets the pattern to which the other heroes must conform. Indeed, in his status as myth beneath history, he provides a fount of energy that the other heroes will find difficult to emulate. Carlyle's familiar images of spiritual unity and growth are once again granted free play. Odin is pictured almost wearisomely in images which show his union with the central fact of the universe and his capacity to make that fact expand and grow in humanity. Like all great men, he is a "living light-fountain" who constitutes a bit of the "marrow of the world's history" (H, 2). He is the "gleam as of a small real light shining in the centre of that enormous camera-obscura image [of paganism]" (H, 26). In contact with the central law behind the universe, he is the thinker who spreads a shadow of himself over the world (H, 34). Without him, the inarticulate darkness, longing to become articulate, would have remained dumb (H, 33).

Hero-worship is the taproot (H, 11) of the life tree Igdrasil (H, 20), the basis of religion (H, 11), a "living rock" (H, 15) upon which all society finds its source and basis. Carlyle's heroes then must possess a common ground, which he establishes by attributing to them

characteristics which depict their union with the central fact of the universe and their diffusion of the fruits of that union. Like the figures of the early essays, these heroes are projections of Carlyle writ large. They are strong, earnest, rugged, and often, in their hatred for artificiality, rude and inarticulate, but they are also sincere, greathearted, wildly affectionate, and deeply sympathetic. Their habitations share similar characteristics with the same proportional dominance of strength over softness; they are Scotland writ large. Odin's Iceland is an island "burst up . . . by fire from the bottom of the sea; a wild land of barrenness and lava; swallowed many months of every year in black tempests, yet with a wild gleaming beauty in summertime; towering up there, stern and grim, in the North Ocean," but this Iceland is tempered, like Odin's strength, with a "rim of grassy country" inhabited by "poetic men" (*H*, 16). Mahomet's Arabia is a land of "savage inaccessible rock-mountains, great grim deserts" (*H*, 47), which leaves him alone with the eternities glaring in on him (*H*, 54), but it too is tempered: "alternating with beautiful strips of verdure: wherever water is, there is greenness, beauty; odoriferous balm-shrubs, date-trees, frankincense trees" (*H*, 47). The actual link between setting and man is made in Luther's case. "I will call [him] . . . an Alpine mountain . . . Ah yes, unsubduable granite, piercing far and wide into the Heavens; yet in the clefts of it fountains, green beautiful valleys with flowers!" (*H*, 142).

The hero, then, by piercing to the heart of nature and her "divine laws," participates in one common essence which endures throughout time.

For at bottom the Great Man, as he comes from the hand of Nature, is ever the same kind of thing: Odin, Luther, Johnson, Burns: I hope to make it

appear that these are all originally of one stuff; that only by the world's reception of them, and the shapes they assume, are they so immeasurably diverse. (H, 43)

I confess, I have no notion of a truly great man that could not be *all* sorts of men. (H, 78)

By sharing in this same essence, all Carlyle's heroes have the potentiality of any shape. Burns, like Mirabeau, could have bellowed away Usher de Brézé; Johnson could have rallied to his country's cause like Cromwell; and Cromwell could have written Shakespeare's plays. As Ernst Cassirer observes:

> By this method the hero of Carlyle became a Proteus that could assume every shape. In every new lecture he shows us a new face. He appears as a mythical god, as a prophet, a priest, a man of letters, a king. He has no limits; nor is he bound to any special sphere of activity . . . . In [Carlyle's] "transcendent" admiration of the great men he sometimes seems to lose every sense of proportion. The differences of our lower empirical world were almost forgotten; the most disparate historical characters were put on the same level.[4]

The metaphysical and metahistorical lack of definition which Cassirer cites is even more intense when Carlyle focuses on the problems of growth and expansion. For Carlyle nature's deepest law is a law of growth. What is true of the individual is true of humanity at large; the meaning of life is to unfold itself (H, 225). In a world where nature sanctions only the true, anything containing meaning must be a step forward in human progress. In positive terms, this attitude allows Carlyle to avoid the omniscient egotism and narrowness of most

4. Cassirer, pp. 242–43.

historians of his age and enables him to grasp the religious truth behind a paganism which he knows could not proceed from quackery or allegory, a Mahometism which he knows could not proceed from deceit and fakery, and a Cromwellian theocracy which he knows could not proceed from lying and hypocrisy. Paganism has a meaning; its worship of valor is incipient and rude, but it is a preparation for Christianity's moral law. From a negative point of view, however, the fact that the theory cannot admit of decay in the hero and his message creates problems. The manner of receiving the hero may fall into its present stagnation (as Nietzsche will likewise say), so that Johnson must live in a garret receiving fourpence-halfpenny a day and Burns must gauge beer, but hero-worship must endure.

Carlyle grants that the vesture of the hero's truth may become obsolete in a scientific age that will not allow belief in his role as prophet or divinity, forms of hero-worship which are "productions of old ages," that "presuppose a certain rudeness of conception," that need a "world vacant, or almost vacant of scientific forms" (*H*, 78). Dante's *Malebolge* is no longer a real place in the middle of a real ocean since Columbus crossed the Atlantic, and Johnson's world of forms is not ours. But the meaning behind these facts of belief endures as truth; the casting off of the vestures, as in *Sartor* and "Characteristics," is progress, not decline. "All death . . . is but of the body, not of the essence or soul; all destruction, by violent revolution or howsoever it be, is but new creation on a wider scale" (*H*, 119).

The problem of decay and decline, of incipient formlessness and chaos, is clearly visible to Carlyle, however. While he does not talk about his response to the problem in his lectures, *Sartor*, the essays, and all the social writings insist that he sees it all around him. When the issue intrudes itself into his account of the historical

243

process, he adopts methods of explaining away his own recognition of incipient decay or chaos as it interferes with progress; a rationalizing tone comes to the fore.

> Does it not look as if our estimate of the Great Man, epoch after epoch, were continually diminishing? We take him first for a god, then for one god-inspired; and now in the next stage of it, his most miraculous word gains from us only the recognition that he is a Poet, beautiful verse-maker, man of genius, or suchlike!—It looks so; but I persuade myself that intrinsically it is not so. If we consider well, it will perhaps appear that in man still there is the *same* altogether peculiar admiration for the Heroic Gift, by what name soever called, that there at any time was. I should say, if we do not now reckon a Great Man literally divine, it is that our notions of God, of the supreme unattainable Fountain of Splendour, Wisdom, and Heroism are ever rising *higher*. (*H*, 84)

Carlyle scorns poetry but he himself is obviously the man of genius in this citation; the man of letters is close to the lowly poet. The real center of feeling, of deep frustration, of doubt, is in the first part of the quotation; the second part ("I persuade myself") is a bald statement not so much of theory as of Carlyle's wish-fulfilling method of escaping both a theoretical difficulty and his own plight.

Disorder, then, in this view belongs to the enemy alone. He is the worshipper of forms which have lost their substance—and hence, their meaning and motive power for inciting moral action. Though the reformer, such as Mahomet, Knox, Luther, or Cromwell, works in the middle of disorder, he strives, Carlyle claims, for progress and order, a return to spontaneous forms containing true substances. Modern history, in particular, is

244

a struggle to attain "wider forms." In Carlyle's rather reductive and schematic concept of historical periods, Luther is the first act of Protestantism, destroying the empty forms of Popery; Cromwell the second, destroying Laudian pedantry and false form; and the French Revolution the third and last, destroying eighteenth-century falsehood and inaugurating a new world of heroes and hero-worship. Even the Three Days of 1830 in Paris are a reminder of the transition to the new state and not further signs of dissolution.

Much of this declaration seems to be rationalization. Carlyle admits that the decline of hero-worship is a fact to which even the French Revolution testifies, but he goes on to claim that this proves that hero-worship exists forever, that Napoleon must come as lightning if not as light, that we are merely in a state of transition from false to true, that a new world of more powerful heroes is a-building. Hero-worship to Carlyle is exactly what he describes it as—a solace, a comfort in an age which evidences only dissolution and decay. It is both a projected ideal which experience tends to negate and a failure to ask further questions, a flight from reality.

> To me, in these circumstances, that of "Hero-worship" becomes a fact inexpressibly precious; the most solacing fact one sees in the world at present. There is an everlasting hope in it for the management of the world. Had all traditions, arrangements, creeds, societies that men ever instituted, sunk away, this would remain. The certainty of Heroes being sent us; our faculty, our necessity to reverence Heroes when sent; it shines like a polestar through smoke-clouds, dust-clouds, and all manner of down-rushing and conflagration. (H, 202)

The indestructibility of hero-worship is "the everlasting adamant lower than which the confused wreck of revo-

245

lutionary things cannot fall" (H, 15). Carlyle's lectures are less an easy declaration that hero-worship is the only unquestioned form in a world where all forms are transitory than a confused and contradictory attempt to prove it so. The weight of the above citation is on the "confused wreck," not the "everlasting adamant."

Carlyle's failure to question the formal indestructibility of hero-worship and the somewhat facile alliance of hero-worship with the eternal law of the world stand out sharply not only in his frequent insistence on the limitations of all forms, symbols, and idols, but especially in his attempts to pierce the eternal meaning and truth behind the obsolete vesture, the archaic rude dialect of an Odin, a Mahomet, and a Dante. In magniloquent language replete with the usual capital letters, Mahomet's Heaven and Hell are metamorphosed from temporal to eternal: "What is all this but a rude shadow, in the rude Bedouin imagination, of that grand spiritual Fact, and Beginning of Facts, which it is ill for us too if we do not all know and feel: the Infinite Nature of Duty?" (H, 75). Similarly, if Knox's sectarianism and obstinacy in setting up a theocracy should be offensive to the modern mind which still seeks the comfort of religious truth, Knox's actions can find its eternal meaning secured by a magic transformation of the word "theocracy."

> But how shall we blame *him* for struggling to realize it? Theocracy, Government of God, is precisely the thing to be struggled for! All Prophets, zealous Priests, are there for that purpose . . . . That right and truth, or God's Law, reign supreme among men, this is the Heavenly Ideal (well named in Knox's time, and namable in all times, a revealed "Will of God") towards which the Reformer will insist that all be more and more approximated. All

true Reformers, as I said, are by the nature of them Priests, and strive for a Theocracy. (*H*, 152)

In all these instances Carlyle never questions the finality of his own dialect, never even raises the possibility that this eternal fact may itself be a dialect. For he knows that if he does this, he too may be involved in the general dissolution of the times. That is why hero-worship is a "solacing" fact.

At one point only, this question seems about to raise itself. In criticizing the nineteenth century's tendency to regard its own insight as final, Carlyle almost qualifies his own insight into the eternal. "Withal, it is an important fact in the nature of man, that he tends to reckon his own insight as final, and goes upon it as such. He will always do it, I suppose, in one or the other way; but it must be in some wider, wiser way than this" (*H*, 120). Here he touches the crucial point but, seemingly oblivious of the problem he has just encountered, turns away for one more of his rhetorical assertions about the eternal.

Are not all true men that live, or that ever lived, soldiers of the same army, enlisted, under Heaven's captaincy, to do battle against the same enemy, the Empire of Darkness and Wrong? Why should we misknow one another, fight not against the enemy but against ourselves, from mere difference of uniform? (*H*, 120)

The two worlds are revealed as absolutely distinct, but the strain in such cases, if it is not apparent to Carlyle, is striking to the modern reader.

This failure of Carlyle to examine his own presuppositions while questioning those of his predecessors or contemporaries has led Cassirer to declare with a faint tone of disenchantment about *Heroes*: "Never before had he made as ample use of mere rhetorical means as

in these lectures." [5] This may indeed be rhetoric, but it is not necessarily, as Cassirer often implies in his chapter on Carlyle, conscious deceit. Carlyle believes in his "solacing fact" as a world theory, and he is often unaware of the sense of strain which he has made inevitable. Later, in *Cromwell*, Carlyle can attain to such belief in Oliver that actions which seem hypocritical to us do not for a moment appear that way to him; deceit, in fact, is precisely what Carlyle wants to erase from Cromwell's reputation, and he hopes to do it by showing us the actions themselves.

The individual dialect is even more pronounced in the descriptions of the heroes that fully tap Carlyle's creative response. Those he really admires are images of himself or a wish-fulfilled self. As "Heaven's Captains," they take part in the great history of the world, the battle of belief against the monsters of unbelief. Luther, Knox, and Cromwell alone among the heroes break into speeches as they smash the idols of falsity. Luther burning the Pope's bull and heroically encountering his inquisitors at the Diet of Worms, Knox tossing over the "pented bredd" of the Virgin Mary into the waters of the Loire, where he is imprisoned as a galley slave, Cromwell defying the king: all three are rebels and revolutionaries, and all three call forth Carlyle's most vehement creative energy. Mahomet can be counted in this company, though direct address is not used to present him: he too is primarily a reformer and corresponds to a basic pattern underlying the portraits of the other three. Each has experienced a conversion similar to Carlyle's "Everlasting Yea" in which the "great Fact" glared in upon him suddenly; each has felt the duty of delivering his message to the world in spite of poverty, struggle, oppression, and total aloneness. All initially desired to

5. Ibid., p. 275.

live quiet lives, did not want to be drawn into the battle and its subsequent disorder.

Luther did not will his notoriety but Rome came athwart him and his "duty." Knox was a tutor but had to respond to his country's call because he could live only according to "fact"; Cromwell was a farmer who felt a similar necessity. Characteristically, though their conversion was early in life, like Carlyle's, their major work began late. Mahomet lived quietly until he was fifty; Knox and Cromwell both lived in peace for forty years. Each was a lonely, isolated man, fighting against idols, the world's pomp and falsity. Each had few adherents at first but was gradually triumphant. Their basic characteristic was the inheritance of Odin, strength and valor. Cassirer and Willey perhaps wrongly insist too fully on their moral character and its predominance. It is true that Carlyle pays service to it and notes its progress over paganism, but his real interest, as always, is in valor. It is as though Carlyle did not need to convince himself of the moral nature of his cause but had only to steel himself for the great battle with the nineteenth century that he felt awaited him.

One other hero, however, appeals so strongly to Carlyle that he becomes a personality despite the slim evidence for his existence. Though Odin has no great obstacle of unbelief to fight against and finds his audience spontaneously, the hero of the Norse folk is the ideal for which Carlyle yearns, a pool of resources, the mythic depth of things. Many elements are peculiar to this lecture: the freshness and spontaneity so constantly mentioned, the imagery of dawn, life, and creative awakening, the sense of wonder and awe, the love of the artless hearty reception given to the hero, the many mythical and giantly humorous tales. Carlyle loves this world, but he sadly knows that it has gone. Odin is not merely a wish fulfillment; he is an escape.

Once these patterns and their relationship to the author have been perceived, it is apparent that the form of the book militates against its content. Even in the last lecture Carlyle is trying to persuade himself that he has written a progressive theory of history.

> We come now to the last form of Heroism; that which we call Kingship. The Commander over men; he to whose will our wills are to be subordinated and loyally surrender themselves, and find their welfare in doing so, may be reckoned the most important of Great Men. He is practically the summary for us of *all* the various figures of Heroism; Priest, Teacher, whatsoever of earthly or of spiritual dignity we can fancy to reside in a man, embodies itself here, to *command* over us, to furnish us with constant practical teaching, to tell us for the day and hour what we are to *do*. (*H,* 196)

The basic form of the book, of course, supports this thesis: the heroes are distributed in a general chronological pattern as well as a typical one, and each lecture may be seen as placed on top of the preceding one, repeating its basic pattern but with typical and chronological variations and progressive development. The last lecture is topmost not only chronologically but also progressively. Thus the literary plan demands that everything conform to its requirements. It is simple and schematic, whereas reality, Carlyle discovers, is not.

Even this form is not of a piece, however. Odin stands somewhat outside history and is not really assimilated into it. He is the emblem of a Teutonic world of myth and dream, at best a kind of Jungian archetype from whom divine energy in all the heroes proceeds. Burns, Johnson, and Rousseau (one wonders what happened to Carlyle's god, Goethe), with their heroic but ineffectual

250

struggles, so undermine the thesis of progressive development and indestructibility of hero-worship that the pattern can be saved only by extending the scale into wider vision, by claiming that their influence is to come, by insisting that the period of skepticism is a period of transition to wider beliefs. But this is vision, not history.

Similarly, the attempt to make Cromwell and Napoleon the new kings and the summary of hero-worship is also fraught with difficulties. Napoleon is a figure that Carlyle cannot really admire, and even the few pages of praise he receives are mixed with blame and strong qualification of his heroism. But Cromwell, who dominates the lecture, is scarcely the modern hero. His presence in the final lecture smashes the general chronological pattern that has been observed throughout. To be sure, there are slight discrepancies in chronology elsewhere in order to consider heroes according to types; but Cromwell, hearkening back two centuries, is a figure of the past whose "dialect" has also disappeared and hence underlines the absence of heroes in the present age. Soon Carlyle will be totally preoccupied with attempting to write a history of Cromwell, presumably intended to function as a model of the warrior king and priestly ruler for the present time, though actually it will be an attempt merely to recover some of the life and meaning of the Puritan past, purely an individual move for Carlyle. Cromwell will soon function as less of an ideal for the nineteenth century than an evanescing past that demands the most minute of historical research to bring it to life in order that Carlyle may live totally within it.

Cromwell's presence here is not so extreme, but it serves to underscore the collapse of the general framework, its inability to come to grips with reality, personal

251

or social, of the nineteenth century. For support, Carlyle begins to fall into the trap which he so narrowly escaped in the later and more immediate *Past and Present;* he retreats into admiration for the heroes of the past as a way of evading the present, and he falls into the language of vision that insists, with a yearning for self-intoxication and delusion, that the total world of heroes is coming in the future. As Eric Bentley observes, "The paradox of Carlyle's vision of the present is that it is all past and future." [6] All other examples of Carlyle's insistence on the indestructibility of hero-worship take on the tone of fright that such should be the truth but may not, in fact, be the actual situation. This insistence is destined to become more frenetic and strident when, outside the confines of the lower pitch demanded by the seriousness of the lecture platform and the historical escape worlds of *Cromwell* and *Frederick,* he feels the intensity of the revolutionary upheavals of 1848, reenters the present in the *Latter-Day Pamphlets,* and creates a world of extraordinary harshness, vicious satire, and delirious power.

Carlyle himself was severe in his criticism of the lectures on heroes. "Nothing which I have ever written pleases me so ill. They have nothing *new,* nothing that to me is not *old.* The style of them requires to be low-pitched, as like talk as possible. The whole business seems to me wearisome triviality." [7] It is doubtful if he realized that in *Heroes* he had given a strong portrait of his own confusion and alienation from the present and that his imagination had created a scheme so remote from the world of present actualities and yet declared with such vigor that the two worlds were identical.

6. Bentley, p. 77.
7. Quoted from a letter in Froude, *Life in London, I,* 208.

CROMWELL AND FREDERICK: PROBLEMS OF POWER AND FUTILITY

that the appearance of an absolute commander for these herd-Europeans, in spite of everything, is a deed of kindness, a relief from steadily more unendurable pressure.

"Thou shalt obey, someone or other, and for a long time; *if not*, you perish and lose your last self-respect" —this seems to me to be the moral imperative of nature.

Nietzsche,
Beyond Good and Evil

Since, as I have already pointed out, neither the four volumes of *Oliver Cromwell's Letters and Speeches with Elucidations* nor the eight volumes (originally six) of the *History of Frederick II. of Prussia called Frederick the Great* offer any significant advance in Carlyle's imaginative development, I shall cover those lengthy works in brief compass. Though they constitute in their research and writing a period of twenty-five years from 1840 to 1865 and should thereby exert a strong claim on our most careful attention as his major statements, they cannot effectively do so. Stylistically, Carlyle's most inventive methods have hardened into mannerisms, and much of the writing, with its omission of subjects and its seemingly aimless sentences, looks like notebook jottings, research that has not yet been controlled by any dominant theme or artistic ordering. Thematically, the core of *Cromwell* is simple, but it is so simple that it cannot contain the difficulties of its own sprawling material and in a bizarre way actually forces these difficulties upon the reader. *Frederick* has a plethora of conceptual themes, but most of them are frequently contradictory, witnesses to the confusion of Carlyle's mind about

253

his book. Though Carlyle frequently complained about the inadequacy of most of his books and the impossibility of writing them, the complaints in the letters and journals about the writing of *Cromwell* and *Frederick* reach a new pitch and constitute the major portion of Froude's *Life in London* at this point. At times they achieve a frightening quality of desperation so intense in their tone as to suggest incipient schizophrenia.

None of this, of course, precludes the possibility of creativity within the works, but those very complaints enter the volumes themselves, and in such attempts at epic they are inadmissible. The first chapter of *Frederick* admits the futility of realizing an epic of Frederick, and the last volume begins with a hazy statement about unrealized themes. No attempt is made, as in *The French Revolution,* to write an epic with a difference that might accommodate some of these problems. Much of *Cromwell* inveighs against the slanderers who have kept his story from reaching the epic realization that is really within it, but much of the inveighing is also against the mountains of "shot-rubbish" beneath which the true picture of Cromwell is buried, against the difficulty of trying to get at that epic picture, and against the impossibility of actually realizing that picture and writing "The Cromwelliad." Again the epic is unrealized. The difficulties of writing, of being creative, of attaining any finality of vision become dominant themes of both books.

Historically, however, both books are of some value, particularly *Cromwell.* G. M. Trevelyan, for instance, praises Carlyle's pioneer effort of overturning the applecart, of upsetting the contemporary version of Cromwell as a liar and hypocrite.[1] Yet, as he also notes, *Cromwell* is far less an objective book than *The French Revolution.* Carlyle's belief in Cromwell is so unqualified as to make one suspect whitewashing. But as a corrective of

1. G. M. Trevelyan, *Carlyle: An Anthology* (London, 1953).

the contemporary view of Cromwell as a consciously deceitful and power-mad farmer, the book offers a valuable reaction that has led to a truer estimate of Cromwell by modern historians. Furthermore, Carlyle's own heroic act of recovering the letters and editing them with such concern is a valuable service in the best modern scholarly tradition, however much he may have felt that these were the efforts of Dryasdust, the gleaner of detail, the historian without vision, whom he despised. Carlyle would not be pleased with qualified endorsement of his pioneering, for it is his interpretation of Cromwell that he hoped would be convincing and which he was sure would emerge if his readers took care in attuning themselves to the "dialect" of the letters. *Frederick*, of course, also represents an exhaustive collection and sifting of sources, but in more specialized areas; its detailed descriptions of the battles have long been admired, and for some time these descriptions were used in the teaching of Prussian military students, thus allowing Carlyle to enter, with Nietzsche, into an oddly oblique relationship with the story of German power and might.

At bottom, however, these two gigantic works are merely treadings of water, the futile heroism of the man of letters without a real appointed task or mission in the nineteenth century, totally alienated from his audience and forced into self-communication, now barred even from the oblique style of Teufelsdröckh. Ultimately they are retreats into a past that cannot effectively be brought back to life, a movement backward beyond the chaos of the present and its origins in the French Revolution, into the puritanism of the seventeenth century and into Carlyle's own childhood roots, and finally into the foundations of Prussian might in the eighteenth century, the last providing more fully than *Cromwell* the tenuous source for a new myth of power in the heroic self. The attempt to connect these worlds with the

present, to revivify them and to furnish them as models, never disappears, but it definitely yields to the fascination of retreating into these worlds themselves, disintegrates into mere contempt for the present and even into disgust for the writer's task which must clear away so much rubbish before the reentry can be possible. In *Frederick,* in fact, the rubbish of documents and sources is so complex and voluminous that, without the aid of the simplistic Puritanism of *Cromwell* to point the way, the reentry is never really made at all. These books, then, are perhaps better viewed not so much as histories (which they certainly are in part) but as pyschosocial documents of the problem of the artist's relationship to society. For Carlyle they widen the gap between self and society, even though that society may venerate him as a sage, and encourage a lofty alienation that soon generates a vocabulary of power and contempt.

The story of the composition of *Cromwell* reveals that gap and is not without relation to the as yet uncomposed quality of the finished book. As already seen, Carlyle's research of Cromwell, which was rather half-hearted from the first, was interrupted by the intense social concern of *Past and Present;* yet he does not seem to have gone further to draw out of this interruption any criticism of his project on Cromwell, which it strongly implies. On the contrary, he sees his project as positive and heroic; he is really rewriting *The French Revolution* in a more heroic, more epic, and more conservative cast. He sees a new role developing as he recalls England to her true roots, as he is "struggling to be the most conservative man in England." [2] His view of the French Revolution now seems to shift as he gradually stresses its destructive aspect, the complete burning up of cant and hypocrisy, and mutes its ultimate hopes and aims. Cromwell's England now seems to provide the real

2. Letter to John Sterling, 4 Dec. 1843, quoted in Froude, *Life in London, I,* 357.

image of the heroic English past, the true epic of action, daring, and belief. Here is no gospel according to Jean Jacques Rousseau: to write "The Cromwelliad" is to connect England, fallen since 1660 and Cromwell's death, with its true roots.[3] As an antidote to the social chaos and complexity of the present period, the absence of all traditions, Carlyle sees himself as a sacred melodious poet resurrecting in his own Homeric manner the glorious past and urging his readers to model their society and selves upon it.

The gap between Carlyle's England and Cromwell's cannot be so easily bridged, however, and the new conservative heroic role is not at all simply fulfilled by a recall to its roots. The last lecture on heroes had already testified by its odd placement of Cromwell to that gap and the real absence, not the presence, of the new kingly hero. *Cromwell* makes that gap conscious. As early as August 29, 1842, in a letter to Emerson, Carlyle complains of the difficulties in applying the seventeenth century to the nineteenth:

> One of my grand difficulties I suspect to be that I cannot write *two Books at once;* cannot be in the seventeenth century and in the nineteenth at one and the same moment . . . . For my heart is sick and sore in behalf of my own poor generation; nay I feel withal as if the one hope of help for it consisted in the possibility of new Cromwells and new Puritans.[4]

A letter in 1843 shows a heightening of the conflict between his creative role and the demands of his social one as prophet.

> After four weary years of the most unreadable reading, the painfullest poking and delving, I have come at last to the conclusion that I *must* write a

3. See Vol. I, Chap. 1.

4. Letter to Emerson, 29 Aug. 1842, *Correspondence of Emerson and Carlyle,* p. 328.

book on Cromwell; that there is no rest for me till I do it. This point fixed, another is not less fixed hitherto, that a Book on Cromwell is *impossible.* Literally so; you would weep for me if you saw how, between these two adamantine certainties, I am whirled and tumbled, God only knows what will become of me in the business. Patience! Patience! [5]

The next letter even more painfully testifies to his creative anguish, his need to get at the epic quality of his material and to find a stable center for both his actions and those of society: "I see and say to myself, It *is* heroical; Troy Town was probably not a more heroic business; and this belongs to thee, to thy own people,—must it be dead forever?—Perhaps, yes,—and kill me too into the bargain." [6] The desperation of his self-convincing points both to the desire to encase himself within his epic material of the past and to the impossibility of that desire. Even as Cromwell begins to emerge as the hero and the parliament is discounted, so that the problems of form analogous to *The French Revolution* disappear, Carlyle's complaints continue to center upon the intractability of his subject. *Cromwell* becomes the "most frightfully *impossible* book of all I have ever before tried." [7] Sometimes he talks as if he had merely hit upon his subject matter as the result of chance and desperation; it is the fulfillment of a Calvinistic need to work, a sense of duty in the profession of man of letters he has chosen. He seems to be acting out a role that he would most gladly relinquish if it did not entail proof of moral failure; contempt for his role and for society actually has the upper hand.

5. Letter to Emerson, 31 Oct. 1843, ibid., p. 350.

6. Letter to Emerson, 17 Nov. 1843, ibid., p. 354.

7. From a journal entry, 2 Feb. 1844, quoted in Froude, *Life in London, 1,* 360.

Finally, as a solution to the problem of Cromwell, he decides to print all his research materials, allowing Cromwell to speak for himself in his letters and speeches. From one angle this decision is obviously a confession of literary failure, but from another it suggests that by such continuous contemplation Carlyle has now translated himself into Cromwell to such an extent that every word of the master has become a revelation and a necessity; to interpret without the presence of the letters would be to falsify. The reader is invited to give himself over to the careful work of absorbing the letters, and he too will presumably be convinced of the social solution of new Cromwells and Puritans.

Even this decision affords no conquest of the material. Carlyle elects to inhabit only the seventeenth-century world of Cromwell; he does not bridge the gap between the seventeenth and the nineteenth centuries. In letting Cromwell do his own talking, he almost admits that his own making of order is an impossible task in the nineteenth century. *Cromwell* marks the failure of the interpretive editorial role: Carlyle seems to confess that as a poor editor he cannot offer an analogy to the really active and militant Cromwell, that he is committed instead to saturating himself in his material or research rather than attempting to translate it or make it viable for his own age. "At least, it is with Heroes and god-inspired men that I, for my part, would far rather converse, in what dialect soever they speak!" (*C, 1, 77*).

The editorial role that previously formed a bridge between personalities, eras, and aspects of selfhood in *Sartor* and *Past and Present* reappears in *Cromwell*, but in a far less creative light and with severe distortions. No dialectic occurs, for the editor can neither get at his epic hero nor reach his audience in nineteenth-century England. Caught in his editorial apparatus, the prophet is removed effectively both from his public and the center

of vision in his hero Cromwell. He must clear away too much debris before he can even barely revivify the original image. The past into which the hero has receded resists revival; it will be scarcely available to Carlyle alone, if attained at all. The dominant image of the writer desperately trying to get at Cromwell and treasuring every nugget of information about him emerges from the book.

Sartor is finally and most cruelly reversed as Carlyle becomes the victim of a hoax, the Squire Papers, letters purportedly by Cromwell in the hands of a descendant of one Squire. The author who had so wittily toyed with the sophisticated literary device of the hoax shows in his eagerness to get hold of every scrap of Oliver's words a fatal guilelessness and gullibility. Carlyle not only prints the letters, despite the fact that their style is rather obviously spurious, but adds a perfectly straight-faced account of the way they came into his hands. He never raises questions that might seem obvious to a more careful editor: Why did the author burn the letters after he had hurriedly copied them out? Why will the author not appear? and so on. His eagerness for new light on Cromwell overrides his critical judgment.[8]

In *Cromwell*, then, Carlyle neither comes to grips with the problems of his age nor succeeds in recapturing the figure of his hero. What he finds instead, perhaps, is the reassurance of his prophetic role, given by the Cromwellian focus, for denouncing the contemporary political and social situation. His hero serves as an ideal figure for coupling the strongly militant faith of his own Puritan childhood, certainly his deepest roots, with the intensity of his need for routing the present quackery of England's government. In short, Carlyle plays Cromwell

8. See Vol. II, Appendix, 339–76, for the text of the letters; also see the introduction to the S. C. Lomas edition of *Cromwell* (London, 1904) for the most substantial critique.

by assuming his heroic mask of Puritanism and militarism.

In letting Cromwell be seen in toto through his letters, Carlyle succeeds in defending his hero against charges of deceit. But in attempting to assume the Cromwellian mask, Carlyle's own elucidations generate further problems, which go against even this clearing of the historical air. As in *Heroes*, his assumption of the language of "eternity" does not leave his own dialect unquestioned, a problem that is not helped by the frequent recognition of Oliver's language as itself a "dialect." Here too the static and endlessly repeated polarity of "heaven versus quacks" and the like is not redeemed by the more complicated aesthetic movement of literary structure, as in *Past and Present*, and ironically leads back again to an emphasis upon a bullying and power-mad Puritan Cromwell that Carlyle sought to play down or disprove. "[Cromwell] if not the noblest and worshipfulest of all Englishmen, at least the strongest and terriblest; with whom really it might be well to comply; with whom, in fact, there is small hope in not complying!—" (*C, 4,* 15). In Carlyle's interpretation, the lust for power seems strangely lurking in the background, and the Bible is always coupled with the sword.

> the Age was Heroic even because it had declared war to the death with these and would have neither truce nor treaty with these ["knaves and quacks"]; and went forth, flame-crowned, as with bared sword, and called the Most High to witness that it would not endure these! (*C, 1,* 84).

Furthermore, Carlyle's glosses usually come most fully to life in Cromwell's speeches where the editor interrupts at the most denunciatory and wrathful moments. He seconds Cromwell's fury in the "Letter to the Irish

Clergy," by such remarks as "Read in your Bibles and consider that!" (*C, 2,* 120) "no cozening here!" (*C, 2,* 126) and "Hear this, Lord Lieutenant!" (*C, 2,* 130). This militaristic and power-hungry image of Cromwell is also abetted by the sheer weight of the letters that deal with battles and problems of ruling, especially of kingship. Significantly, the battle letters stimulate Carlyle's imagination with the greatest vigor, and, equally significantly, Carlyle plays down the role of parliament in the problems of ruling. The major drama of the book—so far as it can be said to have one—is the actual routing of false kingship and the assumption of a true and redefined kingship. The militarism of Cromwell can be intensified into real fierceness and proposed as a social solution for both Cromwell's and Carlyle's age because it is justified religiously—and further justified in its own seeming excesses by the irreligious presence and attacks of quack rulers who are leading the state to ruin.

Ultimately, however, Carlyle, unlike Cromwell, is powerless. In assuming the mask of the man of militant faith, he is what Nietzsche calls him, a "ham actor," a rhetor from need.[9] The strength of Cromwell is only the strength of a mask that leads to no new definition of the self or society. At the end of his "history" Carlyle attempts to connect the end of the historical drama, as he did in *The French Revolution,* with the present moment: Puritanism, like Sansculottism, lives on, and the Destinies intend something higher with it (*C, 4,* 184). But the connection here is even thinner than that in *The French Revolution* and can only disguise the real center of the drama. Its a-historical focus on Carlyle's as-

9. Friedrich Nietzsche, *Beyond Good and Evil,* trans. Marianne Cowan (Chicago, Gateway paperback, 1955), p. 252. The phrase "rhetor from need" is from *Twilight of the Idols,* in *The Portable Nietzsche,* trans. Walter Kaufmann (New York, 1954), p. 521.

sumption of Cromwell's growing power is dissipated with Cromwell's death, and Carlyle must search for another heroic figure as a model for his prophetic needs and identity. The mask must ultimately be removed, revealing the nakedness of the present.

The very note of futility ruins the completeness of the mask but nevertheless provides a note of realism. Carlyle's own inadequacy to play Cromwell is only too apparent to him, and he openly admits the impossibility of the book, the futility of writing it, the inadequacy of the image attained. His awareness of the futility either of speaking to an audience that will not listen or of success in his own enterprise of writing acts as a solvent, reducing the possibility of euphoria and egomania in the assumption of the mask of Cromwell. The awareness of the past as irremediably past acts as a check against the Nietzschean power drive of the book, the glorification of the strong and impulsive hero, the self who will overturn society, who will be a destiny to the ages. The image that finally remains is of a Carlyle closer to Dryasdust, a figure at a writing desk desperately trying to make a battlefield come to life. Often he leaves London and retraverses the famous battlefields, not merely as an act of historical scholarship, but as a devotion and service to his hero. But even here Carlyle is alone, with no armies and—as he frequently notes—only the silent English countryside around him. Ultimately Cromwell sinks far into the past, and the melancholy Carlyle of the writing desk prevails. Within the book itself the letters, the journals, and the attempt to understand the writing of *Cromwell* all merge in an act of self-exploration that is really the enduring strain in Carlyle—not the act of heroic masquerading. That strain will be picked up and redefined with strength in *Sterling*, and it will sustain him as both person and writer in the last years of the *Reminiscences*.

The heroic masquerading, however, never fully died in Carlyle, and *Frederick* is testimony to both its lengthy persistence as well as its long-dying gasps. Researched over a period of fourteen years and published originally in six volumes between 1858 and 1865, *Frederick* intensifies the difficulties of the heroic strain into a state of sheer futility. Where *Cromwell* sags in organization, *Frederick* sprawls; where Cromwell as a figure offered a unitive ideal, Frederick offers too many possibilities, no one of them as strong or central as Cromwell. *Cromwell* had a single theme which it consistently hammered home; *Frederick* has multiple and contradictory themes, none of which is effectively delivered. In *Cromwell* Carlyle recognized the difficulty of writing the action as epic but held onto the ideal; in *Frederick* he dismisses the epic eye as an impossibility at the outset. A caricature of Carlyle and a lowered Teufelsdröckh, Professor Sauerteig, is allowed to express the hope, but Carlyle in his own voice quickly adds, "But he only says, in magniloquent language, how grand it [the epic] would be if disimprisoned" (*FG, 1,* 17). This time Carlyle openly admits, "My hopes of presenting, in this Last of the Kings, an exemplar to my contemporaries, I confess, are not high" (*FG, 1,* 17).

Frederick lies under difficulties far more insuperable than Cromwell did for Carlyle. True, since the libelous picture of Frederick by Voltaire is easily dismissed, the defensive tone of the history can be minimized, but the sheer weight of documents and German pedantry make Frederick a figure who is far more difficult to picture than Cromwell and pose a tremendous task for Carlyle of "sifting the Brandenburg sand." But the real difficulty is with Carlyle, not so much with Frederick. There is no longer any shining beacon of armored Puritanism to lead the prophetic author on, only the vague and undefined image of "a man who was a man" in the eigh-

teenth-century age of cant. In *Frederick* the goal is often missing, or distrusted, or praised with qualifications; the wandering through the sources without the aid of a strong identity and selfhood is therefore all the more uncharted.

Carlyle uses Frederick primarily as an analogue to the new artistic self. The theme is marked at the outset by his confusion of himself with both Johnson and Frederick:

> No wonder they [the world's great powers] thought him worthy of notice. Every original man of any magnitude is;—nay, in the long-run, who or what else is? But how much more if your original man was a king over men; whose movements were polar, and carried from day to day those of the world along with them. The Samson Agonistes,—were his life passed like that of Samuel Johnson in dirty garrets, and the produce of it only some bits of written paper,—the Agonistes, and how he will comport himself in the Philistine mill; this is always a spectacle of truly epic and tragic nature. The rather, if your Samson, royal or other, is not yet blinded or subdued to the wheel; much more if he vanquish his enemies, *not* by suicidal methods, but march out at last flourishing his miraculous fighting implement, and leaving their mill and them in quite ruinous circumstances. As this King Friedrich fairly managed to do. (*FG, I, 5*)

Throughout *Frederick* Carlyle hovers over all these roles: he tries to duplicate the movements of Frederick, and thus vicariously to carry all the world along with him; he tells himstlf that he too is routing enemies, is not trapped by the Philistine mill or the role of a mere writer who produces bits of written paper in dirty garrets. But, as the quotation reveals, he also sees himself as

trapped in a second-rate form of creativity, harassed by enemies and the Philistine world, blinded and tied to the mill. Though he can follow Frederick day by day, his thoughts will not carry the world along with him, as Frederick's actions did. The world of Frederick functions as a model for self-definition far more complex than that of Cromwell, but it also is a retreat, as Cromwell's was, to a world inferior to that of the real Frederick. Frederick will be in chains as Samson-Carlyle-Johnson.

On one level Frederick serves as a model for subsisting personally in the nineteenth century, another age of cant and heir to the eighteenth-century age of cant. Frederick will teach Carlyle who sprang from his century how not to be a liar in the succeeding century of quacks; he will be a more direct tutor than Cromwell; his battles will provide an arena of identification, a projection of Carlyle's own hostility against the quacks, and a stirring sense of power and might. Carlyle will have no authentic battlefields, but the chaos and complexity of the world around him is his analogous artistic battlefield. By subduing in *Frederick* not so much the nineteenth-century quacks directly but, instead, the voluminous and chaotic sources on Frederick, and by duplicating daily the actions of Frederick in writing, Carlyle conducts his own analogous heroic duty in the nineteenth century and thus proves himself the worthy heir to Frederick. Like Nietzsche, he usurps the role of Frederick for a new age; the philosopher or man of letters becomes the leader.

All of this is vaguely suggested—and vaguely distrusted too—as a program. Yet ultimately *Frederick,* like *Cromwell,* is a retreat, and it is a far greater literary failure. Carlyle reaches the end of his book, fourteen years later, a broken man; his victory with Frederick is really a Pyrrhic one, for his book has no unity whatever.

266

The two long volumes devoted to Frederick's background seem out of proportion with the rest, and all the volumes are studded with reams of source materials in their original shape or only slightly transformed by the weak and rather self-contemptuous caricatures of Carlyle, Sauerteig, and Smelfungus. The final volume does not conclude with any real resolution and is openly labeled a "loose Appendix of Papers" (FG, 8, 6). The new self and the new society never really emerge.

As *Frederick* recapitulates and intensifies the agonies of *Cromwell*, the process of finding and treating a subject reminds one of the mutations of the earlier heroic subject, but with a large addition of fright and desperation. Once again Carlyle is looking for a subject upon whom he can perform his interpretive role of man of letters; as most commentators and his own letters show, the choice of Frederick was somewhat fortuitous and probably bad. Froude shows Carlyle meditating on other heroes—the Cid, William the Conqueror, the Norsemen [10]—and ultimately selecting Frederick as the most suitable to teach the age about the need for individuals of great strength. Traill, Carlyle's editor, sees little more in Frederick than a convenient figure to whip the advocates of democracy (FG, 1, xiv). Froude adds reservations about the subject. "Frederick . . . was not a man after Carlyle's heart. He had no 'piety' like Cromwell, no fiery convictions, no zeal for any 'cause of God,' real or imagined. He lived in an age when spiritual *belief* had become difficult, if not impossible." [11] Froude's objections seem relevant, but he does not add that the increased difficulty of the subject, the stronger analogy to the real Carlyle rather than to the mythic image, might provide strong reason for the choice. Car-

10. See Froude, *Life in London*, 2, 83.
11. Ibid., p. 92.

lyle saw himself, like Frederick, living in an age of cant, and he now knew that the Puritan role of *Cromwell* was an impossibility. In short, *Frederick* would be an attempt to found his new myth in a more available past and in more recent historical sources.

Unlike Cromwell, Frederick was realized in contemporary history, and Carlyle was probably attracted to him not merely by chance but by the continuity of the Prussian state as the one centrally stable and masterful human organization around him. Frederick also offered Cromwell's militarism but not his Puritanism, and while one side of Carlyle obviously bemoaned the loss as a deprivation of interest in his subject, another aspect saw in the skeptical but active Frederick a figure far closer to the real Carlyle than Cromwell had ever been. Furthermore, there is little doubt that the stress on battling in *Cromwell* pointed to the centrality of militarism which *Frederick* could unblushingly confirm. Now Carlyle could intensify the militarism (once again the battle scenes are the center of interest) and abandon all the religious language that had led to the potential self-righteousness, megalomania, and remoteness of *Cromwell*. Yet Carlyle could never free himself of an ambivalence about his choice of Frederick: in the voice of *Cromwell* he would have to disapprove of Frederick's lack of any real religious education and depth, but in the more realistic voice of *Frederick* he would have to admire his practicality, action, and panther-like swiftness of decision. This ambivalence never receives any full exploration in the book, for it is part of Carlyle's own larger ambivalence which is constantly intruding.

This division of commitment affects all the problems of writing *Frederick,* of ordering the confusion of the sources and getting at Frederick's image. The difficulties intensify and reach out into all of Carlyle's activities. His journals from the time record him as being cut off from people, utterly without ability to work, his will par-

alyzed and directionless. "My silence and isolation, my utter loneliness in this world, is complete. Never in my life did I feel so utterly windbound, lamed, bewildered, incapable of stirring from the spot in any good direction whatever." [12] This is the language of Craigenputtock, but far more fraught with the real death of creativity. There is no longer the obstacle of society barring the voice from being heard: since the voice has been heard but not listened to, society is best forgotten. Carlyle's *Latter-Day Pamphlets* of 1850, in which he himself played the hero, excoriating the advocates of democracy and philanthropy with a lofty contempt and building a doctrine of a strong new aristocracy much in the manner of the later Nietzsche, had, he felt, alienated him from everyone; but, unlike Nietzsche, he seems to have viewed this alienation as inflicted from without, not as a result of his own choice to play the lofty role of the prophet in the *Pamphlets*. " 'Latter Day Pamphlets' have turned nine-tenths of the world dreadfully against me . . . . Can Frederick be my next subject—or what?" [13]

Carlyle's contempt for man increases: "Oh, I am sick of the stupidity of mankind—a *servum pecus*. I had no idea till late times what a bottomless fund of darkness there is in the human animal." [14] His alienation proceeds apace. His wife's company or solace seems of little avail; *Frederick* is the first of his works she does not read as he composes it. His confusion within is even worse: he has no hope, lives a "strange interior *tomb* life," [15] has horrible dreams of "waste scenes of solitary desolation, gathered from Craigenputtock . . . but tenfold *intensated*." [16] External noises begin to disturb

12. From a journal entry, 3 May 1851, ibid., p. 85.
13. From the journal, January 1852, ibid., p. 97.
14. From a letter quoted in ibid., p. 88.
15. From a journal entry, 28 Feb. 1854, ibid., p. 161.
16. From the journal, April 1854, ibid., p. 167.

him in an outlandish way, intensifying his creative paralysis and making him rage. He complains of the pianoes and barking dogs of neighbors and finally reaches a crisis in the episode of the "demon cocks" which completely hinder him from work. He adds another floor to his house, making it a soundproof room with double walls and light admitted by a skylight so that he is shut out from London and all the noises that threaten to disrupt him mentally.

Ironically, this victory over London is a hollow one, a defeat of sorts. Carlyle is honored as a seer but is himself without direction. He is the prophet of London, but he retreats and escapes into a second Craigenputtock. But this time it is no strategic withdrawal as a prelude to prophetic victory, only a withdrawal of desperation leading to the disruption of his creative power. There in the soundproof room "whirled aloft by the angry elements," [17] he can play Frederick and even chide him, play king to the king and create his own private world of battlefields.

Even by entering the soundproof room, however, Carlyle does not abandon his problems. Instead, as he himself says, he "intensates" them. Like La Pérouse in *The Counterfeiters*, once he escapes from discord in the external world, he begins to hear noises in the bedroom wall, or like the "mole" in Kafka's "Burrow," the castle-keep of art only intensifies the fear of disruption and the need for new self-definition. In all these cases the real discord is inside the self. Thus what might be expected happens: Once inside the soundproof room, Carlyle feels "as if it were like being placed on the point of a spear, and there bidden at once stand and write." [18] "To work! Try to get some work done, or thou wilt go mad." [19]

17. Discussed by Froude, ibid., p. 166.
18. From a journal entry, 16 Sept. 1854, ibid., p. 187.
19. Ibid.

The new heroism of Frederick that suggests itself to Carlyle, then, partakes of the intensity of this alienation. Carlyle's Prussianism is partly the reverse side of his futility: more than a wish fulfillment, it is also a new kind of self and a vision of leadership that can be offered to society as a proto-fascist solution to its turbulence. In the writing of *Frederick* Carlyle could see himself fulfilling this new view of selfhood—the ideal of a real toughening and hardness of self that can be cherished and viewed as a conquest by the heroic individual over the society that attempts to alienate him and kill his prophetic voice. The will is toughened to overcome any paralysis, and the toughening is intensified to counteract any intensity of slackening. The writer's attitude toward himself and his work is duplicated in the hero of the work and the social vision of leadership that evolves. Like Nietzsche's, Carlyle's picture of the new leader and the new society is proto-fascist in its emphasis on master morality versus slave morality, command and obedience, militarism, and strength, even cruelty, as virtues; like Nietzsche's also, the new selfhood and the new society emerge dialectically from the increased loneliness and alienation of the artist who has embarked upon the quest for that very new self and society. More and more emphatic in their conviction of society's final crisis of leadership and organization—of its "latter days," as the title of the *Pamphlets* implies—the projects of both Nietzsche and Carlyle are born as desperate and somewhat hysterical answers to a sense of disinheritance from tradition and fear of the loss of individual and social identity. Socially reified in a simplistic way and taken as their authors' final statements despite the still tentative quality of the original documents, such one-sided and limited aspects of their total views eventually become part of the intellectual background for the dictatorial programs of National Socialism.

One particular episode of *Frederick,* however, does

271

point up the issues of a more complex new self and society and a more subtle relationship with Nietzsche than that which the simplistic and programmatic interpretation of fascist thinkers indicates. This is the great conflict between Frederick and Voltaire, the flare-up at the court, the departure, and the libels of Voltaire against Frederick. In the first volume Carlyle hopes to rescue Frederick's reputation from these libels, just as he had rescued Cromwell from his attackers. But Voltaire is no "Carrion Heath," as Carlyle calls the author of the scurrilous biography of Cromwell, but an old figure from Carlyle's pantheon of heroes, and the most ambivalent one at that. Living in the midst of the eighteenth century, he, like Frederick, lacked religious depth for Carlyle, and his failure to get at the heart of things was the center of Carlyle's early attack upon him. But Carlyle was also attracted by Voltaire's attack upon superstition, by his gaiety, clearness, and satiric wit, and even by his active skepticism. In *Frederick* Voltaire appears with much of his old ambivalence, but there is noticeably little lamenting for his religious defects. The program of the opening volume, the vindication of Frederick over the liar Voltaire, is actually overthrown, so that in Volume III Carlyle explains:

'Voltaire was the spiritual complement of Friedrich,' says Sauerteig once; 'what little of lasting their poor Century produced lies mainly in these Two. A very somnambulating Century! But what little it *did*, we must call Friedrich; what little it *thought*, Voltaire . . . . They are, they for want of better, the two Original Men of their Century . . . . They alone remain to us as still living results from it,—such as they are.' (*FG, 3,* 177–78)

This project, with fewer qualifications and a lessening of the melancholy note, is adumbrated in a journal entry:

My Frederick looks as if it never would take shape in me; in fact the problem is to burn away the immense dungheap of the 18th century with its ghastly cants, foul, blind sensualities, cruelties, and *inanitys* now fallen *putrid,* rotting inevitably towards annihilation; to destroy and extinguish all that . . . after which the perennial portion, pretty much Friedrich and Voltaire, so far as I can see, may remain conspicuous and capable of being delineated (very loosely expressed all this; does not fit my thought like a skin; but, like an Irish waistcoat, it does in some degree) .[20]

Beneath the confusions, qualifications, and indictments of the eighteenth century, there is still a kind of search for what constitutes the contemporary self that is heir to the eighteenth century.

During the major crisis itself Voltaire appears as a satirist, impish, free-wheeling, and unattached, attacking not only Maupertuis but also Frederick himself. The style comes to life at this point: as usual in the book, but with far more vivacity, Carlyle talks to himself, to his characters, and to the reader.

On the whole, be not too severe on poor Voltaire! He is very fidgety, noisy; something of a pickthank, of a wheedler; but above all, he is scorbutic, dyspeptic; hagridden, as soul seldom was; and (in his oblique way) *appeals* to Friedrich and to us,—not in vain. (*FG,* 5, 333)

Fascinated by Voltaire's encounters with that other Carlyle, Frederick, Carlyle uses an exuberant and extravagant parody of his own rhetoric. He juggles with his own style in much the same way that Voltaire juggles with Frederick and his court. The quotation continues:

20. From a journal entry, 28 Feb. 1854, ibid., p. 160.

> And, in short, we perceive, after the First Act of the
> Piece, beginning in preternatural radiances, ending
> in whirlwinds of flaming soot, he has been getting-
> on with his Second Act better than could be expect-
> ed. Gyrating again among the bright planets,
> circum-jovial moons, in the Court-Firmament; is
> again in favour, and might—Alas, he had his *fellow-*
> moons, his Maupertuis above all! (*FG, 5, 333*)

What was in danger of becoming a mannerism, a style
of notebook jottings and gigantic old catchwords, is here
transformed into a source of amusement. The explosive
imagery of *The French Revolution* and the cosmic
imagery of *Past and Present* become material for comedy. The style as process is pushed to extremes: sentences that never really end are interrupted by exclama-
tions, turnings-about, verbal splutterings, and literary
fireworks. Even the narrative sections have a note of
parody: "By degrees matters were again tolerably glorious, and all might have gone well enough; though the
primal perfect splendour, such fuliginous reminiscence
being ineffaceable, never could be quite re-attained"
(*FG, 5, 310*). And later:

> Till, as will be seen, the sensitive Voltaire could en-
> dure it no longer; but had to explode upon the big
> Bully (accident lending a spark); to go-off like a
> Vesuvius of crackers, fire-serpents and sky-rockets;
> envelop the red wig, and much else, in delirious
> conflagration;—and produce the catastrophe of this
> Berlin drama. (*FG, 5, 318*)

Voltaire's appeal to Carlyle crystallizes this creative
freedom of the book, overcomes the dull battle with
sources, the failure of organization and significance that
may have originally prompted this very need for parody
and freedom. In Voltaire Carlyle finds a puckish, impish
figure, dyspeptic and hagridden like himself, but free

from all fetters, a satirist to the core, a hero who wanders where he pleases and, like himself, chides kings, pinpricks them, and sets the whole world in a whirl. The swirling but essentially skipping and light style is the element of victory over sources: Voltaire is in certain respects the analogy to the literary man, Carlyle, who conquers Frederick.

Once again Nietzsche offers a valuable parallel in his treatment of Frederick, which amplifies—and distorts —Carlyle's stresses. The latter Nietzsche, seeing the need for an intensification of the will in the new commander to relieve the deteriorated will of the present, also finds a model in Frederick and, like Carlyle, vehemently disapproves of Frederick's French education and the slackness implied in it, "the pleasurable hedonism of witty Frenchmen." [21] Yet he seems to imply that French skepticism promoted a new kind of skepticism in Frederick, further alienated him from his father, and thus produced the first of a new kind of European, the first man of the future. Is it too fanciful to see in Nietzsche's Frederick a parallel to the merging of Frederick and Voltaire that Carlyle seems to have been looking for with his ideals of action and thought that emerged from the eighteenth-century world and endured?

> Meanwhile a more dangerous and rigorous new type of scepticism was growing in the son—who knows *how* much it owed precisely to hatred of his father and to the icy melancholy of a will forced into solitude? It was the scepticism of bold manliness, closely related to the genius for war and conquest. In the figure of the Great Frederick it made its first entrance into Germany. This type of scepticism despises and nonetheless takes over; it undermines but takes possession; it had no belief but is

21. Nietzsche, *Beyond Good and Evil*, p. 130.

not lost through unbelief; it gives dangerous freedom to the intellect but holds the heart in strict
bounds . . . a *new* concept of the German mind
was formulated, a mind in which the inclination to
masculine scepticism was decisive, whether it appeared as fearlessness of gaze, or as courage and rig-
or of the dissecting hand, or as the tough will to
dangerous voyages of discovery, to spiritual North
Pole expeditions beneath barren and dangerous
skies.[22]

Nietzsche, unlike Carlyle, is untrammeled from his
Puritan faith; he can turn Frederick's skepticism into a
new kind of virtue. Carlyle seems hindered from completely endorsing the truth of Frederick and Voltaire
because he is both attracted to their skepticism as a
strength and repelled by its destructive possibilities. Yet
it is in effect a new truth for him too, since it leaps beyond either the Puritanism of *Cromwell* or the revolutionary ardor of *The French Revolution* to the myth of
the new commander, unfettered by any significant cause
of politics or ideology. But Carlyle would claim only
that enduring remnant of the heritage of the past which
is perhaps all that can be appropriated today. The
euphoric note, the sense of possibilities, is missing in
Carlyle's action of recovery. For him Frederick is the last
of the kings, whereas for Nietzsche he is the first European.

Like Carlyle, Nietzsche not only demands that a new
commander on the order of Frederick appear in society
(oddly enough, both can attain only momentary excitement about the more recent Napoleon) but also implies
that he himself, as a literary man, is the real intensification of Frederick, a more knowing and future-looking
figure. The model of Frederick gives birth to the philos-

22. Ibid., pp. 130–31.

276

opher who is primarily a critic and experimenter, marked by a devotion to skepticism, who will "love to make use of experimentation in a new, perhaps wider, perhaps more dangerous sense." [23] The drive to experiment has been intensified since the time of Frederick by the lower condition of society: "In their passion for new insight, must they [philosophers of the future] go farther in bold and painful experiments than the emasculate and morbid taste of a democratic century can approve?" [24] With a "genuine disgust ready for everything thus rapturous, idealistic, effeminate, and hermaphroditic," "they will admit to a certain pleasure in saying 'no,' in dissecting, and in a certain circumspect cruelty which knows how to handle the knife surely and delicately, even when the heart is bleeding." [25]

Nietzsche, then, goes further in the demonic manner than Carlyle. Aiming to overcompensate and to shock society with his "conservative-radical" proposals, he argues that intense needs demand intense solutions and a new and harder asceticism of the self. "The real philosophers are commanders and legislators." [26] This demonic movement must be given its own experimental designation for a proper perspective, however, as both Walter Kaufmann and R. J. Hollingdale suggest in their books on Nietzsche.[27] The aesthetic freedom in toying with these ideals may indicate that they are not to be reified, but only hinted at to awaken society and to make the self aware of its untapped and slumbering powers. The final pages of *Beyond Good and Evil* suggest this fundamentally aesthetic level of the entire en-

23. Ibid., p. 132.
24. Ibid.
25. Ibid., p. 133.
26. Ibid., p. 135.
27. See Kaufmann, *Nietzsche,* and R. J. Hollingdale, *Nietzsche: The Man and His Philosophy* (Baton Rouge, 1965).

terprise. In the transformation of the tough Frederick with a touch of lightness, the figures of Frederick and Voltaire can be seen, a mixture of the artist as commander and satirist, legislator and skeptic, lawgiver and prober.

> Alas, what are you in the end, my written and painted thoughts? Not long ago you were so brightly colored, so young and wicked, so full of thorns and secret spices that you made me sneeze and laugh—and now? You have taken off your newness; some of you, I fear, are ready to turn into truths.[28]

Carlyle is clearly less aware of the subtlety of the various levels of these ideas, and he is too fearful to spell out their implications. The new self that could have emerged from *Frederick* is never really released, but the self that is hinted at is not very different from the Nietzschean self of *Beyond Good and Evil*. Carlyle's Nietzschean self is more clearly revealed in the *Latter-Day Pamphlets,* written before *Frederick* but, because of their immediate social nature, free from the heroic second worlds of *Cromwell* and *Frederick*. In the *Pamphlets* as well as in *Frederick*, however, the self is marked by a stronger strain of futility and hopelessness than Nietzsche ever admits to and by far fewer aesthetic possibilities that might qualify the fury it expresses.

TOWARD THE TOTALITARIAN SELF

> I always fancy there might much be done in the way of military Drill withal. Beyond all other schooling . . . one often wishes the entire Population could be thoroughly drilled; into coöperative movement, into individual behaviour, correct, precise, and at once habitual and orderly as mathematics in all or in very

28. Nietzsche, *Beyond Good and Evil*, p. 235.

many points—and ultimately in the point of actual
Military Service, should such be required of it!

Carlyle,
"Shooting Niagara: And After?"

In the *Latter-Day Pamphlets,* issued between February 1 and August 1, 1850, Carlyle heightened the voices of both *Past and Present,* which looked toward a visionary society in the future, and *Heroes* and *Cromwell,* which glorified that society in the past, producing a tone that is a mixture of desperation, menace, hopelessness, and fascistic command. Turned toward the crisis of the present, the new tone becomes every bit as important as the thematic material; the heroes of the past are dropped as models, the metaphor of the soldier is reified, and Carlyle, bewildered and terrified by the revolutionary upheavals on the continent in 1848, becomes the wrathful godlike prophet of doom. The *Pamphlets* forecast the creative futility of the lengthy *Frederick* to follow, and the voice, in close touch with immediate social concerns, here acts out to the dead end the impulse behind the heroic roles Carlyle has been playing in an oblique manner elsewhere.

The *Pamphlets* can fittingly be seen as Carlyle's last major social prophecy. Of all his works, they are the most embarrassing to the modern reader. With what Raymond Williams calls their "contemptuous absolutism,"[1] with their harsh insistence upon the use of force in almost any situation, with their contempt for Negroes, prisoners, minority groups, and indeed all humanity, they offer a final distortion of all the positive elements in Carlyle's political vision. Yet they do not represent a complete volte-face from his earlier political and social writings. They may be frightening in both

1. Raymond Williams, *Culture and Society, 1780–1950* (Garden City, Anchor paperback, 1960) , p. 90.

what they say and how they say it, but they are still an outgrowth of Carlyle's earlier social writings. The critic must try to discover what has happened to transform the voice of reform with its social vision in *Past and Present* into the voice of desperation and frustrated power in the *Latter-Day Pamphlets*.

In a certain sense, Carlyle's battle is still basically a noble one: to create the elements of social order in the present anarchic situation. Desperately—and with real love for England—he searches for a political hero who will oust the sham leaders of the present and provide order, structure, and direction for society. His analyses of the failure of the new democratic legislation are not without power or truth. As a moralist condemning the present government's inability to remedy the great social ills, Carlyle is still an imposing figure, and he is even more impressive as a satirist of the strange misdirection, the vagaries of reform, produced by the new legislation. To the modern reader as well as to Carlyle the schemes of Victorian philanthropy reveal a strange lack of proportion, an odd obtuseness, and even some hypocrisy. Philanthropical legislation which seeks first to enfranchise Jamaican Negroes before it provides any real freedom for the "distressed needlewomen" and the millions of Irish paupers that flood England (cf. "The Nigger Question" [2]) is indeed misdirected, even more so

2. Published before the *Pamphlets* in 1840 and later called in a subtitle "Precursor to Latter-Day Pamphlets." Here treated as one of them; found in *E, 4,* 348–83. Though written before *Past and Present* (1843), the essay has all the harshness of the *Pamphlets*. Carlyle's treatment of "colonials," of course, was always somewhat harsh. See, for instance, the handling of the Irish in *Sartor* and especially in "Chartism" (1839) and his celebration of the Paraguayan dictator "Dr. Francia" (1843), the last two both in *E, 4.* Also, without the prompting of imaginative structures to generate complexities as in *Past and Present,* Carlyle tended to state his case in rigidified oppositions.

when it provides for prison reforms of some elegance while around the prison walls lie the dingy houses of the unaided poor who are struggling to keep out of the prison (cf. "Model Prisons"). The irony is further increased when Carlyle notes that these same paupers must pay the taxes to support the new prison reforms which enable scoundrels to live better than any duke in England (*LDP,* 57–58). All these observations wisely direct Carlyle's audience to the larger economic and social problems behind reform and urge some central governmental coordination to meet the complex social intertwining of the difficulties.

One might easily argue against the contempt for prisoners as scoundrels, adding that the two situations Carlyle notes are not quite the same or mutually exclusive, that reform in one area does not preclude reform in another. Carlyle would be willing to a great extent to concede this point, but his major attack remains true: legislation is misdirected and ineffectual in the present social chaos. Since he believes some central control embodied in a hero is necessary, while modern political thinkers might argue for legislation as a basis for or prelude to greater economic and social reform, he actually forces himself into more repressive and conservative measures for instilling order. Nevertheless, his satiric eye, like that of the later Victorian, Samuel Butler, maintains a brilliant focus for exposing this strange amalgamation of earnest concern in one area with total unconcern in another more vital area, certainly one of the strangest feats of the divided Victorian mind. The amalgamation reaches its apex in religious practice, where obtuseness becomes outright hypocrisy, "Jesuitism." Carlyle's picture of people kissing a Bible, characteristically closed (*LDP,* 314), is a telling image of hypocrisy that points toward Butler's satire of the Church as a "Musical Bank" in *Erewhon.* The ultimate concern of these peo-

ple Carlyle describes in the propositions of the "Pig Philosophy" (*LDP*, 315–18) is a vision of the universe dominated by the moneybag and the meat trough (*LDP*, 258).

Carlyle's condemnation of the effects of democracy also seems most just when it approaches the similar and later views of John Stuart Mill and Matthew Arnold. "Hudson's Statue" offers a damning picture of the consecration of ugliness and money and of the encouragement given "an already-ugly Population to become in a thousand ways uglier" by such dreary art (*LDP*, 263). Here Carlyle sounds like Mill in *On Liberty*, awakening to the vast collective mediocrity engendered by the very democracy for which he had fought. His vision also resembles Matthew Arnold's portraits of the Philistines and the Populace in *Culture and Anarchy*.

Such special positive elements of the *Latter-Day Pamphlets* are, however, only a part of their total statement, their constantly reiterated demand for a new structure of command and obedience, for a strong leader and subservient masses, for the social realization of *Cromwell*. Only thus does Carlyle see social chaos capable of being transformed into social cosmos, and here, as in *Past and Present*, he condemns the contemporary chaos, demands and envisions new social order, seeks new leaders, and urges self-reform and the replacement of the money god by the true god of the spirit.

The result is unmistakably a product of Carlyle's vision, but it is different from anything he has ever written. For the first time the commitment to a static reiteration of a viewpoint completely overrides the commitment to process and to exploration of self and society. The editorial role is completely absent, and all the categories that provided interesting means of exploration have hardened. As in *Cromwell*—but even more so—the world becomes a divided camp: the separation between forces is now complete, and there can be no in-

teraction. Ironically, Carlyle can now justify his rigidity, inflexibility, and militarism, as he did in *Cromwell's* world of the past, by what he feels is a prior commitment to a large, almost godlike, vision of freedom. But in this way the totalitarian, absolutist self is born and applied to the present.

The *Pamphlets* offer no literary depiction of the underlying social process and its conflicts that could serve as a basis to an enduring and constantly self-perfecting society. They can only paint in contrasts: a chaotic and fluctuating present society versus an ordered and static future one. Thus, there is no real development from essay to essay or within the essays themselves. A single page may contain three or four "either . . . or" statements of warning or several disjunctive constructions ("unless you do . . .") intensifying the separation of the two worlds. The symbols are never developed as they are in *Past and Present,* as a method of exploring the nature of the social process and its various interconnections.

But perhaps nowhere is the shift from *Past and Present* to the *Pamphlets* more evident than in the changes of the imagery. Never before has Carlyle employed such strong images of disgust and contempt. By comparison, the images of social dissolution in *Past and Present* are mild. The world of the *Pamphlets* is not merely chaotic, but also foul and loathsome, and it is this fact, not the picture of a future society, which occupies the foreground. The social formlessness of this world is now described as ooze, mud, cesspools, choked sewers, kennels, abortions, swamps, peatbogs, dirt, dung, and nauseous odors. Animal imagery is intensified: stupid horses, dead dogs, pigs, owls, rats, bloated drowned asses, foxes, serpents, and slimy creatures crawling on their bellies. To all of these, society and its present leaders are likened, with great contempt and rage.

Such imagery not only signifies the theme of social

formlessness and unreason, but points more dramatically toward a tone of disgust and contempt that becomes paramount. The social visionary himself experiences a horrible alienation from society. Carlyle becomes infinitely removed from any present social situation; if his vision approaches it, it will be defiled. The heroes of the past are studied because the present needs a new strong hero, modeled after Cromwell or Frederick, who, by his special contact with the godlike, like the heroes of the lectures, will descend from above since he has not sprung from below (*LDP*, 142). What is needed is a Sir Robert Peel (often earlier condemned by Carlyle) who will go into the "Augias Stable" of Parliament and Downing Street and reform it by cleaning out the dung that has accumulated there for two centuries (*LDP*, 91–92, 169). This dung, according to the schematic and moralistic theory of history voiced in *Past and Present* and *Heroes* and *Cromwell*, began accumulating when England rejected godlike Cromwell and chose godless Charles and Nell Gwynn. At this point the theory of history fades as all discrimination of insight is blotted out by rage, contempt, and fury.

Far more frightening is the way in which the imagery of contempt sets up a new dialectic, one where no real interaction is possible, only a widening rift heading toward self-destruction and social destruction. For the imagery of contempt easily demands the imagery of guidance, command, and force and the myth of the exalted heroic self, cruel and forcefully commanding. The nine out of ten who are blockheads, the twenty-seven million who are mostly fools,[3] the majority who are stu-

3. It is interesting to watch the commas disappear from this phrase. Pages 115–16 have "the twenty-seven million, many of them fools." By page 209, the phrase has been shortened to "twenty-seven millions mostly fools," in which manner it appears thereafter as a slogan. The loss of commas illustrates the movement from the possibility of real consideration to rejection, contempt, and disgust.

pidity itself, must not be allowed ballot boxes and other well-oiled contrivances to express their will. The ignoble cannot discover the noble; their will is not God's, Carlyle's, and the Universe's.

The minority, even if that minority is only Carlyle, must use leadership, command, and force, if necessary, to effect the vision which it knows is truth. By their very social dissolution, the masses have proved that guidance and command, not enfranchisement with its beer and balderdash and stump-oratory, are what is needed. But Carlyle's vision of society shifts its emphasis to the *means* of vision, force and command, compulsion and power, and the desire for a new social order retreats into the background.

> Glorious self-government is a glory not for you, —not for Hodge's emancipated horses, nor you. No; I say, No. You, for your part, have tried it, and *failed* . . . : and here at last you lie; fallen flat into the ditch, drowning there and dying . . . . And I am to pick you up again, on these mad terms . . . I will not! Know that, whoever may be "sons of freedom," you for your part are not and cannot be such. Not "free" you, I think, whoever may be free. You palpably are fallen captive— *caitiff,* as they once named it:—you do, silently, but eloquently, demand, in the name of mercy itself, that some genuine command be taken of you. (*LPD,* 40)

By a similar line of reasoning, Carlyle decides that Black Quashee of "The Nigger Question" has no right to sit idly by up to his ears in pumpkins and not to work. His real right is "the right . . . to be *compelled* to work as he was fit, and to *do* the Maker's will who had constructed him with such and such capabilities" (*E, 4,* 357). The accent again falls on compulsion, not freedom, and a rigid hierarchy of castes is asserted.

285

There is master morality and slave morality, and since "Slave or free is settled in Heaven for a man" (*LDP,* 248), Carlyle does not see himself doing the settling.

Thus everything that Carlyle envisions becomes godlike. At first, the great consummation seems once again to be the process of making divine order out of chaos, as in *Past and Present.* In "The Nigger Question," for example, God is embodied in the British effort that transforms "mere jungle, savagery, poison-reptiles, and swamp-malaria" into the "noble elements of cinnamon, sugar, coffee, pepper black and grey" (*E, 4,* 374). "The gods wish besides pumpkins, that spices and valuable products be grown in their West Indies" (*E, 4,* 375). But this is less invigoration with the power of labor than intoxication with power alone; the gods in this instance are largely Carlyle and British imperialism. Elsewhere Carlyle again divinizes and mythologizes colonization and imperialism. In opposing Canada's attempts at secession, he declares, "They are portions of the general Earth, where the children of Britain now dwell; where the gods have so far sanctioned their endeavour, as to say that they have a right to dwell" (*LDP,* 152). The appearance of the word "gods" in both statements along with the imperialistic but high-sounding "children of Britain" points to Carlyle's own mythologizing tendency, his own departure from traditional Christian conceptions toward an Anglo-Saxon Teutonic myth, toward "the gods" themselves.

Neither of these assertions really hearkens back to *Past and Present,* however, with its vision of a society and self fulfilled through labor. Though each picks up the excitement of that view of labor, the focus is shifted to command and obedience, to imperialism and colonialism, and to a totalitarian self and society. Those concepts are the true centers of the *Pamphlets,* and of the new society, and the structure they form, not self-

fulfilling labor, is presented throughout as the principal behest of the divine will that is to be actuated. "Gifted souls . . . are appointed, by the true eternal 'divine right' which will never become obsolete, to be your governors and administrators" (*LDP*, 130). This is not even hero-worship, though it preserves some of the earlier doctrine's overtones. Given the focus on forceful command and power, the mob seems scarcely able to do the act of worship; its only task is to quail before the leaders and to do the work that the leader has decided upon.

Carlyle's blessed Paradise is no longer centered on divinized labor but on divinized command and obedience. Only the metaphor of the traditional *Civitas Dei* remains; in "The New Downing Street" the transfer of emphasis is explicit.

> Thou shalt have a wise command of men, thou shalt be wisely commanded by men,—the summary of all blessedness for a social creature here below . . . . Wise obedience and wise command, I foresee that the regimenting of Pauper Banditti into Soldiers of Industry is but the beginning of this blessed process, which will extend to the topmost heights of our Society; and, in the course of generations, make us all once more a Governed Commonwealth, and *Civitas Dei,* if it please God! . . . Wise command, wise obedience: the capability of these two is the net measure of culture, and human virtue, in every man. . . . He is a good man that can command and obey; he that cannot is a bad. (*LDP*, 166–67)

Even this is not without its ambiguities, however, for if the hero has obedience, it is not to the masses and their wishes, but to God—that is, to his own voice in tune with the universe. The masses have only one real task,

to obey, and there is little room for them to command. Furthermore, Carlyle, like Nietzsche, provides no suitable criterion for deciding who belongs to what rank. If the masses suddenly decide to command and thus to question the validity of the commander's commands, they are told that Eternal Laws are ever present, invariable, like the laws of mathematics and physics, "inflexible, righteous, eternal; not to be questioned by the sons of men" (LDP, 236). The use of scientific arguments to bolster tyranny and totalitarian conceptions of society is the inexorable prologue to the scientism and the ideas of biology, instinct, and race in Nietzsche's late philosophy. Both authors begin by attacking empirical science and its limitations but, when pressed for an eternal ground to their assertions, fall into a pseudoscience of instinct and power far more limited than that they sought to remove, far more destructive of any freedom than their original enemy. Both use an argument of eternal validity against the questioning of the masses: against the eternal, scientific, or religious, there is no argument; the drill sergeant is "divine" (LDP, 156).

If the masses choose to go so far as rebellion, then "divinity" will sanction their overthrow. For the visionary leader who sees himself in touch with the Eternal—and perhaps is the Eternal—any use of force is sanctioned to overthrow the followers of Satan, as indicated by the terms and phrases I will italicize in the following quotations. The unworking Haitians receive *god's* revenge, extermination (E, 4, 376). If idle workers refuse to be drilled into real, not metaphoric, soldiers of industry, the new Prime Minister threatens to flog or shoot them (LDP, 46). The *Christian Religion* commands not model prisons for scoundrels, but "fixed, irreconcilable, inexorable enmity to the *enemies of God*" (LDP, 70). Revenge against scoundrels is a *"divine feeling,"* "a monition sent to poor man by the *Maker himself*"

(*LDP,* 78). "The soul of *every god-created* man flames wholly into one *divine* blaze of *sacred* wrath at sight of such a *Devil's* messenger" (*LDP,* 79). The hanging of the scoundrel and the crowning of the new king—but especially the hanging of the scoundrel—constitutes "the *millenium*" (*LDP,* 273). To hasten this millennium, universal cant, Vox as the *god* of the universe, must be dispelled; silence is enjoined; if it is not observed, tongues should be clipped (*LDP,* 181).

It is difficult to believe that Carlyle really intended to implement these brutal suggestions, this absolute usurpation of power in the name of God or the gods. His suggestions might be mere rhetorical exaggeration, the result of excessive anger and alienation, or deliberate jolts to shock and awaken society. Most critics, relying on Froude's description of the *Pamphlets'* composition ("fierce acid," "bilious indignation," "sulphurous denunciation") ,[4] believe that Carlyle meant exactly what he said, but the attribution of total "vitriolism" to the *Pamphlets* should be tempered with a sense of the alienation Carlyle has undergone, with the quality of anguish and torment in the denunciatory voice, and with the pain of disillusioned idealism. If such tempering will not right the picture, it can help to adjust it and to put it in a more proper focus.

All the cruel suggestions, the concentration on command and obedience, and the contempt for suffrage and the masses are really products not only of a more intensely dislocated social situation but also of the receding vision, the failure of the prophet to save society by his message in *Past and Present.* In the *Pamphlets* the hero has gained in power, in absolutism, in titanic will, but this increase is purely theoretical and visionary, for, practically, he has become more powerless than ever.

4. Froude, *Life in London,* 2, 43.

And thus the vision of a future society has become more imbalanced, more fiery, fierce, and intense. Perhaps this reflects the possibility that totalitarianism needs the acute shock of disinheritance and deprivation as a seed-bed for its fiery conception of enemies, its need for victims, and its thrust for power.

Muted behind Carlyle's fiery voice is his full awareness of the receding vision, of his own failure and futility. Futility breaks into the *Pamphlets* much as it had already done in *Cromwell* and as it would in *Frederick*, and the sustained sense of realism, of hopelessness, of the "mask" of the denunciatory voice, and of his role-playing saves the *Pamphlets* from the extremity of Nietzsche's later social writings and prevents Carlyle from toppling into Nietzsche's madness. Carlyle's fierceness, intimately bound up with his sense of isolation and failure, is a desperate means of transforming his futility into courage.

To the whole world's Yes, Carlyle answers No. Like Nietzsche, he dares to be a nay-sayer, but he swears an oath by the Eternal: "I can only say, if all the Parliaments in the world were to vote that such a thing was just, I should feel painfully constrained to answer, at my peril, 'No, by the Eternal, never!' " (*LDP*, 155). In swearing by the Eternal, Carlyle gains the added dimension of being the Miltonic one just man, Abdiel alone against all of Satan and his hosts. But such a No can only intensify and accelerate society's rejection of both Carlyle and his vision, and, indeed, Carlyle seems to invite that rejection as a kind of martyrdom and crucifixion, a proof of his own worth. When destruction by society is essential to the true hero, society becomes more and more contemptible, the vision more affirmative and more intense, Carlyle further and further alienated.

Nevertheless, as in *Cromwell* and *Frederick*, the note of futility insists on intruding itself and dissolving the

heroic vision. Carlyle becomes the one man who stands by Nature and Fact, but he is "felt as a kind of inter-loper and dissocial person, who obstructs the harmony of affairs, and is out of keeping with the universal-suffrage arrangement that has been entered upon" (*LDP*, 274). Thus the nature of the heroic vision, though intensified, falls more and more into the back-ground. In "Stump-Orator," with its study of the method whereby society summons up its talent, Carlyle progressively discovers that, outside of the earnest but mediocre realm of the beaver intelligence, there is no room for the hero in the higher realms of medicine, law, or the church—three careers which he had also tried (*LDP*, 189). Even literature, the choice he had made, which should be the one remaining outlet, the pulpit for a new and dislocated age, has degenerated into a formless "motley flood of discharged playactors . . . a boundless canaille,—without drill" (*LDP*, 191). The self can no longer really be a hero.

The same sense of ultimate futility presents itself in "The New Downing Street." The initial upward move-ment, the return to Veracities, is followed by an aware-ness that getting regimented is "impossible for us"; then, the suggestion that literature will still be a hope is followed immediately by the awareness that it is a "slough of lies." An essay like this, which is typical, re-verses the critical yet visionary movement of an early essay like "Characteristics." "Stump-Orator," however, effects a kind of reconciliation by projecting the vision-ary society far into the future while at the same time al-lowing Carlyle to assert his isolation and the futility of his discourse. Carlyle himself becomes a stump-orator of sorts, though presumably one without hypocrisy.

Brave young friend, dear to me, and *known* too in a sense, though never seen, nor to be seen by men,

—you are, what I am not, in the happy case to
learn to *be* something and to *do* something, instead
of eloquently talking about what has been and was
done and may be! The old are what they are, and
will not alter; out hope is in you. (*LDP,* 213)

This is Carlyle's supreme moment of honesty in the
Pamphlets, his most explicit and pathetic recognition of
his own powerless position.

Even when Carlyle does not explicitly talk about this
powerlessness, it hovers behind the essays. In "The Nigger Question" it is the source of the rather awkward and
painful structural device: a speech delivered by an un-
known orator to Exeter Hall members about the dangers of philanthropy.[5] The interruptions in the speech
that depict the decreasing audience testify to Carlyle's
deep awareness that he represents a minority of one that
is powerless. In "The Present Time" he tries another
method which stems from the same lack of power; he
envisions himself as Prime Minister delivering a speech
to idle workers and regimenting them in the army of
the new era. The militaristic and commanding "I"
comes to the fore in all the essays, here growling at all
new development, there flinging itself into the mouth of
all opposition. But the emergence of the "I," always as
the vehicle of opposition, only underscores Carlyle's inability to implement his power effectively, his need to
fall back on assertion alone. "The New Downing Street"
is supposed to contrast with "Downing Street," but the
description of the ideal contains just as much criticism
of social dissolution as the depiction of the real. When

5. The device of a fictional speaker presenting Carlyle's own un-
popular views was always a crutch for Carlyle, but frequently a
source for creativity too. Sauerteig, who appears in *Frederick* and
briefly in *Past and Present,* made his first appearance in "Biography" in 1832 (*E, 3,* 44–61), where he vehemently condemns fiction.

this inability, this lack of power, does not take the form of envisioned situations of personal power, it becomes gasps of frustration and futility. And the struggle for assertion always goes on under the very feelings of futility: "My friend, I have to speak in crude language, the wretched times being dumb and deaf; and if thou find no truth under this but the phantom of an extinct Hebrew one, I at present cannot help it" (*LDP*, 325).

This same tone of helplessness afflicts Carlyle's final political pamphlet "Shooting Niagara: and After?" written seventeen years after the *Pamphlets*. Long regarded as his most frightful vision, with its picture of a drilled society, the work nevertheless maintains a sense of finality, of last words mixing disgust with weariness and the inability to summon up real energy. Even the positive vision fails to attain power; military drill is by Carlyle's own denomination a visionary "fancy," though we in the twentieth century have lived to see that it is not (*E*, 5, 40). And the presentation of this vision is interrupted by a realization of its futility: "But I forbear; feeling well enough how visionary these things look; and how aerial, high, and spiritual they *are;* little capable of seriously tempting, even for moments, any but the highest kinds of men" (*E*, 5, 45).

The note of wounded pride and the feeling of social rejection show through the lofty declaration. At the end of "Shooting Niagara: and After?" Carlyle is a lonely ineffectual old man, out of contact with the real world and unable to understand its social structure. He has moved from a study of full human and social development in *Past and Present* through the process of spontaneous self-fulfilling labor to a rigid, hierarchical, inflexible scheme conceived in the militaristic and fascistic terms of the structure of command and obedience, a toughened labor of the self.

Nevertheless, while the *Pamphlets* are not saved by

the note of futility and grief, Carlyle himself is. If he represents the new Calvinistic God as a mode of the will to power, his own alienation never leads him into claims of real divinity, or even the glory of great self-exaltation. His concern with immediate social and economic realities—not shared by Nietzsche, who is more interested in, and often obsessed by, the unity of the large philosophical picture—provides a more realistic ballast for reassessing the self. Nietzsche's last works provide once again a commentary on Carlyle, but here the two writers part ways irrevocably. Nietzsche pursues his alienation, his ideas of Dionysos, of master and slave, of extremism, criminality, and immoralism, into madness itself, and in all the later writings there is a deep streak of pessimism, an intense disgust, a lofty contempt, an icy bacchantic laughter, echoing not only lonely freedom but also derangement of selfhood. Only rarely does the personal note of futility appear, for suffering exists as a proof of toughness. The devotion to a toughened will to power refuses the recognition of futility, and thus Nietzsche's self-discovery must go on at the very cost of selfhood. The worsening situation demands only the stronger asceticism of the self, the stronger declarations of independence, success, freedom, uniqueness, and will to power of the self. Carlyle's letters, by contrast, adumbrate the futility that creeps into the *Pamphlets;* they are almost maudlin in their delineation of his alienation, lack of purpose, melancholy, illnesses, and all the problems of being a hero in the futile and complex nineteenth century. Nietzsche's later letters provide no such obverse image to his denunciatory statements but, instead, intensify the image of the philosopher-hero in the writings. Their euphoric tone points to incipient madness, not merely freedom and self-overcoming: "Between ourselves—it is not impossible that I am the first philosopher of the age, perhaps even a trifle more than

that, . . . something decisive and fateful standing between two millenia." [6] Though Carlyle also wants to
hasten the millennium, he never fully attributes this
role and ability to himself.

Other letters of Nietzsche, when not involved in overt
self-celebration, suggest a euphoria that also indicates
mental derangement, a need for self-apotheosis, a failure
in perceiving reality, perhaps in fact the very need to be
deluded and to misread reality: "What is remarkable
here in Turin is the fascination I exercise on people.
. . . When I go into a large shop, every face changes;
women gaze after me in the street." [7] The autobiographical *Ecce Homo*, whose title is presumably designed to celebrate the new Christ who is Christ's reversal, a total *man*, is actually a history of Nietzsche's
heroic role-playing rather than a full study of his personal development. The grandiloquent claims, the self-
divinization, obviously embody a sportive arrogance, a
joy in their own improbability, and a desire to shock;
yet, however rhetorical and experimental they may be,
they nevertheless indicate real mental derangement and
self-intoxication. Their tone is giddy and heady.

Nietzsche's madness, while probably due to organic
causes,[8] is nevertheless associated with his own tighten-

6. Letter to Seydlitz, 12 Feb. 1888, quoted in Hollingdale, *Nietzsche*, p. 232.

7. Letter to Overbeck, Christmas 1888, ibid., p. 237. Also see the
collection of letters in Kurt F. Leidecker's translation of selections
from the Schlechta edition, *Unpublished Letters* (New York, Philosophical Library paperback, 1959).

8. On Nietzsche's madness, see pp. 58–59 of Kaufmann, *Nietzsche*. The whole problem is beset with many difficulties. Most recent studies, intent on rehabilitating Nietzsche, seek an organic
cause and often insist that his thought is quite consistent in its development and unconnected with the problem of his madness.
While it is not necessary to see Nietzsche's thought as leading to
madness, it does seem more reasonable to admit some interrelationship between the thought and the man.

ing of the reins upon himself, his forcing of himself to become his projections, to be his role. Nietzsche needs an apotheosis of self. Thus the chapter headings shift back and forth from the titles of the world's greatest books, those which he has written, to special attributes of self-celebration. While some of them—"Why I am so Wise," "Why I am so Clever," and "Why I write such excellent Books"—are obviously meant to be funny and arrogant, they are also a trifle mad. Nietzsche can see little in his autobiography beyond the role he has played in his books; consequently, the arrangement of his life is according to the books he has published. At the end of *Ecce Homo,* when he can conceive of himself only as a toughened Zarathustra fighting against the whole history of morality, he becomes his own projection—and a rather ugly and limited version of that projection. The final line of "Why I am a Fatality" sums it all up in another set of projections, canceling out one and affirming the other as the total self. "Have you understood me? *Dionysos* versus *Christ.*" [9] Even this is not the Dionysos of either *The Birth of Tragedy* or the somewhat later writings, however, but a tougher, lonelier, more ascetic revolutionary.

Nietzsche pursues his opposition to his age, his alienation from it, into such a furious distortion of his own projections that it becomes impossible to draw the line between artistic role-playing and life.

> I know my destiny. Some day my name will be bound up with the recollection of something terrific—of a crisis quite unprecedented, of the most profound clash of consciences, and the decisive condemnation of all that theretofore had been be-

9. Friedrich Nietzsche, *Ecce Homo* (*Philosophy of Nietzsche*) New York, Modern Library, 1954) , p. 933.

lieved, required, and hallowed. I am not a man, I am dynamite.[10]

The need to make an impact on life, to feel significant, results sometimes in a self-apotheosis that is purely destructive of everything outside the self, that overturns all civilization in a rage; at other times it produces both an overturning and a construction along new lines, but destruction is always dominant. The hyperbole of hope has its side of horror too.

> I am acquainted with tasks of a grandeur formerly inconceivable. Hope is reborn with me. Thus, I am necessarily a Man of Destiny . . . . All the mighty forms of the old society are blown into space—for they all rest on falsehood; there will be wars, whose like have never been seen on earth before. Politics on a grand scale will date from me.[11]

I find it impossible not to see behind these statements some glimpses of a madness provoked by alienation, a desperate desire to play the role of the god he has destroyed. Nietzsche's detestation of religion, mob, and slave morality precludes the role of sainthood and of the suffering self, but the image of the martyr and the crucified Christ returns in a distorted form in the "clown," just as his suffering returns in a kind of bacchantic but pessimistic joy.

In the picture of the clown as the substitute for sainthood, Nietzsche's alienation actually reaches the text of *Ecce Homo*. Yet if it is for a moment analogous to Carlyle's constantly intruding futility, it is immediately checked by qualifications and contradicted by self-apotheosis. Carlyle can never fully realize a moment of apotheosis without qualifying it, while Nietzsche can never reach a moment of unqualified futility:

10. Ibid., p. 923.
11. Ibid., p. 924.

I do not wish to be a saint; I would much rather be a clown. Perhaps I am a clown. And despite this— or rather not despite this (for there has never been anything falser than a saint)—I am the voice of truth. But my truth is terrible: for hitherto *lies* have been called truth. *The Transvaluation of all Values:* that is my formula for mankind's act of highest self-recognition, which in me has become flesh and genius. My destiny ordains that I should be the first decent human being, that I should feel myself opposed to the falsehood of ages.[12]

Though the Nietzsche of *Ecce Homo* is the new Christ and his reversal—"the voice of truth" become terrible, one who has "become flesh" but is the "first decent human being"—the image of the clown nevertheless suggests a martyr, the sense that he is ordained to a fate of decency suggests a passion and a crucifixion, and the title itself, *Ecce Homo*, suggests not merely a reversal of Christ, but a confirmation of Nietzsche in the role of the suffering and crucified Christ. This sense of crucifixion returns in Nietzsche's madness when he signs himself by the opposite of Dionysos in his crazed letters, the Crucified One. What was long denied erupts with a vengeance in his madness.

I have explored this comparison at some length because it seems to me that none of the social proposals of the later Carlyle or Nietzsche can be understood without understanding their own sense of playing a unique prophetic role totally without precedent in religion or literature, their own peculiar social alienation, and their extraordinary reaction to disinheritance, the loss of tradition, and social confusion. Their social goals cannot be fully perceived without a sense of the complex

12. Ibid., p. 923.

dialectic of self and society that provokes the extrava-
gance and harshness of the proposals. Tone is a most
important factor in understanding the later Carlyle and
Nietzsche. The dynamic polarity of the self and its social goals must be kept alive.

Furthermore, Nietzsche, by acting out to the futile
end his alienation, which is so analogous to Carlyle's,
sheds more light on Carlyle than any author in the
nineteenth century. Despite the toying with heroic projections and the need to find the self in heroes, Carlyle
never fully confuses himself with his heroes. He refuses
to pick up his earlier roles and to encase himself in
them. Teufelsdröckh appears but is forgotten, but Zarathustra returns as Nietzsche in *Ecce Homo.* Carlyle
never writes an autobiography of self-exaltation. *Sartor,*
like *Zarathustra,* is an exploration into selfhood, an attempt at self-discovery, but when Carlyle returns to the
autobiographical strain in later years, he discovers himself through the memoirs of others. In Nietzsche's life
and writings other people progressively disappear from
view; Carlyle mourns the loss of his friends, but they are
separated by death, not by his own alienation.

Basically, however, it is the note of futility, of the
voice of the reformer who cannot reform, that protects
Carlyle from Nietzsche's madness. This realistic crucified
Carlyle, the alien prophet to his age, enters his own literature of heroism and shatters the completeness of the
heroic mask. Thus *Frederick the Great,* written after the
Pamphlets, becomes far more than *Cromwell* an odd
mixture—the study of the will to power, the tough commander, the model leader of men and armies, and also
an autobiography of Carlyle's own futile wrestlings with
the sources and subject matter, the confession of a failure to organize a chaos of sources. (Ironically, it was
Nietzsche who wanted to found a city in honor of Fred-

erick, in whom he saw a great atheist and anti-eccle-siast.[13])

This note of futility becomes dominant and finally proves both worthwhile and enduring. The *Life of Sterling* turns at last to a realistically redefined heroism, one that is mild, not harsh, one that foregoes vast social proposals, one that emerges out of the very complexities of the century, one that while always admitting futility turns weakness into strength. Though this strain is muted, recurring only in distorted form in *Frederick* over a period of many years and thus preventing the heroic fulfillment projected in that book, it is nevertheless constant, providing—though not with full satisfaction to Carlyle—the means for self-redefinition in old age. Carlyle's version of *Ecce Homo* is the reversal of Nietzsche's; though marred occasionally by sentimentality and maudlin moments, it is a crucifixion with others, a finding of the self through others, through memory, and through a realistic assessment of the century's disinheritance, not through the lonely and exalted acting out of impossible heroic roles that lead into madness and irremediable futility.

13. Ibid., p. 898.

PART THREE

RETURN TO SELFHOOD

✤ 6 ✤

LIMITED HEROISM:
JOHN STERLING

There are in our existence spots of time,
That with distinct pre-eminence retain
A renovating virtue, whence—depressed
By false opinion and contentious thought,
Or aught of heavier or more deadly weight,
In trivial occupations, and the round
Of ordinary intercourse—our minds
Are nourished and invisibly repaired.

Wordsworth,
The Prelude

The Life of John Sterling (1851), Carlyle's biography of his friend, seems worlds apart from the *Latter-Day Pamphlets*, though it is separated from them by only one year. And it is equally removed from the heroic and militaristic world of *Frederick the Great* which follows it. All the intense concern with social ideas, all the shrill demands for guidance and submission that characterized the *Pamphlets* have now disappeared. *Sterling* is interior in its concerns, casual in tone, and reminiscent in manner; what proposals do arise are muted in their presentation and devoid of shrillness. A new focus has been found: the warm endorsement of true friendship as it manifests itself in the tale of two struggling artists attempting to unfold their talents in a confused and perplexing age. Sterling's struggle is at the center, but, as I shall show, Carlyle's struggle is not unlike it.

303

Sterling is far more than a biography or a memoir. Like the early essays, the subject functions as a mask for Carlyle as well as a figure of whom he has direct knowledge. Carlyle carries his literary exploration of the self into new areas and inaugurates new techniques for understanding himself in relation to his society. Abandoning his lofty but unrealistic preoccupations with heroism in the past, he tries to shape a new and muted heroism for the present. Both the method of writing and the content are introspective: strong heroic codes and dogmas are replaced by richly deep, quiet, and realistic interior values, and a warm and human tone replaces the commanding voice of the *Pamphlets*.

The futility behind *Heroes, Cromwell,* and the *Pamphlets*—that futility which so strongly mars *Frederick* —appears as a central fact and theme in *Sterling*. In facing that futility in the figure of the failed artist, Carlyle redefines his own heroism as well as Sterling's and emerges with a new kind of art. He brings the subject matters of failure and the tone of quietness in the casual writing of the *Journals*, his private voice, to the theme of heroism, his public voice and role. The result is a new autobiography, another *Sartor Resartus*, but also its complete reversal, for the editor no longer struggles for a lofty public voice that will be at one with the private self. Carlyle seeks to understand through Sterling his own failures and weaknesses, including the failure of his own public role; he attempts to plumb the confusions of his century, to know what it means to live without solid social and religious traditions, and, granted this condition of disinheritance, to find out what of value remains, what may be the basis for communication, love, human worth. *Sterling* inaugurates a new kind of memoir writing—one which subsides during the composition of *Frederick,* but not without creating a troubled under-

ground current, the note of futility that destroys the unity of the book and its heroic mask. He returns to this kind of writing again in his final *Reminiscences,* and this method sustains him personally and artistically in his old age, providing a final definition of the self and his central kind of art.

Nevertheless, Carlyle never placed great value on *Sterling;* it was for him a byway from his major task of composing *Frederick,* an interruption of his more important public voice, an interim book done in a few moments of spare time. With his distrust of the imagination, Carlyle could never bring himself to fully endorse the method of memory in *Sterling* as anything but a momentary comfort, a glance backward, and a memento mori, a preparation for his own death, when he felt he would join his departed friend. As an old man editing Sterling's letters, writing the reminiscences of old friends now dead, and particularly reworking the letters and "memorials" of his wife, Carlyle is much like the figure of the old Wordsworth who, his creativity having failed, is occupied with revising *The Prelude.* Each hopes to catch some flicker of life from the original events themselves, distrusts the capacity of art to reveal any self-fulfillment, and is fearful that events may be lost forever.

Though the lack of fulfillment is a dominant theme of all Carlyle's memory literature, he nevertheless attains much of Wordsworth's belief in the creative power of memory. Furthermore, he goes beyond Wordsworth —as I have suggested he moved beyond Blake in *Past and Present*—with his more explicit social and interpersonal concerns in relation to the imagination. His imagination attempts to grasp the complexity of the century, its whirling movements, its failure to provide signposts or directions, all of which result in the failure of

people of all professions, including that of art. In making the failed artist the center of his study, he moves the method of memory into a central theme of twentieth-century literature—the discovery of the truly creative self through the study of the self as other, and as a hopeful, often idealistic, but failed other. In this sense, with Ruskin's *Praeterita* (a book that resembles both *Sterling* and the *Reminiscences,* as well as *The Prelude,* in matter and manner), he anticipates the themes and configurations of Proust in *Remembrance of Things Past,* Gide's handling of Edouard in *The Counterfeiters,* and especially Joyce's treatment of the embittered and idealistic Dedalus in *Ulysses.*

These new and extraordinary concerns, however, do not spring full-blown from *Sterling,* nor do they ever reach a strong level of conscious awareness, affirmation, or solid artistic treatment. Compared with *Sartor, Sterling* suffers from a strong distrust of its imaginative technique, a blurring in Carlyle's attitude toward art as the most fulfilling profession the century affords, and a hazy sense of Carlyle's attitude toward his own relationship with Sterling. Moreover, there is a plethora of stoic platitudes glossed over with Christian phrases, all based on the sepulchral movement of the book, its memento mori manner, a completing of life's task, a step toward the grave. Carlyle cannot reconcile himself to his theme of futility as heroism, and this book is at best a bypath from his other works. Though it picks up themes from them, it remains another kind of duty or task.

Sterling owes its origin, like *Past and Present* and the *Pamphlets,* to an immediate situation, but in this case a personal or at best a quasi-social situation provokes the response. The book is quite clearly a defense of Sterling not against detractors but against friends—in particular, against Archdeacon Julius Hare, to whom Sterling was curate during his brief eight-month's life as a clergy-

man.[1] Hare's biography of Sterling had focused on the curacy and its accompanying religious problems as the center of his life, and Carlyle hopes to rescue Sterling from this misrepresentation.

Carlyle's technique is not to provide a point-by-point refutation of Hare's interpretation, but to shift the basis of argument into a different dimension altogether. By putting Sterling's life into a fuller perspective, at once more tragic and heroic, he transcends Hare's interpretation, leaving it in the religious dust where he feels it belongs. Carlyle succeeds in effecting what he feels Coleridge could not do—really lifting things into a "higher sphere of argument" (S, 59). For the first time in his career, he seems to probe behind and beyond religious values, in fact to push them toward the sanctity of interior states of consciousness. Thus the focus is shifted away from religious controversy altogether and transferred to personal sources of energy, characteristics of feeling and friendship. At the end of Carlyle's somewhat lengthy argument the new source of values is revealed.

> Sterling, I find, was a curate for exactly eight months: during eight months and no more had he any special relation to the Church. But he was a man, and had relation to the Universe, for eight-and-thirty years: and it is in this latter character, to which all the others were but features and transitory hues, that we wish to know him. His battle with hereditary Church-formulas was severe; but it was by no means his one battle with things inherited, nor indeed his chief battle; neither, according to my observation of what it was, is it successfully delineated or summed-up in this Book [of Hare's].

1. Hare's biography appeared as an introduction to his edition of Sterling's writings—*Essays and Tales by John Sterling*, ed. with a memoir of his life by Julius Charles Hare (2 vols. London, 1848).

The truth is, nobody that had known Sterling would recognize a feature of him here; you would never dream that this book treated of *him* at all. A pale sickly shadow in torn surplice is presented to us here: weltering bewildered amid heaps of what you call "Hebrew Old-clothes"; wrestling, with impotent impetuosity, to free itself from the baleful imbroglio, as if that had been its one function in life: who in this miserable figure would recognize the brilliant, beautiful and cheerful John Sterling, with his ever-flowing wealth of ideas, fancies, imaginations; with his frank affections, inexhaustible hopes, audacities, and general radiant vivacity of heart and intelligence, which made the presence of him an illumination and inspiration wherever he went? (*S*, 3)

"Illumination," Carlyle's characteristic religious metaphor, is here linked with and dependent upon the "presence of him." Ideas are only a minor element in a series of personal expressions presented in terms of the "ever-flowing wealth," the sense of life emanating from Sterling, "his vivacity." His "inspiration" is less religious than personal, a testament to his own flow of life and activity. And religion is reduced to formulas, a world without energy and life.

Yet to achieve this inner life of freedom and spontaneity, Sterling, like the young Carlyle, must thread his way through the labyrinth of dead professions, including religion, before he can attain the finality of being a man of letters. The road is much like that of the figures of the early essays whom Carlyle used as masks, and it is not unlike Teufelsdröckh's battle in *Sartor*. Not only must Sterling encounter unbelief and false belief in Radicalism, a version of utilitarianism for Carlyle, but he must also transcend the false religion of Coleridge. In

this respect, *Sterling* goes beyond *Sartor;* it involves a harsher judgment of religion, even Coleridge's Kantian brand, and points toward fundamentals that are elsewhere. Coleridge, in fact, with his religion based on Kant, can be likened to Teufelsdröckh in *Sartor,* and Carlyle's satire on Coleridge can then be seen as a final rejection of what always seemed "tentative" and nebulous to him about Teufelsdröckh as an image of the religious and heroic self.

Both Radicalism and Coleridgean moonshine offer false illuminations that will inevitably beguile and tempt volatile natures like that of Sterling (and of Carlyle), whose one fault is over-hastiness. It is as such a movement through false byways that eventually lead to the clear path of art that Carlyle interprets Sterling's early life. Sterling transcends both Radicalism and Coleridgean religion. Art alone in the nineteenth century is able to provide the true loadstar for one's quest. The image of the loadstar, habitually associated with religion in *Past and Present,* now appears much closer to art, which provides the sole means for Sterling to come into contact with reality. Radicalism and Church offer only the illusion of a means, since they minister to the imagination in a diseased manner.

As an early radical, Sterling helps Torrijos and his Spanish exiles forge the fiery romantic plan of recapturing Spain and liberating their homeland from tyranny. This plan echoes some of Carlyle's early revolutionary themes, but when the invasion ends in disastrous execution of the party at Malaga, Sterling, who had accidentally stayed behind, loses his faith in Radicalism. This is the triumph of fact over diseased imagination, a psychological movement that is akin to the experience of *Sartor,* though perhaps less immediately striking than Teufelsdröckh's conversion. Radicalism may be a valuable antidote to superstition, but it cannot serve as an

"adamantine basis of truth," the means to a noble way of life. In this harsh judgment one can easily see Carlyle's denunciation of his own earlier radical leanings. The "deeper side of the question" must appear for Sterling, and the Torrijos crisis makes it possible. Already Sterling's pilgrimages to Coleridge at Highgate Hill had shown evidences of his religious nature; the Torrijos crisis only confirmed the message that he would "have to struggle inwards and upwards, in search of some diviner home" (S, 90).

Unfortunately, the Coleridgean moonshine poses as a means of fulfilling Sterling's quest for self-fulfillment and stability. His attempt to "find sanctuary in the old Church" (S, 97) by becoming for eight months a curate to Archdeacon Hare at Herstmonceux does not provide the fulfillment he seeks. Carlyle is strong in his condemnation of this move. In a confused epoch when everyone has lost his way, the Church, no longer really alive but continuing to pose as living, becomes, in Carlyle's images, death posing as life, moonshine as sunshine, will-of-the-wisp and meteor as loadstar, dissolution as stability, skepticism as faith. Coleridge is at once the cause of its protracted death-in-life and its proper symbol. The brilliant chapter on Coleridge, certainly one of Carlyle's greatest satiric portraits, reveals the ghastly horror of falsity in both Coleridge and the Church and, at the same time, the terrible tragedy of unfulfilled endeavor in each.

The whole picture of Coleridge emphasizes the discrepancy between his real self and a projected ideal self. Carlyle's criticism tends to remove the sense of ideal projections in heroes or in supernatural realms and to bring the self back to a more realistic basis. Coleridge is indeed like Teufelsdröckh: he poses as the Kantian philosopher who has seen through the veils of things (recalling Carlyle's doubts about Kant as early as *Schil-*

ler), and he perches upon Highgate Hill from which he can observe far-off London significantly covered by the haze below. His talk, with its Kantian distinctions between subject and object, understanding and reason, also bespeaks a testimony of a higher world of clarity, and his presence as the center of the circle at Highgate Hill attests the power of his vision to unify the questing men who come to him. In this picture of Coleridge, however, Carlyle shifts his focus from the figure of Teufelsdröckh to the searching artist figure (Sterling) who visits him.

Coleridge's ideal self is never fulfilled. Everything about him is formlessness. His face, indeed his whole figure, is "flabby and irresolute" (*S,* 54), and he shuffles instead of stepping. His precise talk about objects and subjects is snuffled out as "om-m-mject" and "sum-m-mject" (*S,* 55). Carlyle once again bases his judgment and satire on externals, facts, that he feels mirror a real interior condition, not on the validity or logic of the ideas. Instead of bringing his listeners into clarity, Coleridge leads them into a world of shadows, haze, and mist. The contrast between their expectations and Coleridge's answers points an accusing finger at the philosopher's failure to provide the spiritual clarity he has promised. He fulfills the process of spiritual development he has inaugurated in others by an abrupt decline into illusion and formlessness. The reader travels with him through a spiritual process of greater and greater depth and clarity, only to be tossed suddenly into the snuffling "om-m-mject": "Wait till the Book on the Logos were done;—alas, till your own terrene eyes, blind with conceit and the dust of logic, were purged, subtilised and spiritualised into the sharpness of vision requisite for discerning such an 'om-m-mject' " (*S,* 59). For Coleridge's world—a world where everything loses its direction, purpose, aim, and even individuation—the

swamp is the characteristic image. The listener is "swamped near to drowning in this tide of ingenious vocables, spreading out boundless as if to submerge the world" (S, 55). This is a vast and destructive universe of illusion and unreality, and Coleridge provides not salvation but destruction of the self.

The fault lies in Coleridge himself. His attempt to resurrect a dead Church and to make it into a living one marks his failure in courage. All the formlessness of his being—of his talk, walk, appearance, and speculation—is the "emblem of himself" (S, 60). By thus reducing metaphysical failure to personal failure, Carlyle suggests his own remedy. Once again his ultimate criterion for the possibility of realizing true nobility is the consultation of the deepest self, both eye and heart, as in *Past and Present,* but more than ever before religious anwers are eschewed in this remedy. Sterling is ultimately a glorious example of his times because he has consulted his deepest self, which is centered not in logic and head but in instincts—heart, nerves, blood.

> This man also had said to himself, not in mere Catechism-words, but with all his instincts, and the question thrilled in every nerve of him, and pulsed in every drop of his blood: "What is the chief end of man? Behold, I too would live and work as beseems a denizen of this Universe, a child of the Highest God. By what means is a noble life still possible for me here?" (S, 268)

Sterling discovers, as Carlyle had decided for himself, that the means to nobility, the new religion, lies in art, which reveals both the fullness of universal being and the fullness of his deepest self. Literature becomes at once goal, process, and center whereby the universe and the self receive their fullest articulation and control.

> Such result was now decisively beginning for him;
> the original bent of his mind, the dim mandate of
> all the facts in his outward and inward condition;
> evidently the one wholesome tendency for him,
> which grew ever clearer to the end of his course,
> and gave at least one steady element, and that the
> central one, in his fluctuating existence henceforth.
> (S, 140)

Sterling's application to literature, his discovery of his
role as a poet and essayist, is thus for Carlyle the final
key to any interpretation of his life. It is his triumph
over obstructions, his final clearing away of the debris of
Radicalism and Church. At last, through art, the "fer-
mentation" and "perversions" (S, 62) of Coleridge's
manna, the unnatural, magical process of life, have been
cast out, and the true natural process of life as a coherent and expansive whole with direction, spirit, and
meaning has been asserted. By literature, Sterling constructs his little sunlit island founded on the rocks (S,
234). Just as Carlyle was to view his own conversion to
the new religion of the prophet and man of letters as
final, so he viewed Sterling's to the role of poet and essayist. Beyond that conversion he as biographer saw no
need to delve for the essential interpretation of Sterling's life.

> But these ["foreign journeys, disanchorings, and
> nomadic vicissitudes of household which occupy his
> few remaining years"] cannot be accepted as in any
> sense epochs in his life: the one last epoch of his life
> was that of his internal change towards Literature
> as his work in the world; and we need not linger
> much on these [five journies] which are the mere
> outer accidents of that, and had no distinguished
> influence in modifying that. (S, 156–57)

This statement, then, in many respects merely returns to the movement of the early essays and *Sartor*, but not without certain shifts in focus. The public role is now very much absent; the conversion is primarily a private act, an entry in one's journal. And Carlyle's dismissing traditional religious forms and replacing them by art is now much stronger. In the earlier works the two realms of religion and art were either confused or equated, but in *Sterling* the conversion to art has all the finality of a religious conversion and, in fact, supersedes such a conversion.

Despite the excitement about art as a final choice, however, the image of art cannot contain the problematic action of the book—Sterling's life and his confusions, or Carlyle's. With Sterling's conversion to art, Carlyle once again tries to import a sense of religious finality and transcendence into a realm not habitually associated with religion, but, as usual, he encounters obstacles and discovers that the old stability of religion cannot be easily transferred into new areas. Once the conversion to the stability of art comes about, one might expect Sterling's fluctuating existence to be moderated —or at least to be viewed from a more stable center. Nothing of the sort occurs, however, beyond an occasional declaration on the finality of art. Furthermore, even after Carlyle has explained he will no longer be concerned with Sterling's five voyages because the conversion to literature has marked the final epoch of his life, the attainment of spiritual direction and fulfillment, the rest of the book is composed mainly of extracts from Sterling's letters, which deal only infrequently with literature and almost entirely with scene paintings of Europe, descriptions of voyages, and portraits of English companions that have also flocked to Italy and the Continent—in short, with Sterling's restlessness and wanderings, his continued unfulfillment.

More recent scholarly evidence would also seem to indicate that Carlyle is working against the grain of facts. He wants Sterling's conversion to art to be final, to be a center to his existence because his own choice to be a prophet and man of letters must have that same finality, that same religious assurance. But Anne Kimball Tuell, in her scholarly biography of Sterling, confirms the suspicion that Sterling did not completely cast aside Coleridge and religious problems when he left the curacy.[2] Moreover, Carlyle is even working against the grain of his interests. Sterling's literature is different from his, and he can hardly summon up much energy to praise Sterling's slim and unsuccessful volumes of poetry. He ingeniously explains his adverse judgment of some of the poems by citing Sterling's failure in them to free himself from fragments of the Church.

These attitudes and subjects mar *Sterling,* yet they also have the effect of shifting interest to the personality of the hero, to his interior values, which emerge from his artistic conflict with the century. Carlyle discovers that the obstructions of life have not been erased by Sterling's triumph over Coleridgean moonshine and Radicalism nor by his choice of art as a role. It is Sterling's *dedication* to art that, despite the continuance of a fluctuating existence and the small achievement of his poetry, gives real meaning to his life. This explanation shifts the focus from art as a means to transcendence to personal dedication to art as the means to that transcendence. The real meaning of life lies not in any religious statements of a Coleridge, or in any radical theories of a Bentham or Mill, nor in any artistic dogma or the religion of art, but in the perseverance of the self in

2. Anne Kimball Tuell, *John Sterling, Representative Victorian* (New York, 1941). "Reconstruction of Sterling's religious history shows him more preoccupied with religion than Carlyle will acknowledge and far more than Carlyle knew" (p. 24) .

dedication to the complete unfolding of the self, to full self-realization, despite all the obstacles and hindrances of the nineteenth-century world. In an interior battle weaknesses that come essentially from facing the multiplicity of the century and from being a victim of its confusions and its failures are faced and turned into strengths.

"Poor noble Sterling, he had struggled so high and gained so little here! But this also he did gain, to be a brave man; and it was much" (S, 260). Sterling's bravery, his triumph, is indissolubly linked with his personal tragedy. In the face of worldly failure, of the rejection of his poetry by friends like Carlyle, his perseverance and heroism become more manifest.

> With or without encouragement, he was resolute to persevere in Poetry, and did persevere. When I think now of his modest, quiet steadfastness in this business of Poetry; how, in spite of friend and foe, he silently persisted, without wavering, in the form of utterance he had chosen for himself; and to what length he carried it, and vindicated himself against us all,—his character comes out in a new light to me, with more of a certain central inflexibility and noble silent resolution than I had elsewhere noticed in it. (S, 250)

It is not hard to see in this quotation that Carlyle is steeling himself for the futile heroism of writing *Frederick*, accepting his lonely plight, redefining his militarism in terms of a quiet, more interior battle.

Indeed, as Sterling's awareness of futility increases, so too does his heroism. He does not merely face the disorder and chaos of his century: though he recognizes his inability to alter its basic flux, he can work with that flux to transform it into a modicum of order; he turns

316

his own limited resources into a limited strength. He seems in fact to thrive upon the very disintegration of his world, using this material for a heightening of his creative possibilities. His very "bane" becomes his "antidote" as he finds "disease as health," a viewpoint Nietzsche and Mann were later to echo, and discovers that the unique sufferings of genius lead to unique and higher creations, as Carlyle's *Schiller* had celebrated. Sterling's very unhealth takes on the appearance of health.

> [He] showed a noble fund of natural health amid such an element of disease. Somehow one could never rightly fancy that he was diseased . . . . Such, once for all, were the conditions appointed him. And it must be owned he had, with a most kindly temper, adjusted himself to these; nay, you would have said, he loved them; it was almost as if he would have chosen them as the suitablest. Such an adaptation was there in him of volition to necessity. (*S*, 201, 155)

As Sterling's rejection by the world increases, his perseverance in poetry becomes more evident. (The role Carlyle is preparing for himself becomes apparent here: the rejection of the *Pamphlets* is followed by his perseverance in *Frederick*.) To the last he continues writing, keeping his life and house in order, sending letters to his children.

> For courage, for active audacity we had all known Sterling; but such a fund of mild stoicism, of devout patience and heroic composure, we did not hitherto know in him. His sufferings, his sorrows, all his unutterabilities in this slow agony, he held right manfully down; marched loyally, as at the

317

bidding of the Eternal, into the dread Kingdoms, and no voice of weakness was heard from him. (*S,* 260)

But despite all the language about eternity, the residual Christianity colored with stoic celebrations, his heroic strength remains basically a this-world phenomenon. Transcendence itself now necessarily involves both tragedy and triumph: the tragedy of transiency, of the century's confusions, its disinherited world, and the ultimate mysterious destruction of the self, and the triumph of heroism, bravery, submission in the face of that transiency. The last days of Sterling as revealed in his letters correspond exactly to the eternal moment of his triumph when freed from the world. The afterlife becomes transcendence in this life; religious values become interior states of triumph in spite of and bound up with sadness, failure, and futility.

> These Letters I have lately read: they give, beyond any he has written, a noble image of the intrinsic Sterling;—the same face we had long known; but painted now as on the azure of Eternity, serene, victorious, divinely sad; the dust and extraneous disfigurements imprinted on it by the world, now washed away. (*S,* 258)

Carlyle can say that the history of John Sterling is "beyond others, emblematic of that of his Time" (*S,* 268). His is the one real triumph left to man, and to the artist especially, in a world completely confused and set adrift, a world in which individuals are so isolated and different that the prophetic voice can no longer be heard. To Carlyle he is the image of the only possible triumphs left amid the futility and frustration experienced in the *Latter-Day Pamphlets* with a society that

no longer listens to him. Sterling is thus a "mirror" in which "noble seekers and strivers towards what is highest" may find "some shadow of themselves and of their immeasurably complex arena" (S, 268).

This is not the ultimate conclusion of the book, however. After a break another and quite different final paragraph brings into relief even higher dimensions of meaning. It presents Carlyle's personal application, which I have been noting throughout, but it goes beyond even that and asserts the interrelationships that knit together the process of achieving the new transcendence, the process of human friendship, and the process of memory and biographical writing itself. The themes of *Sterling* are absorbed into a larger living process in which Carlyle appears as both writer of the book and participant within it. After writing finis to his study of Sterling, Carlyle returns once more to himself and affirms the accomplishment of the plans he had stated in the opening pages. In accomplishing his function as a writer, he recognizes that function and its fulfillment in himself, the total meaning of Sterling's life as it relates to his own experience in the past as real and as recalled and recreated by literature in the process of memory.

> Nay, what of men or of the world? Here, visible to myself, for some while, was a brilliant human presence, distinguishable, honourable, and lovable amid the dim common populations; among the million little beautiful, once more a beautiful human soul: whom I, among others, recognized and lovingly walked with, while the years and the hours were. Sitting now by his tomb in thoughtful mood, the new times bring a new duty for me. "Why write the Life of Sterling?" I imagine I had a commission higher than the world's, the dictate of Nature herself, to do what is now done. *Sic prosit.* (S, 268)

The personal tragedy and triumph of John Sterling becomes an interpersonal one. The final valuation comes to rest on personal relationships, which alone seem to rise over the dim millions, over chaos and divisions of the century, even over the new heroism that is compounded of a noble stoicism and Christianity.

It is now clear that from the beginning of the book Carlyle has been active as both writer and participant and that the act of writing, the creative and imaginative exercise of memory, is not merely the discovery of meaning in Sterling's life but also the discovery of meaning in the relationship between the life of Sterling and Carlyle himself. Sterling is a "mirror" for Carlyle: even though he is Carlyle's hero-worshipper, he can also be a special kind of hero. The man who chose art for his career and for spiritual fullness is also the failed artist. Carlyle, as both his editor and the man who walked along with him through the century, finds in Sterling an image of the self as both the artist-hero and the failed artist who makes his own new heroism. The great truths of Teufelsdröckh have been abandoned by the editor of *Sterling*, who sees only an image of himself and his times in the past. A new source of value, a new voice, must now be formed, and this is the task of the method of memory, which can play back over the self and its choices in its relationship with another like it.

The casual style of the book is intended to approximate the method of memory, to be artless. Carlyle's "swift scribbling" (S, 7), in which he is always aware of recalling the incidents and of writing a book, becomes then an appropriate method and not, as Anne Kimball Tuell and other critics contend, a failure in exactness, a sloppy performance.[3] By letting the spirit blow where it listeth, much in the manner of Wordsworth in the opening of *The Prelude*, by involving himself in the

3. Ibid., p. 19.

process of recollection and in the recollected material, and by keeping to a general chronological ordering, Carlyle hopes to discover the pattern of meaning that will unfold in the process of his relationship with Sterling.

> And so, having on my hands some leisure at this time, and being bound to it by evident considerations; one of which ought to be especially sacred to me, I decide to fling down on paper some outline of what my recollections and reflections contain in reference to this most friendly, bright and beautiful human soul; who walked with me for a season in this world, and remains to me very memorable while I continue in it. Gradually, if facts simple enough in themselves can be narrated as they came to pass, it will be seen what kind of man this was. (S, 5)

The process of memory and writing (flinging down on paper some outline) merges with the process of the past (walking with Sterling in this world).

In *Sterling* Carlyle can use this new style of memory because he is in the unique position of being the editor in the present and also a participant in the past action.

From the very beginning of the book Carlyle is eager to see himself as a participant in the action even though he has not yet met Sterling. In giving Sterling's birth and parentage, for example, he associates his own readings for his edition of Cromwell's letters with some rather remote genealogy of Sterling. Despite the obscurity of the connection, Carlyle enjoys the intimations of friendship it suggests, the sense of design amid complexity that it radiates. The insertion itself is made in the typical casual manner, as though only by inserting the material with this casualness can the pleasant sensation of connectedness be attained. "A little bit of genealogy,

since it lies ready to my hand, gathered long ago out of wider studies, and pleasantly connects things individual and present with the dim universal crowd of things past,—may as well be inserted here as thrown away" (S, 9). Other connections between Carlyle's life before he met Sterling and Sterling's are even more obscure. A letter to his mother from Sterling in the West Indies, where he had endured a hurricane, is associated by Carlyle with Goethe's last birthday.

Once Carlyle has met Sterling and actually begins to figure in the story of his life, the pattern of these early obscure connections emerges into clarity. As the parallelism of his own life with Sterling's, only dimly and obscurely prefigured before their first meeting, achieves a reality, both the temporal spans and the significance of the two lives are coordinated. In one of their first meetings, Carlyle strikingly describes the fulfillment of this coordination. The recollected material is immediately brought to a new level of animation as copious talk pours forth from both men in the exchange of "pleasant dialogue" (S, 106). Once again the new valuation is on the life connecting the two men, on interior and realistic values, not on ideas of heroism. It is not what is talked about that is remembered, for Carlyle says, "We talked rapidly of various unmemorable things" (S, 106). It is the walk and the exchange of dialogue that are important, for through this coordination of processes, real union and friendship, which transcends the whirl of the century and the process of time itself, are attained.

Carlyle's primary interest lies not in the difference of opinion that makes a good dialogue but in the "identity of sentiment" attained, which provides the "foundations of a frank intercourse, pointing towards pleasant intimacies both with himself and with his circle" (S, 106). Walking and talking—often by letters—become the two key types of remembrance, the highest material of recol-

lection. For it is within situations where the process of temporal flow brings two beings as close together as possible that the real union effected by an "identity of sentiment" can be accomplished. In such situations the leap which somehow transcends time and remains inexplicable in temporal terms can take place, and what is accomplished endures.

The characteristic image of fulfillment is, as one might expect, the old religious image of light. To Carlyle Sterling is always a "welcome illumination in the dim whirl of things" (S, 127). It is because of this union that Sterling becomes, in a further extension of the displaced religious vocabulary, a "radiant child of the empyrean, clad in bright auroral hues" (S, 2). Sterling's light, however, is not only the essence of his own inner personal being, which he struggles to unfold in literature; it is also the brilliant illumination which he casts upon all those who form a friendship with him. By his enthusiastic endorsement of *Sartor*, he enkindles this light in Carlyle. He produces "deep silent joy," the conviction that Carlyle's battle in the world is not quite mad and futile, but manful, and that thought burns in Carlyle like a lamp, "lighting-up into a kind of heroic splendour the sad volcanic wrecks, abysses, and convulsions of said poor battle" (S, 191–92).

Yet Carlyle is far more acutely aware of disruption and futility than he is of the moments of successful illumination. Even in the past absolute identity remained an impossibility, for "difference of opinion" has always acted as a hindrance to union in times of many worn-out traditions and a variety of new beliefs. But Carlyle sees the chaotic conditions of the nineteenth century and especially time itself as the principal villains. The accelerated movement of the century, its goalless ever-active forces, its divisive movements serve only to sever friends, to victimize them, to thrust them in varying

directions, and finally to submerge them. Even friendship cannot abolish the chaos of the times; the chaotic
disruption characteristic of the nineteenth century hinders closer and more effective union between Sterling and
Carlyle. Artists who could once join together heroically
are now disunited by the kind of art they feel the age
needs; the hero and hero-worshipper must go their separate ways, one to prophecy and the other to poetry. But
by "identity of sentiment" if not of programs they may
unite in recognizing time for what it is, the frustrator of
their hopes and plans, of all their ideals. Friendship can
give them the courage to join heroically in sentiment
even though the century may keep them solitary in their
respective battles. For a brief and flickering moment
Sterling and Carlyle can entertain the heroism of start-
ing a periodical against the "impostures of the time,"
but Carlyle knows that no fighting regiment can be
raised. Each man must fight his solitary battle, and Sterling's being primarily poetic, is not the same as Carlyle's
(S, 221–22). The multiplicity, speed, and divisiveness of
the century militate against the solidity of real union;
the individual must fight this chaos to achieve the glim-
merings of a few moments that endure.

> I had to mount into cabs with him; fly far and
> wide, shuttling athwart the big Babel, wherever his
> calls and pauses had to be. This was his way to
> husband time! Our talk, in such straitened circum-
> stances, was loud or low as the circumambient
> groaning rage of wheels and sound prescribed,—
> very loud it had to be in such thoroughfares as
> London Bridge and Cheapside; but except while he
> was absent, off for minutes into some banker's office,
> lawyer's, stationer's, haberdasher's or what office
> there might be, it never paused. In this way exten-

sive strange dialogues were carried on: to me also
very strange,—private friendly colloquies, on all
manner of rich subjects, held thus amid the chaotic
roar of things. (S, 190)

Despite such moments of union attained in the midst of
a vibrant, whirling city, Carlyle ultimately can see the
sunny islets as mere spots of past time, not as the victory
of the imagination in the present. Confronted with the
acceleration and dissolution of the century, those moments must also dissolve at last, and Carlyle, far more
definitely than Wordsworth, destroys the imaginative
endeavor in rescuing Sterling and the spots of time. Finally, he blots them out altogether, resting in a preparation of himself for the grave or at best modeling himself
after the image of Sterling. The note of futility, regret,
and pain dominates.

So had it lasted, ever since poor John's voyagings
began; his Fathers house standing always as a fixed
sunny islet with safe harbor for him. So it could not
always last. This sunny islet was now also to break
and go down; so many firm islets, fixed pillars in
his fluctuating world, pillar after pillar, were to
break and go down; till swiftly all, so to speak, were
sunk in the dark waters, and he with them! Our little History is now hastening to a close. (S, 242)

Is then the biographical journey of memory a futile
one? Is Sterling only an early version of Reminiscences
which forecasts a gloomy Carlyle already filled with regret and unfulfillment and preparing himself for the
grave? And are the events of the past which memory re-
creates merely transient moments, deceptively masked as
fixed sunny islets but ultimately only part of a dark
undifferentiated chaos that finally engulfs the self? An

325

answer to these questions is difficult and must be mixed. One strongly marked tone of the book emphasizes and underlines these negative implications, which are undeniably close to Carlyle's consciousness. But Carlyle also feels the creative tug of memory, knows that he will discover the depth of the interior self and a new and realistic heroism in Sterling, and the positive brightness and warmth that the book achieves undercuts the plangent note. While throughout *Sterling* memory heightens the sense of transiency and loss, which the century's acceleration and disinheritance has intensified, it also affirms a continuity between past and present and an identity that transcends temporal flow. *The Life of John Sterling* is the process of Carlyle's mind as it discovers not merely the flux of things but also his and Sterling's capacity to transcend that flux, to give themselves some significance, to create friendly dialogues amid the larger babel of the city. The book stands as a real walk again with Sterling, a process of mind and art, of the imagination as memory, that provides a new picture of both Sterling and Carlyle.

As a continuation of Carlyle's endless quest for identity then, *Sterling* is the redefinition of the heroic self on a realistic level, with its center on interior, private rather than public values. No longer are weaknesses cancelled out by asceticism or heroic and tough projections of selfhood; no longer are futilities unfaced by a retreat into the heroic past as a model for the present. In *Sterling* Carlyle makes a distinctly modern advance by offering as a central theme the transformation of certain weaknesses into realistic strengths through a probing of the failed self and its relationship with others in the past. The new realistic heroism that emerges is centered on a rich interior life, charged with spontaneity and self-fulfillment in relationship with the basic nature of others; it is accomplished despite, but with a full aware-

ness of, the barriers of ideology, the confusions of the times, the lack of viable traditions and professions that formerly provided a bridge to understanding and a sense of community, and the increased enmity of time itself, now deprived of any religious hopes.

✆§ 7 §✆

CONCLUSION, WITH A GLANCE
AT THE *REMINISCENCES*

> That was always her way; bright home, with its bright
> face, full of love, and victorious over all disorder, al-
> ways shone on me like a star as I journeyed and jum-
> bled along amid the shriekeries and miseries I
> was myself the most collapsed of men; and had no sun-
> shine in my life but what came from *her*.
>
> Carlyle,
> "Jane Welsh Carlyle"

Carlyle's *Reminiscences* continue the method of memory
inaugurated in *Sterling* but add little to the statement
of its themes. Instead, the note of loss, of futility, is increased, for most of the *Reminiscences* and *Memorials*
were written in deep sorrow immediately after Jane's
death in 1866. The two central pieces of this brilliant
set of recollections, astonishing in their vivid and minute detail and their power of recall, are a memoir of his
wife and another of his friend, Edward Irving, who had
died "thirty-four years ago" in 1834. Again the double
path of memory is traced in each: how memory reveals
the depth of the bonds of affection, how memory retains
that bond, even while it recognizes the loss and intensifies it.

One significant difference in method between "Jane
Welsh Carlyle" and *Sterling* is immediately evident: acting as editor looking over his wife's letters, Carlyle interrupts the process of memory with bracketed com-

ments on his present woe and anguish, recriminations over his unkindness to Jane, cries of futility and loss, and fury at his guilt. The *Reminiscences* then pick up the qualities of journal writing far more than *Sterling* does: "Jane Welsh Carlyle" is in fact written in an empty journal book of Jane's, its progress day by day is noted, and its completion is marked by the end of the pages in the journal. The real journals of Carlyle become commonplace books, a record of opinions or merely a place to moan his loss, his world-weariness. The opinions are noticeably more platitudinous and cover such topics as the increasing anarchy of the world, the horrors of atheism, and the need for faith, Carlyle's central creative activity is focused on the *Reminiscences,* and not until they have been completed, does he talk about them, even to Froude. In these private writings, then, Carlyle redefines himself for the last time, and though the accent is on futility and the loss of the past, the stoic heroism that emerges is not without a certain strength and stability and even an increased self-awareness.

"Jane Welsh Carlyle" reveals new possibilities in the manner of memory, its mythological power. Julian Symons, in his recent biography of Carlyle, has put this matter well: "In the course of writing [the memoir] he created, and came partly to believe in, another Jane Welsh Carlyle, than the tart, witty and frustrated woman whose love for him did not by any means exclude hardness and bitterness."[1] But Symons might have added that the need to create a loving and overpoweringly important Jane could just as easily been prompted by Carlyle's own feelings of guilt, a desire to right his wrongs by memory, and hence even a need to delude himself about the central meaning of his life. Froude, of course, has been challenged precisely on the

1. Julian Symons, *Thomas Carlyle* (London, 1953), p. 278.

remarks he has made in behalf of Mrs. Carlyle's sufferings at Craigenputtock and in London, but they do not
seem without a certain cogency. Carlyle's neglect of
Jane's ill health and loneliness at Craigenputtock [2] is
what his own self-absorption and literary desperation of
the period might have led one to expect. In later years
Froude pictures her "trial" as hard.

> When he was at home, his own discomforts, real or
> imaginary, left no room for the thought of others.

> Carlyle worked all day, rode late in the afternoon,
> came home, slept a little, then dined and went out
> afterwards to walk in the dark. If any of us were to
> spend the evening there, we generally found her
> alone.[3]

If to this neglect are added the fairly well-substantiated
reports of Carlyle's sexual impotence, the reasons for his
need to mythologize Jane, the demanding urge to eradicate his guilt, are clear.

There is, then, an important quality of escape in Carlyle's memoir of his wife, and it may even be seen as a
retreat into a fantasy world far more unreal than *Frederick*. But there is also—underneath the guilt, the maudlin lanuage, and the sentimentality—a real redefinition,
analogous to *Sterling* but far more intense. Carlyle here
openly transfers his religious imagery to Jane and even
redefines the significance of writing *Frederick*, removing
his glory from the struggle in the soundproof room and
celebrating instead the "lucid twenty minutes" (*R*, 139)
of each day's mealtime that Jane provided as salvation
from the room and the book. Jane in fact becomes a
mythical figure, a kind of sun goddess, who is Carlyle's
"one irradiation" against chaos (*R*, 123). This trans-

2. See Froude, *First Forty Years*, *1*, 338–39.
3. Froude, *Life in London*, 2, 252, 253.

formation by memory brings to mind Proust's use of dis-placed religious terminology—of viaticum, the Host, and the rope of grace—in reference to the goodnight kiss and few moments' visit of his mother, which becomes the central act of each day and indeed of his life, the heart of memory. Despite the recriminations and the sentimentality, then, Carlyle actually seeks in the mem-oir another new center for his life, and he finds it in the relationship with his wife, not in his works, his social doctrines, his heroes, or any of his literary roles at all.

The writing of the memoir in Jane's own notebook becomes a symbolic, religious union between Carlyle and Jane and not merely an act of conjugal devotion. This is Carlyle's final and most removed displacement of religious terms, a task in which he has been engaging since the early essays and *Sartor*. With the completion of the notebook, when there is no longer any space in which to write, Carlyle realizes that he has attained a measure of calm and lucidity by his writing.

> It has been my sacred shrine, and *religious* city of refuge from the *bitterness* of these sorrows, during all the doleful weeks that are past since I took it up; a kind of *devotional* thing (as I once already said), which *softens* all grief into tenderness and in-finite pity and repentant love. (*R,* 168–69)

But these moments of quiet transcendence are tinged with pain; the central note is that of heightened futility. Jane's death has plunged him into more than sorrow: it has "smitten my whole world into universal wreck . . . and extinguished whatever light of cheerfulness, and loving hopefulness life still had in it to me" (*R,* 164). The "fatal telegram" announcing her death leaves him confused, crushed, bewildered, in a world without il-lumination, direction, or meaning. "It had a kind of

331

stunning effect upon me; not for above two days could I estimate the immeasurable depth of it, or the infinite sorrow which had peeled my life all bare, and in one moment, shattered my poor world to universal ruin" (*R*, 165).

To soothe himself once the memoir of Jane has been completed, Carlyle turns to Edward Irving, once his youthful friend and later a wildly evangelical preacher of great success in London—but not without madness, as Carlyle regarded him, a strange "double" of what Carlyle himself might have become in London. Again, as in the memoir of Jane, Carlyle enjoyed focusing on the clear, bright, memorable days before London, when all was joyful spontaneous life and the tragedy of unfulfilled hopes and lost friendships remained far off. Inevitably, however, time and the chronological necessity of the thread of the memoir demand that Carlyle bring Irving to his London years. There, though a great popular preacher, he at last becomes a religious fanatic, a man, perhaps not unlike the later Carlyle, whose ideals outrun reality and cannot come into touch with it.

Since Irving's ideas were exclusively in the sphere of religion, Carlyle can here perceive the painful discrepancy. But once again moments of joyful spontaneous confession, even of Carlyle's unbelief to Irving, are quenched, and the movement along separate paths serves as the sad prognostication for the rest of the memoir. The frankness of Carlyle's confession to Irving during their walk on the Glasgow-Muirkirk highway (*R*, 225) cannot be repeated in London, where each has gone his own way, for Carlyle now notices of Irving that "there was a want of spontaneity and simplicity, a something of strained and aggravated, or elaborately intentional, which kept jarring on the mind: one felt the bad element to be, and to have been, unwholesome to the honourable soul" (*R*, 254). As usual, however, he does

not probe his own failings in the relationships, nor does he assess how much he contributed to Irving's uneasiness with him. Again the locus of all value is interior, personal.

Gradually even the attempt at recall becomes painful. As the memoir moves into its final tragic section, the two strands become separated. Carlyle then traces first his own story, then Irving's, frequently wondering in his intrusions why he is following this method, how he has happened to stray from his topic. But even these questionings are signs of an awareness, perhaps not fully conscious, of the dominance of the tragic process of memory, the almost futile attempt to preserve some "identity of sentiment," a closeness of paths.

In the later parts of the memoir on Irving, Jane appears at Carlyle's side, and the frequent intrusions of lament for her show that she is Carlyle's central concern, that everything is assimilated to this tragic process, that he cannot escape the dominance of the tragic mood. The story of the Irving of the past merges into the tragic situation of the present with Jane's death. Thus the memoir of Irving returns once again to the despairing conclusion of the memoir of Jane. In completing it and a short sketch of Lord Jeffrey, Carlyle consciously and explicitly assimilates the two later pieces into the tragic situation of the first memoir. "It was *her* connexion with them that chiefly impelled me" (*R*, 341). Though Carlyle can find no basis for further action in this situation of metaphysical ruin and despair, he has at least found a new center for sustaining himself personally. And he has accomplished this by the creative and mythological power of memory, even though he himself may not be fully aware of it.

The journals and the notes to the *Reminiscences* show Carlyle wrestling with futility, unaware of even the limited victory he has achieved. The two themes, a

resigned stoicism and what Eric Bentley has called a
"wistful defeat," [4] persist side by side. He advises himself in the manner of his old journal roles: "I must
carefully endeavor to find out some new work for myself;—but as yet am quite at a loss. . . . This morning I
feel dreadfully in want of some *Task* again; and cannot
find one" (*R*, 341). Still puritanically disturbed by
idleness, a theme he has maintained from his earliest
works, he offers no evasions or solutions and finally, he
resigns himself to his hopelessness, undertakes some
work even though he can find no basis for doing it.
"Task being undiscoverable, am almost beginning
(Paper laid *out,* all ready) a Quasi-Task, *Reminiscences
of Sundry Notable or Noted Persons*" (*R*, 342). The
note of hopelessness is almost neurotic, but the valorous
attempt to continue playing the artist is somewhat heroic, however desperately it is undertaken. Once begun,
however, these reminiscences are cut short by their as-
similation into the overriding tragic situation of the first
memoir. The past seems exhausted, as does the future.
"Why should I continue these melancholy jottings in
which I have no interest; in which the one Figure that
could interest me is almost wanting! I will cease!" (*R*,
364).

Carlyle does in fact cease. He loses the use of his right
hand, and nothing but a few "quasi-tasks" come from
him by dictation until his death in 1881. The journal
entries cease in 1873, and according to Froude he often
thought of committing suicide in imitation of the ancient Romans. Weary of life, Carlyle lives "mostly
alone; with vanished Shadows of the Past" (*R*, 364).

His public role shows a similar futility. The old
themes are continued, but no one listens. Attempting to
join the committee defending Governor Eyre, the dis-

4. Bentley, *A Century of Hero Worship,* p. 168.

missed ruler of Jamaica, Carlyle admits to wanting to make Eyre "dictator" of Jamaica "for the next twenty-five years"; [5] his defense is courteously received but is rejected. Only the Franco-Prussian War (ironically the very war that gives birth to the soldier Nietzsche's *Birth of Tragedy*) excites him among the events of contemporary anarchy. He bursts out in trumpet tones for a moment:

> No war so wonderful did I ever read of, and the results of it I reckon to be salutary, grand, and hopeful, beyond any which have occurred in my time. . . . Alone of nations, Prussia seems still to understand something of the art of governing, and of fighting enemies to said art. Germany, from of old, has been the peaceablest, most pious, and in the end most valiant and terriblest of nations. Germany ought to be President of Europe, and will again, it seems, be tried with that office for another five centuries or so. [6]

Continuing these thoughts in a letter to the *Times* defending the German demands for Alsace-Lorraine, Carlyle climaxes his strange love affair with Germany, a relationship which began with a love of German literature and German spirituality—of Goethe, Richter, Novalis, and Schiller—and which now ends with a real admiration for contemporary Prussian militarism. *Frederick* and Carlyle's explicit defense here won for him the Prussian Order of Merit, the only real honor beyond the rectorship of Edinburgh that he was to accept. And on this ambiguous note—a gesture of limited social prophecy since it is made in a journal and a letter to the *Times*—Carlyle finished his central public role.

Nevertheless, Carlyle's abandonment of both his social

5. Quoted by Froude, *Life in London*, 2, 390.
6. Journal entry for September 1870, ibid., pp. 428–29.

and personal writings should not be seen as entirely tragic, any more than *Sterling* is. For, as Carlyle himself says, he is at least given the "Shadows of the Past" and taught that the "universe is full . . . of inexorable sterness and severity" yet also "of love." With this knowledge he attains to a certain calm and succeeds in transforming the "wistful regret" into a measure of strength. He finds that he can face the dark world of "eternity" with its mystery, deprived of religious hopes of an afterlife; he can "look into it fixedly now and then" (*R,* 365) and all its terrors disappear. With his "shadows" of memory as companions, he can live "mostly alone" and face the future of "eternity" with stoic composure. The victory of memory is still limited, but it is highly personal and real.

A BASIC BIBLIOGRAPHY

CARLYLE

Primary Sources

Basic Texts

The Works of Thomas Carlyle, ed. H. D. Traill, Centenary ed., 30 vols., London, 1896–1901. I have used an American variant of this edition with the same pagination (Edinburgh ed. New York, 1903–04).

Last Words of Thomas Carlyle, London, 1892. Contains the text of the unfinished novel, *Wotton Reinfred,* discussed in Chapter 1.

Reminiscences, ed. Charles Eliot Norton, London, 1887. My references are to the Everyman's Library edition, London, 1932.

Special Editions

Altick, Richard D., ed., *Past and Present,* Boston, Riverside paperback, 1965.

Harrold, Charles Frederick, ed., *Sartor Resartus,* New York, Odyssey Press, 1937.

Lomas, S. C., ed., *The Letters, and Speeches of Oliver Cromwell with Elucidations,* intro. by C. H. Firth, 3 vols. London, 1904.

Supplementary Material

Two Note Books of Thomas Carlyle from 23rd March 1822 to 16th May 1832, ed. Charles Eliot Norton, New York, 1898.

Froude, James Anthony, *Thomas Carlyle: A History of the First Forty Years of His Life, 1795–1835*, 2 vols. London, 1882.

——, *Thomas Carlyle: A History of His Life in London, 1834–1881*, 2 vols. London, 1884. My references are to a later edition (London, 1911).

Collections of Letters

Correspondence of Carlyle and Emerson, ed. Charles Eliot Norton, 2 vols. London, 1883. Recently reedited as *Correspondence of Emerson and Carlyle*, ed. Joseph Slater, New York, Columbia University Press, 1964.

Correspondence Between Goethe and Carlyle, ed. Charles Eliot Norton, London, 1887.

Early Letters of Thomas Carlyle, 1814–1826, ed. Charles Eliot Norton, London, 1886.

Letters of Thomas Carlyle, 1826–1836, ed. Charles Eliot Norton, London, 1889.

Letters of Thomas Carlyle to John Stuart Mill, John Sterling, and Robert Browning, ed. Alexander Carlyle, New York, 1923.

Bibliography

Dyer, Isaac Waton, *A Bibliography of Thomas Carlyle's Writings and Ana*, Portland, Me., 1928 (by date of publication).

Moore, Carlisle, "Thomas Carlyle," in *The English Romantic Poets and Essayists, A Review of Research and Criticism*, ed. Carolyn Washburn Houtchens and Lawrence Huston Houtchens (rev. ed. New York, MLA, 1966), pp. 333–78.

Tennyson, G. B., *Sartor Called Resartus*, Princeton, 1965. The appendix contains "Chronologies of Composition for the Works of Thomas Carlyle, 1814–1833," pp. 329–42.

Secondary Sources

Bentley, Eric, *A Century of Hero Worship: A Study of Heroism in Carlyle, and Nietzsche, with Notes on Wagner, Speng-*

ler, Stefan George and D. H. Lawrence, New York, 1944; rev. ed., 1957. A bold and very original book which offers a valuable comparison between Nietzsche and Carlyle in their treatment of "heroic vitalism." While often speculatively brilliant, however, the book nevertheless appears as a potpourri of politics, depth psychology, and biography. Ultimately, it seems to be contemptuous of its major figures and to reduce their ideas to their neuroses.

Calder, Grace J., *The Writing of "Past and Present,"* New Haven, 1949. Examines the various manuscript drafts.

Cassirer, Ernst, *The Myth of the State,* New Haven, 1946. My references are to the Anchor paperback edition, Garden City, 1955. Contains an interesting chapter on Carlyle's myth of heroism.

Froude, James Anthony. See the *First Forty Years* and *Life in London* previously cited under "Primary Sources." Froude's interpretation of Carlyle is not particularly deep and penetrating, but it is marvelously detailed and well balanced. The criticism of his detractors does not strike me as warranted. The controversy over Froude's *Life in London* and his edition of the *Reminiscences* is well summed up in a book that is biased toward Froude but unpolemical in tone—Waldo H. Dunn, *Froude and Carlyle,* London, 1930 (see esp. Chap. 16, on Carlyle's impotence, pp. 204–17).

Geyl, Pieter, *Debates with Historians,* New York, 1958, Meridian paperback, 1958. A historian criticizes Carlyle.

Grierson, Herbert J. C., *Carlyle and Hitler,* Cambridge, 1933.

Harrold, Charles Frederick, *Carlyle and German Thought, 1819–34,* New Haven, 1934; reissued, Hamden, Conn., 1963. A richly detailed and thorough investigation of Carlyle's intellectual development in a particular area. A good introduction to the early Carlyle.

——, "Carlyle's General Method in 'The French Revolution,'" *PMLA, 43* (1928), 1150–69.

——, ed., *Sartor Resartus,* New York, Odyssey Press, 1937. Much intellectual background and extensive—perhaps too extensive—footnoting.

Holloway, John, *The Victorian Sage,* London, 1953. Attempts —with rather limited results—to bring New Critical imag-

istic reading techniques to Carlyle; two chapters offer an interesting treatment of controlling metaphors and styles in *Past and Present, The French Revolution,* and *Frederick the Great.*

Houghton, Walter, *The Victorian Frame of Mind, 1830–1870,* New Haven, 1957. Examines Carlyle's major themes in relation to the framework of Victorian society and thought; uses Carlyle as a touchstone for most of the central concepts of Victorianism.

Neff, Emory, *Carlyle and Mill,* New York, 1924; *Carlyle,* New York, 1932. Biographical, with a stress on the economic and social aspects.

Ralli, Augustus, *Guide to Carlyle,* 2 vols. London, 1920. A popular and helpful handbook, but rather rhetorical and traditional.

Roe, Frederick William, *Thomas Carlyle as a Critic of Literature,* New York, 1910. Rather obvious.

Shine, Hill, *Carlyle's Fusion of Poetry, History, and Religion by 1834,* Chapel Hill, 1938. Sees the synthesis but tries to account for it within the traditional methods of intellectual history.

Tennyson, G. B., *Sartor Called Resartus,* Princeton, 1965. This book, unfortunately not published until after my manuscript was completed, is the first full-scale attempt to treat Carlyle as an imaginative artist. The works up through *Sartor* are closely analyzed, and in many cases Tennyson anticipates and parallels my own remarks on them.

Trevelyan, G. M., *Carlyle, An Anthology,* London, 1953. Good selections well arranged with a fine introduction; author pays homage to Carlyle, especially to *The French Revolution.*

Wellek, René, *Confrontations: Studies in the Intellectual and Literary Relations Between Germany, England, and the United States During the Nineteenth Century,* Princeton, 1965. Reprints two early essays of Wellek on Carlyle which are of varying quality but often suggestive in their connections: "Carlyle and German Romanticism" and "Carlyle and the Philosophy of History."

Williams, Raymond, *Culture and Society, 1780–1950,* Garden

City, Anchor paperback, 1960. Carlyle treated among the literature of social analysis.

Willey, Basil, *Nineteenth Century Studies,* London, 1955. A good chapter on Carlyle's redefinition of religious terms.

Young, Louise Merwin, *Thomas Carlyle and the Art of History,* Philadelphia, 1939. Suffers from the same confusions of Wellek by trying to square Carlyle's theory with his practice. Much more limited in its treatment.

THE IDEA OF THE MODERN

Ellmann, Richard, and Charles Feidelson, Jr., eds., *The Modern Tradition: Backgrounds of Modern Literature,* New York, 1965. An anthology of statements by philosophers and artists on the modern; the classifications and interrelationships of the introductions to each section have been very helpful.

Heller, Erich, *The Disinherited Mind,* New York, 1959; Meridian paperback, 1959. Concerned mainly with the loss of faith and replacements for that loss.

Langbaum, Robert, *The Poetry of Experience: The Dramatic Monologue in Literary Tradition,* New York, 1957; Norton paperback, 1963. A good reevaluation of the concept of Romanticism and a wise extension of it.

Mann, Thomas, *Essays of Three Decades,* New York, 1947. Mann always relates the works of the past to some central intellectual and artistic trend.

Peckham, Morse, *Beyond the Tragic Vision: The Quest for Identity in the Nineteenth Century,* New York, 1962. Slapdash and popular, but very original and exciting.

Spender, Stephen, *The Struggle of the Modern,* Berkeley, 1963. One essay, "The Modern as Vision of the Whole," is particularly valuable.

Trilling, Lionel, "On the Modern Element in Modern Literature," *Partisan Review,* Jan.–Feb. 1961. Stresses the irrational and negative element.

———, "The Fate of Pleasure: Wordsworth to Dostoyevsky," *Romanticism Reconsidered,* English Institute Essays, New York, 1963. Studies the shift to negative transcendence.

(This and the article directly above are now collected in Trilling, *Beyond Culture*, New York, 1965.)

BLAKE, NIETZSCHE, MARX

Blake

Texts

Selected Poetry and Prose, ed. with an intro. by Northrop Frye, New York, Modern Library, 1953. Sufficient for most of my needs.

Blake, Complete Poetry and Prose, ed. Geoffrey Keynes, London, 1961. Contains the complete text of *Jerusalem,* abridged by Frye in the Modern Library edition.

Criticism

Bloom, Harold, *Blake's Apocalypse,* Garden City, 1963; Anchor paperback, 1964. The best guide to all of Blake's poems; especially good on the later prophetic visions.

Price, Martin, *To the Palace of Wisdom,* Garden City, 1964; Anchor paperback, 1965. Studies in order and energy from Dryden to Blake. Ties Blake in with the eighteenth century and offers criticisms and problems muted in Bloom's more doctrinal treatment.

Nietzsche

Texts

A standard edition exists (*The Collected Works of Friedrich Nietzsche,* ed. Oscar Levy, 18 vols. London and New York, 1909–13), but both the translations and the editing are poor. I have used more recent paperback versions for my purposes.

Beyond Good and Evil, trans. Marianne Cowan, Chicago, Gateway, 1955.

The Birth of Tragedy and The Genealogy of Morals, trans. Francis Golffing, Garden City, Anchor, 1956. A spirited translation with a good introduction that compares Carlyle and Nietzsche.

BIBLIOGRAPHY

Ecce Homo, in *The Philosophy of Nietzsche,* New York, Modern Library, 1954.

The Will to Power, New York, 1960. From the Levy edition; this is not a true Nietzsche work, for it consists of aphorisms, some of them discarded and later assembled (as the philosophy of the will to power that Nietzsche projected) by his sister, who worked her own distorted will upon her brother's material.

Thus Spoke Zarathustra, trans. R. J. Hollingdale, Baltimore, Penguin Books, 1961. An excellent introduction. Another good translation is in *The Viking Portable Nietzsche,* trans. and ed. Walter Kaufmann, New York, 1954.

Twilight of the Idols, in Kaufmann's *Portable Nietzsche.*

Criticism

Hollingdale, R. J., *Nietzsche, The Man and His Philosophy,* Baton Rouge, 1965. Derives from Kaufmann but is much weaker on the philosophical analysis; its value is in its biographical detail and the translation of letters unavailable elsewhere in English.

Jaspers, Karl, *Nietzsche. An Introduction to the Understanding of His Philosophical Activity,* Tucson, 1965. A translation of the famous philosopher's 1935 opus; attempts to understand Nietzsche in terms of Jaspers' *existenz* philosophy; good in that it stresses the active quality of Nietzsche's thought, his sense of a task, a role.

Kaufmann, Walter, *Nietzsche: Philosopher, Psychologist, Antichrist,* Princeton, 1950; New York, Meridian paperback, 1956. A pioneering reevaluation that corrects the Nazi distortions—perhaps overcorrects them. Still the best book on Nietzsche in English.

Marx

Text

Economic and Philosophic Manuscripts of 1844, Moscow, 1961. A new edition has been released under the title, *Karl*

BIBLIOGRAPHY

Marx, Early Writings, trans. T. B. Bottomore, New York, 1964.

Criticism

Tucker, Robert, *Philosophy and Myth in Karl Marx,* Cambridge, 1961.

INDEX

Albion, 187-88, 217, 225

Altick, Richard, 337

Apollo, 171-75

Arkwright, Richard, 213

Arnold, Matthew, *Culture and Anarchy*, 282

Ashley, Earl of Shaftesbury, 219

Bentley, Eric, *A Century of Hero Worship*, 238-39, 252, 334, 338

Bible, 184, 186-87, 189, 194, 213-18, 230, 261-62, 281

Blake, William, 27, 59, 62, 65, 79, 171, 174, 176, 184, 188-89, 207, 213, 221, 224-25, 233-34, 305, 342; *The French Revolution*, 165; *Jerusalem*, 186-88, 217, 230; *The Marriage of Heaven and Hell*, 61, 86, 164-70, 175, 186; *Milton*, 183; "A Poison Tree," 230

Bloom, Harold, 186-88, 234, 342

Bottomore, T. B., 343-44

Brewster's Encyclopedia, 19

Brindley, James, 213

Browning, Robert, 338

Bunyan, John, 184, 192

Burns, Robert, 241-43, 250

Butler, Samuel, *Erewhon*, 281

Byron, George Gordon, Lord, 31-32, 66; *Childe Harold*, 47

Calder, Grace, 184, 339

Carlyle, Alexander, 338

Carlyle, Jane Welsh, 53, 269, 328-36; *Memorials*, 328

Carlyle, Thomas
I. WORKS
LONGER WORKS
Cromwell, 11, 28, 185, 210, 239, 248, 252-64, 268, 276, 278-79, 282, 284, 290, 294, 304

Frederick, 11, 210, 239, 252-60, 264-78, 290, 294, 303-04, 316-17, 330, 335

French Revolution, 28, 62, 118, 121-86, 191, 210, 221, 237-38, 254, 256, 258, 264, 274, 276

Heroes, 55, 151, 181-82, 236-52, 261, 279, 284, 304

Latter-Day Pamphlets, 10, 210, 229, 252, 269, 271, 278-94, 299, 303-04, 306, 317-18

Past and Present, 13, 182-235, 256, 259, 261, 274, 279-80, 282-84, 286, 293, 305-07, 312

Reminiscences, 110, 263, 305-06, 325, 328-36

Carlyle, Thomas
I. WORKS
   LONGER WORKS (continued)
   Sartor Resartus, 8-12, 17,
      21, 23, 31, 34, 38-39, 42-
      44, 49, 53, 55-56, 61, 63,
      65, 67, 69-118, 121-23,
      127, 130, 134-35, 178,
      181-82, 219, 237-38, 243,
      259-60, 299, 304-09, 314,
      323
   Schiller, 24-31, 216, 229,
      310-11, 317
   Sterling, 10, 13, 263, 300,
      303-30, 336
   Wotton Reinfred, 44-56,
      80, 93
ESSAYS
   "Biography," 292
   "Characteristics," 5, 17, 56-
      68, 83, 104, 122-23, 127,
      243, 291
   "Chartism," 182, 214, 280
   "Diamond Necklace," 12
   "Dr. Francia," 280
   "Downing Street," 292
   "Edward Irving," 332-33
   "Goethe," 30-33
   "Hudson's Statue," 282
   "Jane Welsh Carlyle,"
      328-31
   "Model Prisons," 281
   "New Downing Street,"
      287, 291-92
   "Nigger Question," 280,
      285-86, 292
   "Present Time," 292
   "Richter," 38-40
   "Shooting Niagara: And
      After?" 279, 293
   "Signs of the Times," 38,
      56-68, 104
   "Stump Orator," 291

   "Thoughts on Clothes,"
      70
   "Voltaire," 40-43
   "Werner," 40
LETTERS
   Correspondence of Emer-
      son and Carlyle, 9, 12,
      69, 134
   Early Letters, 44
   Journals, 304. See also
      Froude
   Letters, 1, 17-19, 22, 70
   Letters to Mill, Sterling,
      and Browning, 141
   Memorials of Jane Welsh
      Carlyle, 328
   Two Note Books, 24
II. PRINCIPAL THEMES
   aesthetic element, 1, 13-
      14, 39-40, 58, 67-68, 90,
      100, 109, 112, 115-17,
      127, 172-73, 175, 180,
      189-90, 202, 224, 227,
      230-31, 233, 277, 304-
      06, 309, 312-14, 319-20,
      326, 333-34, 336
   alienation, 3, 7-11, 18, 27,
      63, 80, 87-88, 102, 107-
      08, 189, 190-93, 222-24,
      252, 255-56, 263, 271,
      284, 289-300, 304, 317-
      18, 325-28, 331, 333
   army, 161-64, 210-11, 214,
      228-32, 261-62, 266, 268,
      279, 288, 292-93
   captains of industry, 203,
      210, 219, 230
   change, 2-3, 18, 62, 66, 89,
      127, 131-39, 192, 243
   editorial role, 23, 34, 63,
      88-98, 101-02, 116, 259,
      282, 304-05, 320-22
   energy, 62, 165, 167, 172,

307-08, 312. *See also*
force
epic, 139-52, 154, 159, 177,
    188, 254, 256, 258,
    264
fascism, 10-11, 189, 221,
    229, 271, 286-88, 290
force, 5-7, 26-28, 59-62,
    130-31, 142, 146, 151,
    163, 188, 210, 284-85,
    288
heroism, 3, 7, 10, 13-14,
    19, 49, 67, 85, 110, 151-
    53, 164, 178, 197-98, 209,
    219-20, 228, 235-52, 259,
    266, 271-72, 280-84, 290-
    94, 299-300, 304, 306,
    315-26, 334-36
history, 28, 60, 118, 121-23,
    138-39, 160, 169, 173-77,
    180, 225-26, 237-39, 245,
    250, 254-55
humor, 12, 31, 34-35, 39-
    40, 57, 94, 111-12, 150.
    See also irony
industrialism, 2, 18, 185,
    189, 203-08, 225
irony, 40-41, 133-36, 148-
    50, 170, 181. *See also*
    humor
labor, 188-89, 197-98, 203,
    206-18, 221-24, 227-32,
    286
man of letters, 18, 19, 22,
    25, 27, 41, 219-20, 244,
    258, 266-67, 308
medievalism, 59, 203-04,
    227-28
multiplicity, 3, 11-13, 25,
    29, 61, 92, 94, 126, 132-
    33, 136, 138, 153, 157,
    305, 310, 316, 318, 323-
    24, 326-27

mysticism, 38, 47, 75-76,
    86, 89, 200-01, 311
myth, 13-14, 74, 84-85,
    106, 110, 130, 140, 143-
    44, 240, 249-50, 255,
    268, 276, 284, 286, 330
nature, 64-65, 75-76, 78-79,
    86-87, 89, 100, 103, 109,
    122, 129-30, 143-44, 166,
    172-79, 194-98, 201, 207,
    226
order, 12, 38, 96, 112, 146,
    159, 161, 196, 208-09,
    229, 234, 244, 259, 280,
    282, 316
organicism, 5, 18, 71-72,
    89, 127, 131-32, 194-200,
    242, 313
prophetic role, 3, 7, 11,
    17, 21, 104-07, 181, 184-
    86, 213, 216-17, 223, 227,
    230, 232-34, 260, 270-71,
    278, 289, 294, 298, 318,
    335
Puritanism, 22, 27, 124-25,
    148-49, 160, 178, 185,
    189, 227, 251, 255, 259-
    68, 334
religion, 2-3, 18-20, 28, 32-
    33, 75, 84, 125-26, 137,
    144, 194-95, 200-18, 247-
    49, 261-62, 268, 272,
    288, 297, 307-14, 318,
    330-31
selfhood, 2, 4, 8-9, 13-14,
    21-23, 29, 52-53, 77, 81,
    84-85, 92, 109-10, 113,
    181, 189-202, 207, 211-
    12, 224, 248, 263, 265,
    271-73, 278, 283, 293-99,
    304-06, 310-12, 326
skepticism, 3, 6, 9, 19-20,
    32, 38, 41-42, 54, 60, 82,

Carlyle, Thomas
  II. PRINCIPAL THEMES
    skepticism (continued)
      93, 96-99, 102, 106-07,
      110, 176-79, 251, 272,
      275-77
    style, 6, 24-25, 34-37, 135-
      38, 173, 202, 253, 273-
      74, 321
    unconscious, 5-7, 54, 62-64,
      122, 127-29, 144, 179.
      See also force, selfhood
Cassirer, Ernst, 249, 339; Myth of
    the State, 238-39, 242, 247-48
Christ, 85, 150, 207, 214, 218,
    220, 240, 295-98
Coleridge, Samuel Taylor, 93,
    307-15
Conrad, Joseph, Nostromo, 175-
    81
Corday, Charlotte, 153, 166
Craigenputtock, 18-20, 23-24, 69,
    269-70, 330
Cromwell, Oliver, 7, 10, 48, 151,
    182, 203, 210, 231, 242-45, 248-
    49, 251, 254-65, 267, 272, 284,
    321

Dante, 139-40, 243, 246
Danton, 140, 151-53, 163-64
Dickens, Charles, 192
Dionysos, 43, 171-73, 294-98
Döring, Heinrich, 40
Dostoyevsky, Fyodor, 107; Notes
    From the Underground, 29;
    The Double, 155
Dryasdust, 255, 263
Dyer, Isaac W., 338

Edinburgh, 8, 19, 335
Edinburgh Review, 19
Edwards, Jonathan, 64

Ellmann, Richard, 1, 341
Emerson, Ralph Waldo, 2-3, 8,
    12-13, 88, 184, 338; Correspon-
    dence of Emerson and Carlyle,
    69, 121, 257
Engels, Friedrich, 184
Eyre, Governor, 334-35
Ezekiel, 186-87, 190

Feidelson, Charles, 341; Symbol-
    ism and American Literature,
    88, 95, 100
Fellini, F., 8½, 117
Fénelon, François, 33, 41
Forster, E. M., Passage to India,
    175
Fraser's Magazine, 70
Frederick the Great, 7, 10, 151,
    182, 264-78, 284
Freud, Sigmund, 111
Froude, J. A., 8, 267, 289, 329-30,
    334, 338-39; Thomas Carlyle:
    First Forty Years, 43, 74; Life
    in London, 185, 237, 252, 254,
    256, 269, 270, 334
Frye, Northrop, 80, 234

German authors, 2, 7, 19, 21, 23,
    72-73, 93, 123, 152
Geyl, Pieter, Debates with His-
    torians, 238, 339
Gide, André, The Counterfeit-
    ers, 40, 113-17, 270, 306
Goethe, J. von W., 20, 22, 30-33,
    41, 43, 85, 250, 322, 335, 338;
    Sorrows of Young Werther,
    47, 49-50, 52, 55; Wilhelm
    Meister, 31, 52, 55
Greene, Thomas, "The Norms
    of Epic," 141
Grierson, H. J. C., Carlyle and
    Hitler, 238, 339

Hare, Julius, 306-07, 310
Harrold, C. F., *Carlyle and German Thought,* 20-21, 70, 337, 339
Hartman, Geoffrey, 106
Hebrew prophets, 213, 240
Hegel, G. W. F., 222-23, 225
Heller, Erich, 341
Heller, Joseph, *Catch-22,* 57
Hirsch, E. D., 100
Hollingdale, R. J., 277, 343
Holloway, John, 339
Homer, *The Iliad,* 139-40, 142, 144, 146, 173, 257
Houghton, Walter, *The Victorian Frame of Mind,* 32, 340
Hume, David, 6, 20, 207

Irving, Edward, 53, 328, 332-33

Jaspers, Karl, 343
Jeffrey, Francis, 19, 333
John, St., 214
Johnson, Samuel, 241-43, 250, 265-66
Joyce, James, *Ulysses,* 13, 306
Jung, Karl, 7

Kafka, Franz, "The Burrow," 270
Kant, Immanuel, 20, 25, 38, 43, 46, 61, 310
Kaufmann, Walter, 42, 113, 277, 343
Kierkegaard, Soren, 55
Knox, John, 244, 246, 248-49
Kubrick, Stanley, *Dr. Strangelove,* 57

Lafayette, 136-37, 140, 145-46, 179
Langbaum, Robert, *The Poetry of Experience,* 42, 86, 105, 341

Lawrence, D. H., 6, 10, 107; *The Plumed Serpent,* 7
Leidecker, Kurt, 295
Levy, Oscar, 342-43
Locke, John, 6, 20, 190
London, 8, 12, 23, 104-05, 188-89, 208, 263, 270, 311, 324-25
London Magazine, 24
Louis XVI, 129, 135, 140, 142, 153, 156, 162, 167, 178
Luther, Martin, 241, 244-45, 248-49

Mahomet, 241, 244, 246, 248-49
Mailer, Norman, 7, 107
Mann, Thomas, 113, 317, 341; "Schopenhauer," 66-67
Marie Antoinette, 151-53
Martineau, Harriet, 237
Marx, Karl, 122, 184, 188-89, 207-08, 214, 228, 230, 233-35, 343-44; *Economic and Philosophic Manuscripts of 1844,* 190, 221-28
Melville, Herman: *Billy Budd,* 55; *Moby Dick,* 40, 55, 100-01, 113; *Pierre,* 88
Mill, John Stuart, 2, 338; *On Liberty,* 282
Milton, John, 36-37, 99, 139, 184, 220, 290; *Paradise Lost,* 106, 140; *Samson Agonistes* 265-66
Mirabeau, 125, 140, 151-52, 162, 242
Montaigne, Michel de, 19
Montesquieu, 19
Moore, Carlisle, 338
Mumford, Lewis, *The City in History,* 58

Nabokov, Vladimir, *Pale Fire,* 40
Napoleon, 162-64, 210, 238, 251, 276

INDEX

Neff, Emory: *Carlyle*, 238, 340;
Carlyle and Mill, 238, 340
Newton, Isaac, 65, 190
Nietzsche, Friedrich, 7, 10-11,
40, 176, 222, 228, 233-34, 255,
263, 266, 269, 271-72, 288, 290,
294, 317, 342-43; *Beyond Good
and Evil*, 253, 275-78, 300;
Birth of Tragedy, 42-43, 164,
166, 170-75, 221, 296, 335; *Ecce
Homo*, 295-300; *Thus Spoke
Zarathustra*, 107-13, 118, 231,
299; *Twilight of the Idols*,
236, 262
Norton, Charles E., 337-38
Novalis (Friedrich von Harden-
burg), 23, 38, 61, 335

Odin, 238, 240-41, 246, 249-50
Overbeck, Franz, 295

Paine, Thomas, 207
Paul, St., 201, 214-15; *Epistle to
the Ephesians*, 214-16
Peckham, Morse, 341
Peel, Sir Robert, 284
Plugson of Undershot, 192, 210,
226
Poe, Edgar Allen, 55
Pope, Alexander, *The Dunciad*,
57-58, 146, 191-93
Price, Martin, 342
Proust, Marcel, *Remembrance of
Things Past*, 306, 331

Ralli, Augustus, 53, 340
Richter, Jean Paul Friedrich,
33-40, 42-44, 91, 112, 335
Robespierre, M., 140, 149-50,
153, 156, 178
Roe, Frederick, 340

Rousseau, Jean Jacques, 125,
144, 181, 250, 257
Ruskin, John, 2, 126; *Praeterita*,
306

Samson, Abbot, 196, 200, 202
Sansculottism, 125-26, 129, 145-
46, 159-62, 164, 262
Sauerteig, 269, 272, 292
Schiller, Friedrich, 20, 24-30, 43,
229, 317; *The Robbers*, 27;
Don Carlos, 27
Schopenhauer, Arthur, 66, 81,
107, 173-74; *The World as
Will and Idea*, 58, 65
Scotland, 33, 241
Scott, Walter, *Ivanhoe*, 205
Sewell, Elizabeth, 91
Shakespeare, William, 242; *King
Lear*, 72-73
Shaw, Bernard, 126
Shine, Hill, 340
Socrates, 43, 166, 171
Spender, Stephen, 341
Squire Papers, 260
Sterling, John, 95, 110, 117, 303-
27, 338
Sterne, Laurence, *Tristram
Shandy*, 40
Stevenson, R. L., 55
Symons, Julian, 329

Tennyson, G. B., 338, 340
Terror, the, 154-55, 157-62
Teufelsdröckh, 11, 23, 34, 38-39,
43-44, 63, 70-118, 299, 308-11,
320
Tillich, Paul, *The Courage To
Be*, 83-84, 99
Titans, 142-43, 145, 151, 167, 171,
173-74
Tolstoy, Leo, *War and Peace*,
175

350

Traill, H. D., 124, 267, 337
Trevelyan, G. M., 254, 340
Trilling, Diana, 7
Trilling, Lionel, "The Fate of Pleasure," 89, 107, 341-42
Tucker, Robert, 344
Tuell, Anne K., 315, 320

Virgil, 139-40
Voltaire, 33, 38, 40-44, 60, 93, 181, 264, 272-76, 278

Wagner, Richard, 171
Warren, Robert Penn, 180-81

Weimar, Duke of, 219
Wellek, René, 340
Werner, Zacharias, 66
Willey, Basil, Nineteenth Century Studies, 238, 249, 341
Williams, Raymond, Culture and Society, 279, 340
Wordsworth, William, 86, 99; The Prelude, 105-08, 303, 305-06, 320
Wren, Christopher, 213

Young, Louise M., 341

CARLYLE AND THE IDEA
OF THE MODERN